The
North Yorkshire
Village Book

D1324252

THE VILLAGES OF BRITAIN SERIES

Other counties in this series include

*Most are published in conjunction with
County Federations of Women's Institutes*

The
North Yorkshire
Village Book

Compiled by the North Yorkshire
Federations of Women's Institutes from notes
and illustrations sent by Institutes in the County

Published jointly by
Countryside Books, Newbury
and the NEYFWI, Thirsk
the NWYFWI, Harrogate

First published 1991
© North Yorkshire Federations of Women's Institutes 1991

Countryside Books
3 Catherine Road
Newbury, Berkshire

ISBN 1 85306 137 9

Cover Photograph of Askrigg
taken by Andy Williams

Produced through MRM Associates Ltd., Reading
Typeset by Acorn Bookwork, Salisbury
Printed in England by J. W. Arrowsmith Ltd., Bristol

Foreword

With its dramatic coastline, historic York, the world heritage sites of Fountains Abbey and Studley Royal, the attraction of 'Herriot Country' and the Spa towns of Scarborough and Harrogate, North Yorkshire has something for everyone all year round.

It boasts two great National Parks, the impressive grandeur of the North Yorkshire Moors in the east and the incomparable beauty of the Dales in the west.

Although the A1 runs north/south through the middle, the rural areas with scattered farms and small market towns protect the peace and quiet of the beautiful countryside.

Castles, stately homes and historical battle sites are of interest to many tourists.

Only some of the many hundreds of villages can be featured in a publication of this size but we hope the reader will enjoy the delights of an excursion through our beautiful county.

Sylvia Foxton
County Chairman of North Yorkshire West
Margaret Wood
County Chairman of North Yorkshire East

Richmond

NORTHALLERTO

Hawes

THIRS?

SETTLE

HARROGATE

SKIPTON

NORTH YORKSHIRE WEST
WI
FEDERATION

Acknowledgements

The NYEFWI and the NYWFWI wish to thank all Institutes whose members have taken part in this book by providing material and illustrations for their villages, with special thanks for the co-ordinators of this project, Olive Whittingham and Joan Wilson.

County Map drawn by Mary Tym

St Mary's Church, Kirby Fleetham

Ainderby Steeple 🦢

Ainderby is three miles south-west of Northallerton. The existence of this hamlet, with a church, is recorded in the Domesday Book. St Helen's church, built on the highest point, was enlarged and rebuilt during the Middle Ages. It was thus the social and visual focus of the village and the surrounding countryside – and still is. Farming families throughout the parish traditionally support it; of the four current church wardens, three are farmers.

The church itself is a handsome Gothic building of stone in the decorated style. The church had a steeple from about 1316 (when the village seems to have become known as Ainderby Steeple to distinguish it from Ainderby Quernhow and Ainderby Myers in the same county), but the steeple was replaced by a belltower in the 15th century.

None of the three 'big' houses, Ainderby Manor, Ainderby Hall and the former vicarage, is easily visible from the road. The Manor and Hall were extensively altered during the late 18th century when local land-owners were benefiting from enclosure and agrarian reform, but part of the old Hall was demolished in 1949. An architectural practice now occupies the site.

In 1976 it was decided to make Ainderby Steeple a conservation area. There are many mature trees because of extensive planting carried out in the 19th century, and the two greens are full of spring bulbs to delight the eye. Although the village contained no buildings of outstanding merit, the greens and trees together formed an attractive whole worthy of conservation. A tradition still kept up is that of the huge bonfire on the larger green on 5th November.

There is now no industry in the village except the architectural practice and the farm, and no shop or post office. In 1913, Kelly's Directory listed a blacksmith, a carpenter, a grocer with a post office, another shop-keeper, two dressmakers, a dentist, a branch of the Yorkshire Penny Bank Limited and market gardeners. There is one public house in the village, the Wellington Heifer.

Airton 🦢

Airton, as its name implies, stands on the river Aire. It is some nine miles north-west of Skipton and many walkers know it mainly as a village on the Pennine Way.

A corn mill at Airton was mentioned in the deed of gift to Fountains Abbey in 1198. Corn was gradually replaced by sheep farming but in the 19th century Airton mill, like many others in the southern dales, was converted to cotton spinning. The wool produced locally was then collected for the rising wool industry in the towns, by 'broggers' and drivers who brought their pack horse trains through the dales. Dewhirsts owned the Airton mill, amongst other similar mills in the dales, and this provided the main source of employment, apart from farming, until it became more economic to move the industry to the steam-powered mills in Skipton. The mill has had a chequered history; it was used to make Dettol during the Second World War, then to house chickens and now, like many other Yorkshire mills, has been converted to flats.

Pendle Hill can be seen from the village and Airton became a Quaker community, based on the meeting house built in 1700 on a plot of land near the village green given to the Friends by William and Alice Ellis, well known Quaker weavers, who lived in the cottage opposite. The meeting house still stands and is used for occasional meetings. There is now a hostel attached and in the grounds are the graves of well known Quaker families.

There are many old houses grouped around the village green – the oldest of them is probably Vipoint House, which still retains its original spice cupboards and beehive oven, and until recently was the village post office. The village school, naturally, was on the green but this is now closed. Also on the green there is an old squatter's cottage and the remains of the old stocks. Perhaps because of the Quaker influence there is no inn and now there are no shops either, but there has long been a Wesleyan chapel in the village, and the present chapel, which overlooks the Aire, is almost a hundred years old. It is the chapel hall which has acted as a village meeting place over the years. There have been some new houses built and old barns converted in the last few years but the essential Airton remains unchanged.

Aislaby 🦢

Aislaby, a small village between Middleton and Wrelton, on the A170 road from Pickering to Helmsley, is mentioned in the Domesday Book as Aslachesby, the homestead of Aslac, the Dane. It would appear that Aslac dwelt on the site at present occupied by Aislaby Hall.

For several centuries the Hayes family lived at the Hall. The Hayes property comprised all of the village of Aislaby and much of the surrounding land, apart from Home Farm, directly opposite the present Hall. Stories are told of the 'wicked Captain Hayes', a name earned by immoral dealings in the West Indies during his time at sea. The night he died, the watchers heard the sound of a coach and horses coming up to the door and going away again. Rushing out, they saw a black hearse and four black horses. Next morning the coffin was found to be empty.

In 1893 William Cooper of Gledhow Hall, Leeds, bought the Aislaby estate, much reduced in size but still about 1,000 acres. He was a remarkable man, excelling at everything he did, including work as a naturalist, horticulturist, horseman and big game hunter.

As well as the Hall and its pleasant, historic gardens, the present village is a compilation of stone-built cottages, some brick-built houses, farmhouses and outbuildings. The Blacksmith's Restaurant, the Wheel House, the Pottery and a large modern residence in landscaped gardens complete the picture.

Aldborough

Nowadays Aldborough is in a backwater lying between the A1 and the river Ure, though visited by tourists who come to see the English Heritage museum and the Roman remains. In Roman times, it was a thriving walled town, Isurium Brigantum, the capital of the Celtic tribe of the Brigantes, which flourished until towards the end of the 4th century. Now all that can be seen are two pavements and a section of the town wall, and a display of artefacts and information in the museum. Other pavements are known to exist under outbuildings and floors of occupied houses and one large paved area was removed and is on display in York.

There are relics of a more recent past to be found in the 'Hustings' – a stone staircase attached to a building at the top end of the green near the restored village stocks. From here the 60 or 70 electors of Aldborough chose their two Parliamentary representatives before the Reform Act of 1832.

Aldborough Village

The church of St Andrew was the mother church of an extensive parish, which in Saxon days stretched from the Wharfe to the Ure. It stands in a large and ancient burial place in the heart of the Roman town. The present church, the third to be built on this site, was erected in 1330 and is well worth a visit. It is believed to have been the site of a Roman temple, dedicated to Mercury, for a statue of the god (now inside the church) was found nearby. The windows in the north wall are the oldest and most valuable and have recently been restored.

Many people remember visiting this village before the Second World War and for some years after it to sample Miss Mudd's justly famed teas at Aldborough Dairy. As well as her excellent catering, Miss Mudd became famous for her success in butter and cheese making. There are many photographs and certificates on show in the Dairy, along with some interesting items of dairy equipment. No teas are served now but the shop is still in the family and it is a post office and general store.

The centre of the village is the green, with its maypole which has been in use every year since its revival in 1964. The May Day celebrations are held on a Sunday in mid May and provide a variety of traditional entertainments for visitors and residents.

The river Ure has always played an important part in the life of this village. In Roman times it was the main thoroughfare and is still navigable for some miles further upstream, so has a constant traffic in summer weather. It is well used by anglers and is approached by two lanes at either end of the village.

Aldwark ✿

The Saxons gave the village its name, which means 'old fort' and referred to a fort probably built by the Ninth Legion of the Roman army about AD 71–74.

The church, dedicated to St Stephen, was consecrated on 27th November 1854. Special permission, however, is required for marriage ceremonies. Windows, mouldings, arches and all ornamental work are of magnesium limestone from West Hartlepool. All the materials for the church were brought up the river by barge.

From Roman times the river was the chief form of transport and flat-bottomed keels sailed as far as Boroughbridge. With the addition of locks from Linton through to Ripon, trade flourished well into the 20th century. Lead, minerals and farm produce were shipped downstream, with lime and coal the main cargoes upstream. There was a coal yard and warehouse near Aldwark toll bridge.

There was a public house at the bridge called the Anchor Inn and the village boasted its own brick kilns, a blacksmith's shop (now the post office), another public house and a school, and held a Feast day on the weekend nearest to 5th November.

The Manor, built in the 1860s is now an hotel and golf course. In the grounds is the Conjuring Stone, which after various ceremonies and exorcisms was used to fasten the spirit of a witch who was said to haunt this place.

Aldwark in more recent years became known in the National Press as 'the village that tried to buy itself', when the owners, a trust of the late Lord Ancaster, put the village on the market. The tenant farmers, some of the villagers and a business group put together a bid but it was unsuccessful and the village was sold for a sum in excess of £3 million to the Society of Merchant Venturers in Bristol.

Allerston ❧

This small rural village, of some 180 souls, comprises a cluster of old stone cottages now protected by a conservation order and a sprinkling of modern houses. The village is fortunate to be set at right angles to the main A170 Thirsk to Scarborough road and has a Methodist chapel, church, village hall (once the village school), post office cum general store and, of course, a public house – well served for souls, stomachs and spirits!

The village has a private spring water supply administered by the parish council, and has therefore always had the benefit of cheap water power. At the top of the village, the spring was dammed in order to drive a water wheel at the estate saw mill. From there it was collected at the mill dam, to be used at the corn and flour mill, and again collected in the water gap to drive an iron water wheel at Low Farm. The same water thus served three functions. Subsequently the water wheel at the mill was replaced by a water turbine and later still by electricity when this was installed in the 1950s. Sadly the mill ceased working in 1975.

At the bottom of the village street, immediately adjacent to the old railway station, is a small walled enclosure containing a stone-lined pit, long used as a sheep-wash but known to older inhabitants as 'Tempit' – surely a version of 'T'hemp pit'. Hemp was required in quantity for the fitting out of sailing ships.

Apart from hemp production, Allerston also possessed a linen-weaving industry; a number of paddocks lying to the west of the village street behind and below the forge and Methodist chapel were known at one time as the Bleaching Garths and were the enclosures where linen was laid on the grass to bleach after steeping in alkaline lyes and sour milk, a long and tedious process.

At the end of the First World War, land and farms belonging to the Cayley Estates were sold, and the bottom half of the village was purch-ased by the North Riding County Council who split up the large farms into smallholdings of around 50 acres. Small parcels of land were added to cottages to be used as poultry farms. All tenants had to be ex-servicemen who had served in the war. These families breathed new life into the village, the number of children at the school rose from 16 to over 30.

Inevitably, like many other villages, Allerston has changed and is no longer mainly a farming community. Since the 1950s the school has closed but the number of houses has almost doubled, many occupied by in-comers from diverse parts of the country, who are finding warmth and neighbourliness in a North Yorkshire village which is beyond price.

Alne 🌿

> Said a gloomy young fellow of Alne,
> I wish I had never been balne,
> For my girl's run away
> With my pal and my pay
> And the neighbours will laugh me to scalne.

It is how you say the name that gives the game away. Visitors pronounce it 'Alnee', locals say 'Awn'.

Years ago Alne was an alder swamp. Today it is a pretty village with a long curving main street, its houses and cottages set well back behind long front gardens, with neat clipped hedges and some interesting iron gates and railings. Geese, cows and sheep once grazed these gardens, before enclosure, when they were the common field.

A winter scene at Alne

At the crossroads to the west of the beautiful tree-lined Avenue is the Plague Cross, traditionally the site where goods and money were left for exchange during one of the plagues that raged in the area.

The church of St Mary the Virgin dates from the 12th century. Of special interest is the Norman doorway decorated with pictures of animals and signs of the zodiac. Inside is the Virgin's Crown, preserved in glass in 1893. It was carried before the coffin of a maiden who 'had triumphed over the strongest allurements of this life and regarded it as an occasion of joy rather than grief'.

Any young couple marrying in Alne church would do well to be acquainted with the local custom, and come to church with an ample supply of coins to 'buy' their exit from the churchyard through gates tied and decorated by the local children.

Alne has had its share of characters, including Anne Wilkinson who in 1670 was charged with, but later acquitted of, witchcraft by sticking pins in an effigy and causing Mary Earneley to fall into a 'virulent and sicke fitte . . . for one houre or more'.

Amotherby & Swinton

Amotherby appeared in the Domesday Book (1086) as Aimundrebi, which derives from Eymund's farm. As the name suggests it was originally a farming community but over the years other industries have taken up residence in this village lying between Malton and Hovingham.

The church is dedicated to St Helen. The first written reference to a church in Amotherby was in 1218 in the charter of Pope Honorius III to St Albans Abbey. Except for the tower, the church has been almost entirely rebuilt, in common with many others in the neighbourhood.

Many burials were found under the church, the most interesting being of a young woman lying under a heavy stone slab carved with a female face. This slab now lies in the porch. At the head of this grave, apparently on the same level and about two ft within the old foundations, was a stone pavement. The stones were burned red about halfway through and were covered with two to three inches of burnt matter and a large quantity of charcoal. An iron blade was also found, greatly corroded. This has led people to believe that it could have been an Anglo-Saxon burial.

The most interesting of the effigies in the church is that of Sir John de Bardesden, who died in 1329. He was a turbulent character, excommunicated in 1303 for a time and involved in considerable disputes with the Prior of Old Malton over rights of pasturing. His effigy is one of only seven known which show a knight wearing a surcoat with sleeves. Most do not have sleeves.

The village of Swinton (Swintune in the Domesday Book, meaning pig farm) lies between Amotherby and Malton. As far as can be surmised there has never been a church but two Methodist chapels were established in the early years of the 19th century. The Wesleyan chapel (1816) is now the band room and worship moved to the present building at the end of the 19th century. A brass band was formed in 1936 and continues to this day. This busy group plays at local schools, galas, carnivals and at local tourist attractions such as Rievaulx Abbey.

Appleton le Moors ॐ

Appleton le Moors lies on high ground just inside the southern boundary of the North Yorkshire Moors National Park. At the top of the single street which, unusually, runs north to south, is the vast expanse of the moors, while to the south where the land falls away there is a far reaching view over the Vale of Pickering to the wolds, which are in the East Riding.

The numbers of sheep which graze the verges are determined by the common right of stray attached to some properties in the township of Appleton. With Hutton le Hole, Lastingham, Rosedale and Spaunton this forms the Manor of Spaunton which has existed since the Norman Conquest.

The present name and spelling of Appleton le Moors is probably Victorian. Delving into the records has produced ancient variations, one of which, Dweldapilton, has recently been adopted by the hotel (to the discomfiture of the visitors who have difficulty with its pronunciation). The hotel was once the Hall, a building whose grandiose appearance reflected the wealth and status of its owner in the late 1850s, Joseph Shepherd. He was born in Appleton of poor parents. Like many of his contemporaries in the district, he went to sea and prospered in the whaling business. In due course he made a fortune and came home to enjoy it.

Shepherd wanted to give the villagers access to things he, as a boy, did not have – education especially. He did not live to accomplish this ambition; he died unexpectedly in 1862 while riding down the village street.

Shepherd died opposite the house in which he had been born. As soon as she was able, Mrs Shepherd bought it and, 'with a loving regard for the spot', erected a school building and a school house, complete with vaulted roof, decorated windows, a little spire and a turret. By way of contrast she gave the commission to build a church to the celebrated High Victorian architect, J. L. Pearson (who went on to build Truro Cathedral). Christ Church has been called 'a little gem among moorland churches' by no less an authority than John Betjeman. It is remarkable for its style which is French Gothic, and for its soaring spire which was cleverly placed to command attention for miles around.

Besides the church there is a Methodist chapel built in 1832, a pub, two bed and breakfast establishments, seven farms, three of which are in the village street, a light engineering works, and a post office.

Appleton-le-Street ❧

Appleton-le-Street appeared in the Domesday Book as Apeltun, which is of Anglo-Saxon origin. The 'le-Street' refers to the Roman road on which it stands, which ran from Malton to Hovingham. There is one pub, the Creswell Arms, a post office and several farms.

The church, with its 11th century tower and rounded windows, is an excellent example of Saxon architecture, one of the finest in the North of England. It is dedicated to All Saints, and originally belonged to the Benedictine abbey of St Albans in Hertfordshire. Within the church there are several reminders of the lords of Appleton in the 14th century. Among these are the effigies of two ladies, one is believed to be that of Alienore de Boulton and the other Hanorse de Boulton. This latter effigy has been moved from its original position and now partially covers the tomb of Jane Thompson who died in 1782.

The fair and show held at the Gales was once so popular that a siding was put on the railway so that cattle could be unloaded for it but alas, like the show, the railway has gone. Appleton is still a farming community but not as self-reliant as it once was. In the village there is a dovecote which is to be preserved.

Appletreewick ❧

Appletreewick, a name of Danish origin and better known to the locals as 'Aptrick', dates back to monastic times. It lies between bleak brown moorland and the banks of the river Wharfe. It is one hilly street, looking in one direction to Simon's Seat, one of the dale's best loved hilltops at 1,550 ft, and in the other direction to Thorpe Fell, a 'must' for all fellrunners. Lead was mined on the fells all around Appletreewick but when that failed so too did the economy of the village, and today it has only a few farms straggling its hillsides.

Many of the houses date from the 16th and 17th centuries and are in yeoman style. Mock Beggar or Monks Hall was so called because it was a resting place for monks travelling between Fountains Abbey and Bolton Abbey.

High Hall was built by the Craven family. William Craven, known as the Dick Whittington of the Dale, was born in one of the cottages at the top of the narrow street (now the church of St John, more correctly a chapel of ease). Born in 1548, he went to London as an apprentice to a mercer and eventually in 1600 he was made the Sheriff of London and later the Lord Mayor. He returned to the area after this, restored High Hall and endowed much in the next village of Burnsall. Although it was rebuilt in the 17th century, the style is Elizabethan.

The village has grown very little from its original size and has few modern houses, but a number of 'restored' barns. In summer it is very popular with caravanners (despite its narrow approach lanes) and also with swimmers and sunbathers, as the river bank in parts shelves down to sandy pebble beaches. But in winter it reverts to what it really is, a very quiet dales village, which has no shop or post office but two pubs!

Arkendale

Arkendale is a small rural village situated one mile from the A1, four miles from Knaresborough and three miles from Boroughbridge. Being in the Vale of York it is surrounded by rich farming land.

In the 1920s most families farmed or were engaged in agriculture. Most cottages had at least one acre of land and outbuildings to keep a pig, a cow for milk and hens. There were a number of larger farms and the men on the smallholdings did casual work for them, such as haymaking, harvesting and threshing.

There were two chapels in the village and standing in the middle was the beautiful Gothic-style church of St Bartholomew which was rebuilt in 1837; before that there was a small chapel of ease dating back to the 1400s. Originally there was a butcher's shop, the estate joiner's shop, a post office and village store. In 'low' Arkendale there was a blacksmith's shop, where the blacksmith from Coneythorpe forge used to come two days a week to shoe the cart horses.

In 1882 when Arkendale estate was sold by Mr Eden to Joseph Nussey, it was a highly important agricultural and sporting property of 1,056 acres. The estate included almost the entire village, five farms, several dwelling houses and buildings and a fully licensed public house called the Bluebell. On each side of the street stood a magnificent avenue of trees, which were sadly cut down in later years. These have now been replaced by the parish council with new young trees.

The Bluebell inn has always been the hub of village life. In the early days it was only two small rooms with cottages and buildings attached, and it is said that Cromwell visited the Bluebell during the Civil War when soldiers were probably billeted in the village; two soldiers died in Arkendale.

Arncliffe 🦌

Arncliffe is in Littondale – its ancient name being Amerdale, which comes from Saxon times.

The eight mile long river Skirfare runs the length of the valley. All this area once belonged to the mighty Percy family. A small village with only 55 on the electoral roll, it is situated around a magnificent village green, the setting similar to many northern villages, where livestock could be driven onto the green when the menace of an attack from the Scots was evident. Most of the houses surrounding the green are listed Grade II buildings and most of the village is a conservation area.

The church of St Oswald has a plaque with names of the men of Amerdale who went to Flodden Field. This church and the pub, the Falcon, featured in the TV series *Emmerdale Farm*, in its earlier days. Charles Kingsley wrote *The Water Babies* at Bridge End, having the inspiration at nearby Malham.

The area is totally agricultural, mainly sheep farming, the terrain being too rocky for crops or dairy herds. Arncliffe has six farms and one within the parish but out of the village. None of these employ full time labour. As yet, there are no holiday homes and everyone works within the village.

Askham Bryan 🦌

Askham Bryan is a small village situated five miles west of York, a short distance from the A64 York to Leeds main road. Many people journey along the A64 and do not realise that behind the large agricultural college, built in the 1930s, lies the village of Askham Bryan, with its Norman church and delightful village pond with ducks and willow trees.

The oldest building in the village is the church of St Nicholas. The church still retains much of its Norman architecture. There is a vesica piscis (or fish) window at the east end – one of three in the country. In the year 1597 it was recorded that the vicar was severely reprimanded for using the vicarage as an alehouse to supplement his income.

In 1600 Askham Bryan was a thriving village, having 16 tailors, 15 shoemakers, ten millers and blacksmiths, nine butchers, five publicans, three bricklayers, two wine merchants, plus farmers. By 1860 most trades had disappeared, leaving only twelve farmers, a blacksmith, a butcher, a miller and two pubs. Today it is a sad story; we have lost the school, vicarage, post office and shop.

Over the years many stories have been told about characters in the village. One such story was of the time when a Mr Swan lived at Askham Hall. A stranger to the village met a boy driving some geese. 'Whose geese are they?'. 'They're Swan's.' Thereupon the stranger, thinking the boy uncommonly stupid, asked 'Where are you driving them to?' 'Askham', was the reply. The stranger, with puzzled look, soon left.

A number of new homes have been built in the village in recent years and soon start to blend in. Some of the old houses still remain. One such is the Doctor's House, built in 1750, a good example of Georgian architecture. Only one public house remains, the Nag's Head. This was originally two houses and the pub, one house being a shop and post office, but in the 1970s the houses were made into a restaurant.

Askham Richard ✒

The picturesque village of Askham Richard, complete with church, school, duck pond and pub, is situated off the A64, some six miles south-west of York.

Sir Andrew Fairbairn purchased the Askham Richard estate in 1879. He built the present Askham Grange and embarked on a building programme which included Park Cottage, houses in the village and the pump house on the green, which served as a communal water supply. Moved by compassion for the little ones he saw wandering across the fields on cold and bleak days to Askham Bryan, some mile and a half distant, he gave a piece of land and built and equipped a school and schoolhouse.

After the Second World War the Fairbairn family sold the Grange to the Home Office and on 6th January 1947, it opened as the first open prison for women in the country, under Miss Mary Size as Governor, with three inmates.

St Mary's church is first recorded in 1076. Its parish registers are intact from 1578. The church was restored in 1879. The stained glass east window, cross and two brass candlesticks on the altar were given in memory of Sir Andrew Fairbairn. A Roman coffin stands outside the church porch. It was discovered in a field in 1838 where it was being used as a cattle trough.

In the 20th century skeletal remains were found in the village when excavations were being dug for a new dairy. They are believed to be those of soldiers from the battle of Marston Moor in 1644.

Over the years the social life of the village has dramatically changed. Once there were musical concerts, whist drives, dances, a flourishing ladies' and men's cricket team, tennis, football and darts, sports days, the WI Choirs Festival in York Minster, a women's club and village library. A travelling yearly fair on the green stayed two or three days. All these events no longer take place. Instead, the highlight is a yearly fair on the green to raise funds for the church and village, together with the sale of tea and cakes on Saturdays and Sunday afternoons.

Askrigg 🐾

The village today has changed very little in the last 200 years. The three-storeyed 18th century town houses on either side of the main street climb up the hillside and give the impression of a huge stage set with the hills towering to the north behind them.

The two waterfalls at Mill Gill and Whitfield have been tourist attractions for centuries. Turner visited, sketched and painted local scenes and William Wordsworth and his sister were both impressed by their splendid surroundings. At one time the biggest beck provided the power for three different mills and as early as 1908 the corn miller produced electricity for the village using Mill Gill Falls as the source of the supply.

In the early part of the 19th century there were five inns but the village itself was losing its importance at the top end of the dale as Hawes grew in size. The market is no longer held but the old market cross still stands in a prominent position in the cobbled area in front of St Oswald's church.

The North Eastern Company brought the railway to Askrigg in 1877 and a year later it was linked to the Midland Company's line to the west. The tourist trade which had been negligible before that date developed very quickly. There were day trippers and others who came to stay in the guesthouses and inns for longer periods. Askrigg's popularity as a holiday centre was well established before the BBC brought it to world-wide prominence in *All Creatures Great and Small.*

It is a working village with two farms within its boundary. The sheep and cattle associated with them move lazily around the high pastures during the summer months and stay at a safer, lower level when winter approaches.

Despite the increasing number of second or holiday homes there is still a strong community spirit in the village and all locally-organised events are well supported.

Askwith 🐾

Askwith is a small village on the north side of the river Wharfe between Ilkley and Otley.

Although the parish church is in the neighbouring village of Weston, the vicarage has been in Askwith since the early 1860s. The best remembered of its occupants is the Reverend Charles Tweedale, a celebrated spiritualist and noted musician, remembered today for the many fine violins he made.

On entering the village, a left turn down Back Lane leads to the

Quaker meeting house, now a private house. The burial ground is still in evidence, dating back to the 1600s.

The Wharfedale Steadfast Lodge is still flourishing, celebrating 150 years in 1993. This 'Sick Club' was formed by local people, and ensured members of a weekly sum when ill, and a payment on death to ensure a 'decent burial'.

Askwith has a busy village hall, and whilst there are no shops, there is a post office and a hostelry, the Black Horse. The village has changed very little, with only a few new houses, old people's bungalows and farm dwellings.

Askwith has had its share of characters. One, Charlie Holmes the mole catcher, when asked on a television interview why he had never married, replied 'Eh I hadn't time, me moles kept me busy'.

Austwick 🌿

Austwick parish is an agricultural area of some 12,000 acres; it includes the hamlets of Wharfe and Feizor, with Lawkland and Eldroth on the opposite side of the A65. An attractive village, Austwick nestles between limestone hills, one of which – Oxenber – is conspicuously wooded.

The ancient base of a market cross is to be found on one of the greens. Records show that an annual cattle fair took place here on the Thursday before Whit Sunday until the end of the 19th century.

Austwick is the home of some 317 people. The character of the village has changed little despite recent house building. The most venerable building, Austwick Hall, is mentioned in a document of 1573 as being a small fortified manor house. The other old houses are easily recognised, having Tudor-style chimneys, mullioned windows and, a great boon to the historian, dates over the doorways.

The parish church was consecrated as 'Church of the Epiphany' by the Bishop of Ripon in 1841. Originally, there was a gallery – a feature that was removed when an eastern extension took place in 1883.

Each February, the parish hall is the meeting place of the stint-holders of three local pastures, who gather here to discuss matters of mutual interest. A 'stint' represents the pasturage of a sheep and stints were awarded to neighbouring farms to control the rate of stocking. This meeting, the Herd-Letting, is so called because at one time shepherds were appointed. The minute book, bound in calf, was begun in 1814.

Austwick has a post office and shop combined, a garage, two residential guest houses and the well known Game Cock inn.

Aysgarth

The village is situated on the main A684 road from Northallerton to Sedbergh. Until 1954 it had a railway station and two mills in operation. The older mill generated electricity until 1948; the other mill, originally a cotton mill, became a flour mill until it too closed in 1965.

The village has two hotels, two resident doctors with a surgery, a garage, a Methodist chapel and a police house. There is still a post office, though the remaining shops are more orientated to the tourist trade. The village blacksmith retired in 1954. It is still a farming area but without arable as it is hill country; the milk from the cows is taken to a large dairy in Hawes.

There was a Friends' meeting house in Aysgarth from 1703 to 1863 and the burial ground is still there, but the meetings are now held in Carperby. The old school building was a sanatorium from 1907–1947 and is now a youth hostel. The Methodist chapel was built in 1900 by one George Dougal and today still has services each Sunday and a Sunday school.

The church of St Andrew stands near to the famous Aysgarth Falls. The Jervaulx Treasures – the vicar's stall – is made from the exquisitely carved bench ends once part of the abbot's stall in Jervaulx Abbey. The bell tower is 14th century, and has a peal of six bells.

Aysgarth is a very pleasant place to live with friendly people and the most delightful walks and paths to explore. In the old flour mill is a tea shop, a craft shop and the carriage museum, and the old village school is now being made into a medical centre.

Bagby

Bagby, which lies approximately three miles south-east of Thirsk in rich farming land, boasts one church, one shop with sub post office, one pub, one garage, a cricket field and, just to be different, one airfield. The main street, overlooked by the Hambleton Hills, winds its way up rising ground from the York to Thirsk road, through a mix of housing and farm buildings, some ancient, some modern, most in mellow red brick.

The Methodist chapel is closed but the church, formerly in the parish of Kirby Knowle and of a very early foundation, was completely rebuilt in 1862. St Mary's church, Bagby, finally acquired full parish status in 1990. As a priest of Baghebi was mentioned in the Domesday Book, it had waited a long time for this. Unfortunately, the school is closed but the building, dated 1891, is now the church hall and much in use.

Most of the property used to belong to Thirkleby Hall, which provided the main employment, but some farms were sold off in 1919 and 1926. Two pumps served the village, water being carried to the houses.

For many years, a major landmark was the sycamore tree which stood on the A19 outside the Griffin inn (now a farmhouse). It was pointed out by stagecoachmen as the finest between Edinburgh and London. Sadly, it had to be felled in the 1940s, as it was badly rotted.

Bainbridge

In the early Middle Ages the forest area in the whole of Upper Wensleydale lying to the south of the river Ure was known as the Forest and Manor of Bainbridge. The village itself was established in the latter part of the 12th century when it became the home of twelve Foresters. In the 17th century trustees became responsible for the manor and to this day the Lords Trustees, local freeholders, have jurisdiction over all but two of the hamlets in the area and are responsible for the care and upkeep of the green, which is such an attractive feature of the village, nestling as it does under the fells.

The village is sheltered on the east by Brough Hill, the site of a Roman fort excavated extensively from 1926 to 1931 and again in the 1950s and 1960s. A Roman road can still be seen leading west from the village straight over Wether Fell towards Lancashire.

In medieval times when guides were often employed to show travellers the way, a horn was blown at Bainbridge in the evening to assist wayfarers to safety before nightfall. The most recent one can be seen in the Rose and Crown during the summer months, but during the winter months the custom is continued and the horn is sounded at 9.00 pm from the Feast of Holy Rood to Shrovetide. Various members of the Metcalfe family in Bainbridge have carried out the duties of Hornblower for over a century.

There is a friendly, neighbourly atmosphere in the village to which visitors return year after year. The old Independent church has been converted into houses but the Methodist church, which was opened in 1836 and replaced an earlier one on the same site, still has regular services. There is a Friends' meeting house built in 1836 with its own small burial ground, while across the road stands the Rose and Crown, hostelry for travellers from early times, standing beside an 18th century Richmond to Lancaster turnpike road on the north side of the village.

The dreaded workhouse of olden days, built nearly 200 years ago, still stands in the village but it has now been refurbished and renamed High Hall and provides a home for elderly people close to a modern sheltered housing complex.

A grammar school was founded by Anthony Besson in 1601. It moved to a neighbouring village in 1931 but its old premises are now occupied by the staff of the Yorkshire Dales National Park.

Baldersby 🦋

Just off the A1 between Thirsk and Ripon, the village of Baldersby and its handsome 'great house' are nearly three miles apart. Between them the beautiful spire of St James' church in the village of Baldersby St James stretches heavenwards.

The great house was built by Colin Campbell in 1720 for Sir William Robinson and is an early example of Palladian revival in England. It was bought by George Hudson, the Railway King, in 1845 and sold to Lord Downe in 1854. Hiding in its park of 200 acres, the Hall is now a school.

Lord Downe was responsible for building the feudal-type village of Baldersby St James. He commissioned the well known Victorian architect, William Butterfield, and the result became a 'model village'. The main feature is the way in which the buildings are graded according to the social standards of the Victorian era. First the church and the vicarage; opposite is the school and schoolhouse and further up the village the workers' cottages and the almshouses. The village is visited by many students of architecture. All the Butterfield buildings are now listed as of outstanding architectural merit. Lord Downe died in 1857 a week or two after he had laid the first stone for the church. The slender tower and spire rising 160 ft above the surrounding farmland can be seen for miles around.

Butterfield's work can also be seen in Baldersby – The Hill, a private residence now, was the estate agent's house, the village shop and cottages opposite. Butterfield worked mainly in the south of England, and these Yorkshire villages are some of the few examples of his work in the North. Near the shop is a mission room built for church services and as a reading room. A door connected it to the attached house, which was the home of the curate. The door has been bricked up now, and the house is privately owned.

Balne 🦋

Balne is an agricultural village consisting of nearly 3,000 acres of land, 23 miles of road and a population of 270 in 1991. The river Went flows through, and the London to Edinburgh railway intersects the parish. The church of Pollington cum Balne, St John the Baptist's, is a brick building erected by the late Viscount Downe. The register dates from the year 1854.

The parish room, which is now used for local functions, was in the early days a small schoolroom for the village children. The children were employed to break up stones that were dropped nearby, carted by farmers from Askern and Womersley, at the rate of seven shillings a load. It was then spread on the road by workmen whose wages varied from a farthing to tenpence a day.

Two public houses, two shops, a Methodist chapel, a blacksmith's shop and a railway station used to be operational, but unfortunately only one public house remains open, the rest of the facilities have been lost.

A number of acres locally were woodland, and a gamekeeper lived nearby. In spring when the woods were yellow with daffodils he would let the local people pick a bunch on Good Friday.

Barkston Ash 🌿

Barkston Ash is a farming village of about 250 inhabitants, with nine farms most of which have been farmed by the same families for many generations. There is one shop which also serves as the post office.

A landmark in the village is an ash tree. The tree stands on a grassy knoll at the top of the Main Street where it joins the Tadcaster to Ferrybridge road (A162). The present tree is over a hundred years old and the successor of a number of ash trees planted in the same place. Legend claims that the trees were planted there to mark the centre of the county of Yorkshire. Although there are some who dispute this fact, aerial photographs show that the tree is the centre of the county to within about one mile.

Sited on the south-western slopes of the Vale of York, the village is sheltered by this rising land from prevailing winds. Spring water is plentiful and the good soils are mainly sand and clay, all excellent for agricultural development.

There is a small church built in 1880, which was previously a chapel of ease but was consecrated in 1974 as Holy Trinity church.

The Ash Tree inn, named after the famous ash tree, stands beside the old coach road from London to York (now the A162) and was built in 1769 when the turnpike was made. It served as a coaching inn for travellers north and south. The old blacksmith's shop and the joiner's shop still stand, though now not in use.

One of the most interesting farmhouses is Turpin Hall with its old oak panelling and mullioned stone windows. Dick Turpin, the highwayman, is reputed to have stayed here.

Barton Hill 🌿

Barton Hill is a tiny hamlet set on and divided by the A64 coast road. Nowadays most people fly through without even noticing its existence but in days past its significance was much greater. It lies at the bottom of Whitwell Hill, now just one of the uphill stretches on the road east, but in earlier days horse-drawn coaches would stop at the Old Spitalbeck inn at Barton Hill to collect two fresh horses to help the existing team haul its load to the top of the then much steeper hill. In earlier times part of the building which became the inn had been used as a hospital for Cromwellian soldiers during the siege at Scarborough Castle and similar local action during the Civil War.

The 20th century saw the arrival of the motor car and the railway, and the local railway station at Barton Hill served as a vital link for surrounding small villages to centres such as York, local market towns like Malton and the coast. As the crossing at the station was somewhat less than level, the old coach house and hay store was turned into a garage to serve the motorist with petrol and replace his springs – victims of the crossing.

A brickyard also existed in the hamlet but is believed to have gone out of existence with the demise of the handmade brick. All that exists now are the workers' cottages, the yard itself having had many later uses, from railway goods yard to potato store to bus museum. Now sadly it lies idle.

Beckwithshaw

A village true to its name, being originally bounded by streams and woods, the latter now unfortunately decimated somewhat. From a hamlet of a pub, a few cottages and scattered dairy and sheep rearing farmsteads, it grew with the addition of Moor Park Hall with its parkland, estate cottages, farm and workshops for a farrier, a joiner and a cobbler. Then came a shop with post office and a Methodist chapel, dedicated in 1848, built on to an old malt kiln which later became its Sunday school. In 1865, a weekday school replaced an upstairs room at the pub, reached by an outside flight of stone steps, which had formerly served the purpose.

Just over 100 years ago, the lord of the manor, Mr Henry Williams, built St Michael's and All Angels church, with beautiful stained glass windows and a splendid peal of six bells named individually after members of his family, the heavy bell being 'Henry'.

Gone are the shop, the chapel (now a private residence), the Hall (a wartime Land Army hostel, now derelict) and the original workshops. The vicarage and old fashioned country pub are now modernised eating places and infilling has produced two groups of up-to-date residences for commuters and pensioners.

There is a legend that John O'Gaunt promised a cripple, John Haverah, as much of the historic Knaresborough Forest as he could hop round between sunrise and sunset. He acquired about seven square miles by throwing his crutch the last few yards as the sun set. Haverah Park contains the remains of 'John O'Gaunt's Castle' and 'Pippin Castle', said to be its chapel and burial ground, also the Boar Holes, relics of former hunting days.

Bedale 🐚

Bedale is not very far from the A1 and many people turn off at the motel to pass through the village on the way to Wensleydale. Bedale was granted a charter in the reign of Henry III for a market to be held and this is still held every Tuesday.

Bedale has been in existence for many centuries. Roman stones were found in the church wall. The early Saxon church points to a relatively thriving township before the Norman invasion. It was a very busy industrial town before the Industrial Revolution really began, and in the latter half of the 1700s some of the town's industrial wealth was spent on improving buildings and conditions. The Bedale you see today is still very much of that time.

The chemist's shop on the corner of the Wynd and looking into the Market Place was a public house called the Boar's Head up to the 1920s and the buildings behind the shop date back from the 14th century.

Bedale Hall is a Georgian house, standing just across from St Gregory's church. It now belongs to the community and a committee have full charge of the building, where the Tourist Information Centre is situated.

St Gregory's church is mentioned in the Domesday Book, and inside the double gates there is a small double-fronted stone building which was the old grammar school. This existed before the Dissolution of the Monasteries in 1536. The building is now used by the church as a church shop run by volunteers and tea and coffee is also served.

The 14th century cross is mounted on six stone steps with a stone shaft and surmounted with a cross, and undoubtedly marked the centre round which the town has grown.

Going along by the beckside the stream branches off and this feeds Aiskew mill. We then come to the harbour, in reality a canal basin, which was to be part of linking Bedale to the river Swale and onto the river Ouse. The iron mooring rings are still to be seen on the harbour walls. The navigation was commenced in 1768 and was never completed because of a lack of money.

Bell Busk 🐚

Bell Busk is situated about a mile from Coniston Cold on the Otterburn road. It did not appear on the map until 1627, when it probably consisted of one house on the east bank of the river Aire between the old bridge and the ford. The house lay near the track for packhorses between Skipton, Settle and the North and a bell is thought to have been hung nearby in a conspicuous bush and rung as an indicator of the route to be taken or as a warning after dark if the water was high. This is probably how the village got its name; a bell hung in a busk or tree.

The village is one of the earliest seats of Quakerism in Yorkshire. A

Toleration Act licence was granted in 1689 and Quaker meetings were allowed to be held. There was also a Wesleyan chapel, which is now a garage for a householder, but Bell Busk has no parish church.

In 1781 Peter Garforth, the grandfather of James Garforth, built the silk mill on the river at Bell Busk. It was a huge building and gave employment to many persons from the surrounding area. The cottages in the village (some of them back to back) were built as dwellings for the employees and a four-berth toilet was constructed across the road for their comfort. Now not in use, it is a listed building. There was also a communal wash-house, now converted into a cottage.

The bell which must have called the employees to work can still be seen on the end gable of one of the rows of cottages. The last time it was officially rung was for the Queen's Coronation day in 1953.

An old Roman road which commences just over the bridge on the Coniston Cold side of the village is known as Granny Lane and connects Bell Busk with Gargrave.

Beningbrough 🦢

Beningbrough is an ancient settlement on the banks of the Ouse, at the edge of the great forest of Galtres. The parish is bounded on two sides by the river Ouse while the Nidd, joining at the elbow, completes the union of the three dales rivers.

The tiny hamlet standing on a high bank above flood-level is the oldest part of the settlement, one mile from the Hall and two miles from the nearest village, being only a small collection of houses of various styles but all built of brick. Only two houses have been built in this century. It has remained an agricultural area, though farming practice has changed with the times, from stock rearing and grazing to modern mixed farming.

The river has played a significant part in the development of the area, water transport being important from early times. Before the advent of the railways produce was loaded at the landing to be taken to the markets in York, Hull and further afield, while coal, lime and other goods were brought from the West Riding. There was a communal sheep wash for all the local farms.

Fewer people are engaged in farming today and people from outside have joined the community. Beningbrough is now a very popular venue for anglers, and at weekends the village street is lined with cars.

The rural peace was broken in the 1970s when, after years of drought, the Yorkshire Water Authority decided to build a water extraction plant on the opposite bank, to feed water into the reservoir at Eccup. However, nature has taken over again, and animals and birds have returned.

Early in the 18th century John Bouchier decided to replace the Manor house his family had occupied for 150 years, with a new and much grander one. The Hall and park are now the property of the National

Trust and attract many visitors, who are able to view the fine entrance hall rising through two floors to a height of 32 ft and admire the magnificent carving for which the house is famous.

Bilton ❧

Many people believe Bilton to be a suburb of Harrogate. This is not so. In fact Bilton existed as a village for centuries before the health-giving qualities of the spring waters resulted in the growth of Harrogate Spa.

At that time Bilton was a mining village, producing coal for the public gas supply which had by then reached Harrogate. Soon more coal was needed than could be mined in Bilton, so this was brought to Bilton Crossing by the newly opened railway and transported from there through Bilton on a narrow gauge line to the gas works at New Park. These narrow gauge lines disappeared when houses were built on the site of them, but to this day there are reminders in the naming of such roads as Old Barber (after the Barber line), Old Trough Way, and Spencer's Holt.

A short distance from Spruisty Bridge can be found a flight of tiny steep steps cut into a sheer rock face. These are said to have been used centuries ago by monks from Fountains Abbey when they came to minister to the people of Bilton.

In 1793 two local landowners, Richard and Francis Taylor, endowed the first school in the village. Since both Taylor brothers were unmarried, the area around the school became known as Bachelor Gardens. The school became a listed dwelling house when a new Richard Taylor School was opened.

By 1857 Bilton had a fine parish church. The church of St John was financed by another local benefactor, William Sheepshanks. At this time Bilton had only a few hundred inhabitants, mostly farmers, stone workers and textile workers, but the building of Bar Methodist chapel soon followed.

The heart of Bilton has the ancient Gardener's Arms at one end of the lane and the more recent Dragon Hotel at the other. A little further away, where until 1981 Knox House Farm stood, is the Knox Arms. The listed farmhouse was retained while the barn became a country inn, with the old granary being available for use as a meeting place for local groups.

Birstwith ❧

Nestling in the fold of the hills, in the delightful valley of the Nidd, can be found the one-time estate village of Birstwith. It has a long and varied history. The discovery of a Neolithic axe head suggests an early Stone

Spruisty Bridge at Bilton

Age settlement – the first of many to make an inroad into what was to be known as the Knaresborough Forest.

Apart from quarrying, coal mining and corn milling, Birstwith also had a cotton mill by the river. An attractive relic from this time is the weir, which was constructed to produce a good head of water for the mill-race, ensuring the mill wheel was constantly turning.

The Greenwood family, mill owners in the Keighley area of Yorkshire, bought Wreaks Mill in 1805, and established themselves as squires by acquiring land and building Swarcliffe Hall, an imposing home overlooking the village. This is now a private school for boys.

A notable visitor was Charlotte Bronte, who came to Swarcliffe Hall in the early 1840s, staying for six months as governess to the children. It is said that the idea for *Jane Eyre* came to her after visiting a country house in the area.

The 17th century saw a very strong Quaker influence, with a meeting house and burial ground along by the river. With the decline of the Quakers came the Methodists, Primitive and Wesleyan. Workers of this persuasion were given every encouragement to settle, because of their reliable and hard-working characteristics. In 1857 Frederick Greenwood, an Anglican, built up on the hillside the lovely village church, with its slender spire and imposing ring of bells.

The very fine packhorse bridge is a really beautiful monument to past art. The monks from Fountains Abbey travelled this way with their packhorses, weighed down with wool for the mills of Yorkshire and Lancashire, returning with cotton and supplies for their needs.

In its heyday Birstwith boasted a busy blacksmith's forge, a sweet shop, a tailor's, a cobbler's, a butcher's, a cycle shop, and general store and post office; in fact, quite a busy place. Unfortunately, only the latter remains.

The old Greenwood estate is no more; properties were sold by auction in 1949 to meet death duties, many of the sitting tenants buying their homes and land. Land became available for building, and new properties sprang up, bringing new people to the village.

Bishop Monkton 🦋

With a beck running the length of the village and trees on the grass verges, Bishop Monkton is acknowledged as a most desirable place in which to live.

As its name implies this village had for centuries ecclesiastical connections, beginning with the first recorded date of AD 661 when the township became part of the monastic community of Ripon. Early in the 13th century a manor house was built where the Archbishop of York was known to stay when he travelled around on his episcopal duties. The manor house was replaced by Monkton Hall on the same site and demolished in 1850.

The earliest record of a cornmill (former flax mill) is 1304. Eventually, destroyed by fire, it was rebuilt in 1784. It still exists as a substantial building, not any longer used for corn milling, having been taken over by a pine furniture business.

Another building, now housing industrial paint, was for many years a flourishing paper mill. A special kind of paper was made here and exported to many parts of the world. These mills of course provided employment locally.

In 1840 the first Noncomformist chapel was built and in 1878 the present Anglican church was erected. Another asset was the building in 1859 of the Mechanics Institute, with a clock tower added later. It provided a meeting place, with educational facilities, such as a library and supply of newspapers and a programme of lectures of wide range. The social side was catered for by concerts.

The population increased from 11 in 1086 to over 700 now. The statement of the village elders that 'it isn't the same!' is true and bound to be so. Old occupations have died out and many who live here commute to Ripon, Harrogate or Leeds and houses change hands frequently. Army vehicles regularly pass up and down from a nearby bridging site. New people have brought new life and there are plenty of activities available. One old custom which has survived is the locking of the church gate at weddings until the bridal couple on leaving throw coins for children.

A notorious scandal concerned the time when whist drives were illegal, but were held here at Bishop Monkton. Crowds of people used to come from Leeds to take part, giving this place a reputation as 'a hot-bed of gambling!'

Bishop Thornton & Shaw Mills ✤

The parish of Bishop Thornton has always been an area of dispersed settlement with no main village, just hamlets. Its natural boundaries are streams which in the past have provided the source of power for corn, woollen-fulling, flax and silk mills. Thomas and William Shaw, millers at the time of the Hearth Tax 1672, are supposedly the reason for the name Shaw Mills.

In 1871 (population 505) the mills employed 61 people producing silk yarn. The new owners, Robert and John Threlfall, replaced many of the original mill cottages of 'one-up, one-down' with more commodious dwellings. In 1890 High Dam was made to increase the water power for spinning. Largely due to the Threlfall's sponsorship and local enthusiasm, the present Methodist church opened in 1904 to seat 150 people. Shaw Mills boasted four shops, a post office and the Nelson Arms, whose landlord thereby supplemented his cordwainer's income. Until the advent of bottles, milk was sold through the inn's central hatch. The workers were very proud of their fine spinning and boasted that 'they spun the silk for Kaiser Bill's underwear'.

Falling trade led to the closure of the mills in 1921, but over the years they continued to be used for the manufacture of various products. In the 1990s Low Mill became a housing complex, following earlier council properties on Sunny Bank.

Bishop Thornton covers a wider area, but until the 'stunted common' was enclosed in 1758 it consisted mainly of isolated farms. The old bridle road skirted the common and passed the church of St John the Baptist, built circa 1460 by John Walworth, the Archbishop of York's forester, as a chapel of ease in the centre of the parish. Only the tower now remains and the new church of St John the Evangelist was opened in 1889 standing on the new turnpike road, one of two which crossed the original common.

Raventofts Hall – for many years the home of the Walworth family – had a mass room over the kitchen wing, and a convenient 'Headless Nun' walking the orchard at midnight no doubt deterred visitors when the resident priest was about. The Hall was largely rebuilt in the 17th century by Peter Ingilby, but remained one of the centres of Roman Catholicism in the district from the Reformation until 1790.

Dual occupation remains vital to the local economy with tourism, particularly farmhouse holidays, replacing the more traditional manufacturing industries.

Boltby ✒

Boltby, five miles from Thirsk, has the Hambleton range on the east and the huge bulk of Blackamoor on the north.

The chapel of ease situated in the middle of the village was rebuilt in 1855 and consists of a nave and chancel with a bell gable at the west end. There is also a burial ground attached to the present chapel, now Holy Trinity church. This is the third building on the site.

There were two public houses. The Johnstone Arms is now a trekking centre and summer tea-rooms, run by the family of the last landlord. The Carpenter's Arms is now a private house, and the village shop and post office have gone the same way.

The parochial school was erected about 1860 for 30 children; it closed after the Second World War and the building was recently bought by the villagers and modernised for use as the village hall.

The population in 1851 was 295 persons over 3,834 acres of land. In 1991 there were about 140 people, who nearly all own their own houses as the result of the sale of Mr F. E. Walker's estate. School holidays, evenings and weekends will find the village resounding with the voices of the children playing. It is not a village of holiday cottages deserted in the winter, the way so many have gone. On the contrary, wood smoke rises from the chimneys and as one passes the windows a warm glow seems to beckon you in.

Bolton Abbey ✒️

Situated just within the Yorkshire Dales National Park and five miles from Skipton, Bolton Abbey comprises a group of small hamlets. Bolton Abbey village itself has a population of about 50 persons. The village is at the bottom of a valley formed by the river Wharfe, the surrounding hamlets of Storiths, Hazlewood, Deerstones and Halton East nestle in the hills overlooking the valley.

The village's greatest claim to fame is its historic priory founded by the Augustinian canons in 1155, where it flourished until dissolved by Henry VIII in 1539. The nave of the church was fortunately allowed to be retained as a parish church. Apart from the present church, which contains features from earliest days, the ruins of the priory have been preserved in reasonable condition and the remnants of the more important buildings associated with the church are easily traced.

Successive owners have loved and cared for the area, which is still a working estate with a large wood yard, forestry department, pheasantries and tourism office. Many of the houses are occupied by estate workers and the surrounding farms are tenanted. Although a few houses in the hamlets of Beamsley and Halton East are privately owned, the greater number are occupied by workers employed on the estate, either on the land or in the hotel, shops and restaurants. The character of the village has therefore been maintained and we still retain the village school. Growth however, in the form of new housing is very limited due to the controlling influence of the Dukes of Devonshire.

Down the river from Bolton Abbey is the much photographed Bolton bridge, where the A59 crosses the river Wharfe. Ferry House, nestling virtually under the bridge, is thought to stand on the site of a chapel for wayfarers.

Upriver from the priory the river Wharfe runs through a narrow gorge called The Strid, at its narrowest point but three ft wide when the water is low. This beautiful spot has seen many tragedies, the gorge being a tempting leap to the unwary.

Bolton-on-Swale ✒️

Bolton-on-Swale, or Bodelton as it appeared in the Domesday Book, is a small hamlet housing only 46 people situated about six miles south-east of Richmond. For such a small community it has had more than its fair share of notable characters.

In the 1600s the house of John and Kit Wright stood in what is now part of the churchyard. John and Kit were co-conspirators with Guy Fawkes in the Gunpowder Plot of 1603, who were caught and put to death without trial for their part in it.

The village is also famous as the burial place of one Henry Jenkins who reportedly lived to the ripe old age of 169. When he was about ten or twelve years old it is said he was sent with a horse-load of arrows to nearby Northallerton on the first leg of their journey to the battle of Flodden Field. He carried out his employment as a fisherman on the river Swale for 140 years and was still able to swim across the river with ease at the age of 100! He died in 1670 and was buried in St Mary's churchyard.

Bolton Old Hall next to the church started life as a pele tower and was later extended into a dwelling. The old pele tower, which is now the drawing room, is reputed to be haunted by a 'lady in grey' and also houses a secret panel revealing the entrance to a passage which ran from the pele tower to the home of John and Kit Wright. In the 18th century Bolton Old Hall became the dower house for Kiplin Hall, the local seat of the gentry, which was built for Sir George Calvert who later became Baron Baltimore.

Bordley 🌿

Bordley, with a population of only 21, is three miles from Hetton. There are six farms about half a mile apart, and ruins and old coal shafts can be found in the area. The road through Bordley goes to Malham, and further up the valley and to the right is Bordley Town. Here there is a big stone where the market square used to be.

Just beyond Bordley Town is what is thought to be an old Roman settlement. It would have been in an ideal position, sheltered, facing the sun and with running water. Some distance away and near to the road going to Skirethornes, is 'The Druids Circle'.

Boroughbridge 🌿

Boroughbridge stands on the river Ure, where in 1562 the main bridge was built after the collapse of the bridge at Milby. Boroughbridge became a port for boats loading timber, wine and lead from the dales and linen from Knaresborough.

Boroughbridge was also a stage coach stop on the London to Edinburgh run. In 1989, the centenary of the first mail stage coach to stop, the High Street was transformed back to that time with horses and coaches only for the day.

The yearly horse fair known as Barnaby Fair was held the second week in June, when travelling people bartered their wares and gold, cut glass and Crown Derby brought colour to stalls as horses were galloped down the High Street to show their pace. This was held until the 1980s when drink and damage became profuse.

There was a flour mill on the weir, in use until the 1950s. It was burned down in a great fire in 1961 and the land has now been reclaimed for houses. The train service from Harrogate to the main line at Pilmoor was withdrawn in 1950 and the station is now an industrial site.

The church in St James' Square was replaced in 1851 by the church that is still in use today on Church Lane. A monumental fountain, was built on the old church site in memory of the Lawson Tancred family, and was used to pump water for the town in early days.

Market Square still has the old butter market building where the farmers' wives sold their products. The war memorial contributed to by Boroughbridge people and placed there by the British Legion, stands in the centre of this square, and there was also a German gun to commemorate a VC award to Captain White in 1916, but it was taken to provide metal for further guns in 1939.

Borrowby ✺

Borrowby is situated west of the A19 on the junction of four minor roads. The original stone-built houses each had a field to the rear, and many of these long narrow strips can still be seen as you drive along the A19. At one time the village hosted a variety of crafts and professions – shoemaker, joiner, blacksmith, cartwright, fishmonger, tailor, miller, shopkeepers, post office and two public houses. Today there is one public house and a part time post office.

Borrowby also once had a thriving weaving industry with over half of the 400 inhabitants being employed. Linen was made from the blue-flowering flax, the bleaching mill was at what is now called Cockstride House, and the weaving took place in Brittons Row. The corn mill situated at the southern end of the village next to Broad beck, which leads into the Cod beck, stood unused after its closure until converted into a luxury family home.

A small Quaker burial ground can be found behind Ryecroft House. The Wesleyan chapel dates from 1879 and is still in regular use today. The Primitive Methodists also had a chapel, built in 1882, but only the base of this now remains.

The church of St Mary is to be found on the opposite side of the A19 slightly to the north. A discovery in the churchyard in 1852 of a large quantity of human bones heaped together supports the theory that the original church was destroyed by the Scots at the beginning of the 14th century.

A public footpath leads to the church from the village through what is known as Leake Greens. Leake was a village, thought to have been of considerable importance before the Norman Conquest when it was completely destroyed. Leake Hall is the only remaining building of the village of Leake and was formerly the manor house of the Danby family.

Bossall 🦢

Bossall is situated on the west bank of the Derwent, about ten miles from York. Although it is now only a small hamlet, it was once an important centre for secular and religious leaders of the nation. The palace of King Edwin, the first Christian king, was at Bossall. There are many tales of battles and assassinations surrounding his court.

When Edwin decided to move his court into York, he donated his Hall at Bossall to the Church and became a Christian. He erected a wooden shrine on the site of the present York Minster, and was baptized there at Easter AD 627. The first church at Bossall was erected soon after this, in the south-west of a field now known as Old Bossall, and dedicated to St Botolph. The third Bishop of York, Boza, took up residence in the Hall in AD 678, and it was probably from him that the village took its name. The present church was erected between 1180 and 1185 by Paulinus de Bossall and his wife Julianna, and much of the original fabric remains; particularly the superb crossing arches and piers.

The inhabitants of the old village were wiped out, possibly by the Black Death, in 1349 and many grass covered mounds are all that remain to show where the village stood. The Hall, church and old vicarage, with a few scattered farms and cottages, a total of less than 100 residents, is all that is left of a once important place, but its influence will not be forgotten. In 1632 the marriage is recorded of Thomas Shephard, a clerk in Holy Orders, at Bossall, and Miss Margaret Tutville. Three years later they sailed with other Pilgrim Fathers to America, and in 1636 Mr Shephard became the co-founder of Harvard University.

The churchyard of St Botolph's was declared a Site of Special Scientific Interest in 1988 because of the variety and profusion of flowers there, particularly in early spring – snowdrops, wild daffodils, primroses, violets, cowslips and many lesser known varieties. The view over the surrounding countryside is spectacular, with a lovely patchwork of colour spreading out across the wolds.

Bradley 🦢

Bradley is a friendly village in an attractive setting, half a mile off the A629, and a little over two miles south of Skipton – the gateway to the Dales. Approached one way by a swing bridge crossing the Leeds–Liverpool canal, visitors do not have to be in a hurry. They may find they have to give way to one or more of the gaily-painted pleasure boats or slow down while some of the resident duck population take a stroll along the road.

Bradley is divided into two parts – High and Low, collectively known as Bradleys Both. Long ago however, it went by the name of Bradleys Ambo. In 1965, a new estate was built between the canal and heath virtually doubling the size of the village, and grafting onto the close-knit community an influx of newcomers. Happily, the two communities have merged successfully and any divisions have disappeared.

The Bradley section of the Leeds–Liverpool canal was completed c1775. A coal business was eventually established on the left of the swing bridge complete with wharf and weighbridge, while a coal stay and canal wharf occupied a large area to the right. Coal barges pulled by boat horses were a regular sight.

Most of the essentials of village life can be found here – it has a pub, a school, post office-cum-newsagent's, butcher's shop, village store and hairdresser, plus a Methodist chapel, an Anglican church and a well-equipped village hall, to serve a population of about 1,000. But it was not always so; the population figures have shown considerable fluctuations over the years. For example, in 1801 there were 315 inhabitants, while in 1831 some 614 people lived here.

Quarrying supplied slate and stone for building, but most of the villagers were engaged in hand-loom weaving in their own homes. Some were wool combers.

In the mid 1860s, industry came to Bradley in the form of spinning and weaving mills, providing much needed employment. One of the mills, at Cross Lane, is now divided into several small units and craft workshops, but weaving is still carried on at Rose Shed.

Brandsby

Brandsby is a small village of warm sandstone cottages with pantile roofs and larger more impressive homes, including the Georgian Brandsby Hall. The village is situated on the wooded slopes of the Howardian Hills overlooking the Vale of York.

The village now comprises two separate settlements connected by a broad avenue of limes. The houses formerly clustered around Brandsby Hall but over 200 years ago the lord of the manor demolished them and replaced them out of sight at the other end of the estate. The church too was resited when the ruinous Norman church adjoining the Hall was demolished. All Saints' is an unusual church, the only one in the district built in the Classical style, with an impressive open cupola and an interesting set of monuments to commemorate the Wiley family, who pioneered stockraising and sent cattle to Argentina. The tradition of stockraising still continues, as lorry loads of sheep and cattle leave the village daily.

A founder member of the village hall was Joseph Crawhall, the painter, who lived in Brandsby from 1903 till his death in 1913. He left a legacy of animal and hunting paintings, unusually painted on linen, mostly now to be found in the Burrell Collection. Another famous painter associated with Brandsby was John Sell Cotman, watercolourist of the Norwich School. Francis and Theresa Cholmeley became his patrons from 1801 and for three summers when he was a young man he resided at Brandsby Hall and painted some of his best works.

Brandsby school was closed in 1966 and as there is no pub the focal point of the village is the shop and post office. Brandsby estate was sold a few years ago but the farming tradition remains. There is some diversification into soft fruits, plant propagation, tourism and horseracing. Although very much a village of individuals the Village Hall Committee does manage to gather in most of the population for the yearly not too ancient tradition of punch drinking.

Brawby 🌿

Brawby is a small village situated in the heart of Ryedale. To the north are the Yorkshire Moors and to the south the Howardian Hills.

The market towns of Malton, Pickering and Kirkbymoorside are all approximately eight miles distant. The village is bordered by the rivers Seven and Rye and until the river banks were built up about 40 years ago, flooding of the low lying cottages was a frequent occurrence.

Farming is the main industry with the old established firm of agricultural engineers, J. Thackray & Sons, now owned by the fourth generation, still providing employment.

The original school built in 1859 closed in 1909 when a new school was opened. This also closed in 1984 and the children are now taken by coach to Amotherby and Malton. The original school is now used as a village hall, and the 1909 school has been converted to a dwelling house.

The Primitive Methodist chapel was built in 1838 and is still in use. An open air service, formally known as 'The Camp Meeting' is still held each summer.

Brearton 🌿

Evidence has been found of man's existence here as far back as 2000 BC, with the discovery of a scraper of the Bronze Age. A Roman road is thought to have been constructed which skirted Brearton and Copgrove, heading for Aldborough, no doubt to assist the movement of military and supplies through forest and marsh.

Today, Brearton has one of the finest medieval landscapes in England, with some excellent examples of the manorial system. Fields were ploughed in long, narrow strips between a quarter and a half acre in size, and soil heaped up in ridges, in part as boundaries and to assist drainage. The plough teams were cumbersome, usually eight oxen yoked in pairs: to turn the oxen at the end of each strip a double curve developed, examples of which can be seen in the hedges and fields of Brearton in Back Lane.

In 1861 'the township of Brearton' had 63 occupied properties with farming the principal employment. The community had a grocer's shop, a butcher, shoemaker, cordwainer, a market gardener, two school-teachers and a dressmaker. There were two inns, one of which, the Malt Shovel, still flourishes, probably the oldest surviving building to be seen in the village. The church of St John was erected in 1836.

There is little evidence of the past to be seen, but the plan of the village is old, the main street leads in a direct line to the village green and had farms on either side. Population figures have decreased and the architecture changed. In recent years the blacksmith's forge has been converted to a family house, infilling in the main street has included six new properties where cottages existed, and barns have been dismantled to make room for residences. No shops have survived for today's villagers' needs.

Brompton by Sawdon ✣

Brompton by Sawdon lies in the valley of the river Derwent equidistant from Scarborough and Pickering. To the north, the land rises steeply to the North Yorkshire Moors National Park and across the valley to the south are the more gentle slopes of the Yorkshire Wolds.

There has been a village at Brompton since early times and for more than 450 years it has been associated with the Cayley family. Exactly when the association started is not known but a Cayley was lord of the manor in 1572 and there are memorials in the church to many Cayleys since that time.

William Cayley was created Baronet in 1661 but it is probably the 6th Baronet, Sir George Cayley (1773–1857) who is the most widely known. He was a great aeronautical pioneer who designed and built flying machines which were the forerunners of the modern aeroplane. Sir George lived and worked at Brompton Hall and conducted his flying trials in Brompton Dale. In 1853, he sent his coachman across the dale on what is said to be the first true glider flight in history – the coachman afterwards gave in his notice. Since Sir George's day there have been many changes. Brompton Hall is now a school for children with special educational needs and Brompton Dale is part of a prosperous modern farm, but the family still maintain their connections here.

Despite modern trends, weddings are still very popular in the village. They are regarded as village events and people gather outside the church to wish the couple well. Presumably, there were people outside the church when Mary Hutchinson of Gallows Hill Farm and William Wordsworth, the poet, were married in 1802.

It seems appropriate that Wordsworth should have been married at Brompton where daffodils flourish. When the horse chestnut trees which commemorate Queen Victoria's Jubilee are opening and the ducks and other water birds are pairing on the lake and becks, daffodils bloom everywhere. The horse chestnut trees grow on the green known as the Butts which is said to have been the area where the men practised their archery in medieval times. Now the Butts is a favourite place for visitors who bring picnics to share with the ducks and wander by the streams on summer afternoons.

The flourishing farms do not employ as many people as in the past but there is a small engineering company, a wholesale and retail butchery business and a top class restaurant to offer further employment. The post office, shops and the pub supply most needs and the village hall, which used to be a reading room, is heavily booked by clubs and societies.

Brompton-in-Allertonshire ༄

Brompton-in-Allertonshire is recorded in the Domesday Book, but a lovely mosaic found by a house builder in the 1930s indicates that the Romans had some interest here. On the border of the village is an ancient boundary stone, possibly 11th/12th century, marking 'Bruniton Liberty'.

The most interesting event in Brompton's history is the Battle of The Standard on the 22nd August 1138. On this day King David with the Scots were defeated by King Stephen and the English, a mile or so outside the village. It was said that thousands of Scots were slain and buried in a spot which has since been known as Scot Pit Lane. Land nearby is known as Red Hills because of the blood which flowed there, and the nearby farm is known as Standard Hill.

It is believed that as early as the 7th century 'a simple structure of wood and thatch was erected' as a church at Brompton. Now it is an ancient stone building in Gothic style, having several lovely stained glass windows, one of which is dedicated to John Kettlewell who died in 1695. He bequeathed the residue of his estate, including Low Farm in Brompton (now known as Kettlewell Farm), for the benefit of Brompton and Northallerton. This formed a charity known as the Kettlewell Trust which is still administered to provide religious books, to promote education and for the relief of need.

For a long time linen manufacture was the chief industry of the village – first with hand-loom weavers employing some 300 men and women in their own homes. The subsequent introduction of machinery and the adoption of the factory system concentrated the trade in two mills which continued manufacturing until after the Second World War.

Natives of Brompton are staunchly loyal to the village and those who have come to live here have soon developed a great affection for the place. When the present vicar came here he was told by one old 'Standard' (as the real locals are known) that he would have to live here for 20 years before he could empty his teapot into the beck.

Brompton-on-Swale 🌿

The two main influences on the development of Brompton-on-Swale have been the road through its centre and the river Swale. Both lend geographical definition to the village, which has no clear centre but follows a linear lay-out.

The modern plan can be traced to medieval times – a wide street with a row of house-plots and long narrow gardens on either side. The earliest buildings would have been of timber and thatch, but from about the 17th century these materials came gradually to be replaced by locally obtained stone – mostly river cobbles from the Swale. It is the character of the buildings and of their material, rather than any comely village lay-out, which gives Brompton-on-Swale its attractive appearance today.

It was not until the first half of the 19th century that Brompton-on-Swale acquired for itself the trappings normally associated with the English village: St Paul's church was built in 1838 and the first school in the village also dates back to 1838. The Swale is reputedly the fastest flowing river in England, and records reveal many occasions from earliest times when homes and roads have been damaged by it. But it was with the 'Big Flood' of 1884 that Mother Shipton's prophecy – 'Brompton will wash away by Swale when God sees good' – might best be said to have come true: two roads were destroyed and the water reached as far as the upper floors in some of the riverside cottages.

The mill, which was the descendant of the first mill reported in the Domesday Book, finally closed in 1947, and the brewery which had been set up in the former manor house closed in 1956. New housing estates have been built, a new school, and, with the closure of the railway, people now are more reliant than ever on the road.

Broughton 🌿

Broughton, on the A59 west of Skipton, is a farming community and owned by the Tempest family of Broughton Hall.

The Tempests have been associated with the village for the past 800 years. The Hall is open to the public on Bank Holidays and in June each year the grounds attracts thousands of people to the Game Fair devoted to all manner of country sport and pursuits. The gardens of the Hall are now a thriving garden centre and the stable block and Home Farm buildings have been converted into a business complex. Another of the farms on the estate is now an equestrian centre visited by members of the Royal Family. The Hall and its grounds are frequently used by film makers.

Until 1930 there was a working quarry in the area, the stone being taken away by train on the well known Settle line. There was also a mill which produced linen and when this ceased it was converted to make gas for the Hall. The village school closed in 1906.

Bulmer ✑

Bulmer, with a population of 160, is a farming village in the Howardian Hills overlooking the Vale of York. It lies two miles from the A64 road, 13 miles from York. Its buildings are often likened to those of the Cotswolds, with which it shares part of the same geological band of limestone.

The church of St Martin stands out as the oldest and most important building in the village. The Domesday Book tells us that people worshipped at 'Bolemere' over a thousand years ago, but that was in a different building. The effigy to Sir John Bulmer, Knight Templar, is one of the oldest in Yorkshire. He died in 1268.

The Slip inn stood opposite the church but this was closed by the Countess of Carlisle, a fervent abstainer. There is now no public house. Records show that a schoolmaster lived in Bulmer in 1823. The village school was founded in 1827 by the Carlisles and closed in 1947. This building is now the village hall and is the centre of many village activities. The Old Rectory, a fine old house and listed building, was built in the early 18th century.

There is still a village shop and post office and inasmuch as it still has eight farms Bulmer is still a working village. As it is now a designated conservation area and one of outstanding beauty, the properties recently built have to blend in with the older houses.

Because Bulmer is a breezy village standing at the top of a steep hill known as Bulmer Bank it is described by villagers as being 'a top coat colder' than its neighbouring village of Welburn.

Burn ✑

Burn is a small village on the A19 about three miles south of Selby. It has a population of about 450 inhabitants and has not grown much over the years.

A Wesleyan chapel was built in 1846 on land given by Mr W.

Webster, a local preacher, who had established a woodyard nearby in 1837. The woodyard is still a thriving business in the village, with the chapel being incorporated into the joiner's shop, where craftsmen still make handmade wares. Originally a steam engine was used to drive the saw for cutting the wood. In 1894 a Primitive Methodist chapel was built across the road and is still in use today. There were two blacksmith's shops in the village; the ruins of one can be found at the southern end of the village. The village had two public houses, the Shoulder of Mutton and the Wheatsheaf, the latter being the one remaining. In 1857 a plague struck the village, and deaths occurred in every house.

In 1940 Bells Wood and Hagg Bush Wood to the east of the village were chopped down to build an airfield, the 578 Squadron flying Halifax bombers from here from January 1944 to March 1945. An enormous number of bravery awards were gained from this small airfield. In 1983 the Burn Gliding Club moved onto the airfield and established their headquarters there.

In the will of Elizabeth Ashton in 1709 the sum of £3 was given to help the apprenticing of young people in Burn. This is still awarded today, along with vouchers for widows and the elderly from the Burn and Brayton Charities.

One of Burn's present day respected villagers is Mr Arthur Gregory, who along with his son breeds the famous Poplar Burn herd of pigs. He exports these famous pigs worldwide, as well as around Britain.

Burneston

An attractive village just off the A1, Burneston has a long history, going back to the days of coach travel when Oak Tree Farm was a recognised stopping place for travellers.

According to the census of 1891 there were three inns – the Farmers Arms, the Travellers Rest and the Woodman, but of these only the Woodman remains. There was a post office, two shops, two butchers, a blacksmith, a stonemason, a dressmaker, a schoolmistress, an organist, a draper, a nurseryman, an organist and verger, the vicar, a tailor and eleven farmers, out of a population of 253. They have all gone; there is now only a post office and general store and the butcher from a nearby village comes round twice a week. There are no market day buses now to take the wives to market with their baskets of eggs and butter and poultry.

A great deal of new building has taken place over the years, but part of the village is now a conservation area. This includes a row of six small cottages, Burneston Hall (once the vicarage) and the church. St Lambert's church is a very fine building which has been described as a mini-cathedral, with its high beamed roof and carvings. The earliest mention of a church on this site was in 1089 but the present church was started in 1390. The almshouses in The Square were originally built as a free grammar school and six dwellings known as the Hospice were founded in 1680 by Matthew Robinson BA, vicar of Burneston, and maintained by a charity trust he set up.

The old red telephone box has been retained even though it has a modern handset inside.

Burneston has had its share of sporting vicars in the past, the most famous being the Reverend J. T. Hartley, who became vicar in 1874.

A very keen tennis player, he won the Wimbledon final in 1879 and went on to successfully defend his title the following year.

Burniston 🦡

The Three Jolly Sailors wave a welcome to Burniston visitors approaching the village along the Scalby Road from Scarborough. In the time of Queen Victoria's Jubilee so much food was provided there for the children's party that they had to come back after school for a week to eat it up. In the bad winters of those times the snow reached the lintels outside the windows and two ghosts were seen in the back bar; Aloysius Tredegar, an old English gentleman was one and a little beggar boy with his trousers tied under his knees with string was the other. It was reported that neither of these ghosts was frightening and that they had been seen by many people.

Up the road from the 'Jollys' lived Mr and Mrs Chew. He was a blacksmith, a kindly man taken to wearing his wife's cardigans tight across his torso and adamant his house was 17th century. His wife was a great character and had a 'thing' about painting her house and surrounding fence in bright colours. Sometimes she used to tie a rope round the brass bedstead and then round her ample waist so she could lean out of an upstairs window and paint everything bright red. She housed five evacuees during the Second World War and they all went back to visit her.

Burniston had one Methodist church and one Baptist chapel. The Methodist is still going strong but the Baptist chapel was pulled down a few years ago, only to find the original water in the bath used for total immersion. The small gothic windows now grace a stone cottage beyond the village hall.

There were smugglers in Burniston and Cloughton during the early years of the villages, and a smuggling murder at 50 The High St in 1823, when William Mead shot James Law of Staintondale from the upstairs window of the cottage.

Quarrying for sandstone provided work for the locals, as did the lime kilns which can be seen round the villages, getting their lime from Suffield. This was mixed with coal and wood and burnt in the kilns leaving slaked lime for fertiliser.

Burnsall

Burnsall is a small village situated on a bend of the river Wharfe with the dramatic backdrop of Burnsall Fell. The village has 111 permanent residents and consists of 67 houses, two hotels, a general store cum post office and a cafe. The village has changed very little in the last century.

The oldest building in the village is thought to be the 12th century church. Before AD 700 a wooden building had been established by Wilfrid, who was the Bishop of York. Prior to his building the church he was reputed to have preached on a rock now known as St Wilfrid's Pulpit situated along the riverbank not far from the church. The only part of the original wooden church which still exists is the font, which is at the back of the church today.

Probably the most famous feature of the village is the bridge. It is said to be a typical Dales bridge with its five stone arches. The original bridge across the Wharfe at Burnsall, and the road connecting Burnsall to Appletreewick (his birthplace) were the gift of Sir William Craven. The foundations of the original bridge still remain but since then the strong waters of the Wharfe in flood have demolished the arches several times. The people have however always rallied round and rebuilt the bridge, not only out of necessity as the only other crossing places are a distance of three miles in either direction, but also out of affection for this impressive piece of architecture. It is from the bridge that the 'Classic Fell Race' starts every year on one of the last Saturdays in August.

Burnsall is very much an agricultural village, with most of the farm-land being owned and worked by three families; sheep and dairy cattle are the major elements, but some grass for silage and winter feed is also grown. As in many country areas tourism is also becoming a growth industry and is probably the second largest source of income.

Burrill-cum-Cowling

A five minute walk separates Cowling from the nearby village of Burrill. There is a 17th century manor house in Burrill and the houses stand along either side of the road, with the small Victorian church among them.

Cowling, with its half dozen dwellings, stands on the edge of the escarpment looking east across the Vale of Mowbray to the Hambleton Hills. On a clear day with the right light, the towers of York Minster, which is 45 miles away, can just be seen.

The village is said to have been a convent in medieval times and the Queen Anne hall is built on the remains of a much earlier construction. Across the road is a walled paddock with an old stone gateway at the top end. A pair of arched stone windows have been placed on top of the gateway so that they can just be seen over the brow of the hill. These are known as 'Dr Dodsworth's spectacles'.

In the early 19th century, Cowling was given to John Croft of Portugal (and port) by the Rev Dr Dodsworth. John Croft gave valuable help to Wellington during the Peninsular wars – spying on Napoleon's activities – and, upon his return to England, was made a baronet. He later moved to Kent, where the Crofts of Cowling still live.

Burton-in-Lonsdale

Burton-in-Lonsdale in the valley of the river Greta, a tributary of the river Lune, is dominated by the spire of All Saints' church, which stands beside the village green close to the Norman castle mound at the western end of High Street. Four streets form a rectangle on the northern valley side and are bordered by mainly 18th and 19th century cottages and houses built of sandstone.

The pottery industry developed in the 18th century using local clay and coal. The hummocks and hollows on the south side of the river, between Faccon Farm and Park Foot, are the remains of the coal and clay pits. The mine owners of the 18th century were the Foxcrofts of Halstead and in the 19th century, Thomas Hodgson of Greta Bank. Burton's potteries were family affairs centring round the master potter's home and the craft was handed down from father to son. Everyone from the master to the boys who turned the wheels, was in contact with every process, digging clay out of the hillside, bringing it home in the cart, refining it, 'throwing' it on the wheel, stacking the green or unfired pots on shelves and on flat tops of garden walls to dry, glazing, firing, and taking finished pots to market. Mass production from Staffordshire and the advent of the railways (Burton being off line of either the neighbouring routes), was the reason for the decline of the local industry. Richard Timperley Bateson, now in his nineties and still living in the village, closed the last Waterside Pottery in 1944.

A local benefactor, Richard Thornton, gave the schools and school houses. He died in 1865 leaving £2,800,000 beside valuable real estate, by far the largest fortune of the century to that date. His nephew, Thomas Thornton, joined him in business and inherited a large part of his estate and it was he who built All Saints' church on the site of his and his uncle's birthplace.

Burton Leonard

The village of Burton Leonard nestles between the Great North Road (A1) and the busy Harrogate to Ripon road (A61). The holly trees found on either side of the road approaching the village are reputed to have been planted by the monks of Fountains Abbey, who traded with the village during the 14th and 15th centuries.

On reaching the village, one looks down onto the first of its three village greens. In 1926, all the greens were purchased by the village from the Duchy of Lancaster 'for the sum of five pounds'.

The village church is the third church on the present site. The first St Leonard's church dated back to 1220 and lasted over 500 years until it 'fell down' around the year 1780. In 1878 the present church was built, thanks to the generosity of James Brown of Copgrove Hall.

The Methodist chapel is found on the north side of the Low Green. There have been three chapels in the village, the first, built at the turn of the 19th century, was for the Wesleyan Methodists. This eventually became the village smithy around the year 1870, and the building can still be seen on the right as one leaves the village on the road to Copgrove. The village school, which lies on the south side of the High Green, was built around the year 1815.

On the southern edge of the parish boundary is one of the old lime quarries, now taken over by the Yorkshire Wildlife Trust, which has listed over 200 different species of plants in the quarry area.

Up to the end of the 19th century the village boasted three public houses – the Royal Oak, the Hare and Hounds and the Crown. Before the days of trains and motor travel, the Crown inn provided stabling and feed for horses and accommodation for the weary traveller. The Crown is now a nursing home, but the other two pubs continue to provide a meeting place for villagers.

Byland 🌿

A community of Cistercian monks established themselves at the abbey here in 1177. They were able farmers, clearing, draining and cultivating the rough ground and developing the wool trade with their flocks of nearly 8,000 on the great sheep runs of the north country. It was the centre of importance and activity in the area until the Dissolution of the Monasteries in 1538, when there were 25 monks besides the abbot.

The site was granted to Sir William Pickering in 1540 and came eventually to the Wombwells (of nearby Newburgh Priory). In 1924 it passed into the care of the Ministry of Works. The now ruined abbey has a particularly splendid west front with a great rose window 26 ft across, half of which still remains.

Today only an inn, two farms, a house and two cottages remain near Byland Abbey. Abbey House was a timber yard and then a dairy farm. A few years ago it had another wing built on and it is now a private house. The inn was a typical country inn with the cellars still in use until 1987, when it was modernised and enlarged.

Calcutt 🌿

Calcutt, which lies on the outskirts of Knaresborough, includes Blands Hill, Thistle Hill and Forest Moor Road in its environment.

Blands Hill starts at the bridge over the river Nidd where there is the Mother Shipton inn and the entrance to the Long Walk, the petrifying well and the cave where the prophetess Mother Shipton lived in the 15th century. Off Blands Hill is a lane called Spitalcroft – once the site of a hospital, possibly a leper colony.

Formerly there was a row of old weavers' cottages in Calcutt; some were back-to-back, some had cellars, all had communal toilets and cobbled yards. They were pulled down some years ago and the occupants rehoused in Knaresborough. By contrast there is now Whiteway Head, an estate of modern detached houses and bungalows built on land formerly farmed by Jimmy Proctor, our jovial milkman.

There used to be a mission church in Calcutt, belonging to Holy Trinity church. This ceased to be used in the 1970s and is now a private house. Next door is the Union inn, also drastically changed over the years. Behind is the cricket field, used first by Calcutt Cricket Club, latterly by Knaresborough Forest Cricket Club. It is a pleasant venue in summer, situated in a field which runs down to the river.

Thistle Hill is best known for its hospital. This was an isolation hospital for infectious diseases, particularly diptheria which claimed many young lives. Fortunately immunisation wiped out the disease and the hospital now has been modernised and is a private nursing home. The southern bypass will cross the top part of Thistle Hill on its way to join the A1. This will pass through part of Birkham Wood, much to the disapproval of conservationists.

A little white house on Forest Moor Road is reputed to have been the home of Blind Jack of Knaresborough – Jack Metcalf – a giant of a man who became very famous as a builder of roads although he had been blind since childhood.

Caldbergh 🌿

Four miles beyond Middleham, on the way to Kettlewell, lies the hamlet of Caldbergh – 'Cold Hill'. Mentioned in the Domesday Book of 1086, it is situated 800 ft up on the south side of the river Cover.

In one direction it looks across Coverdale Pen Hill, while behind it Flamstone Pin dominates the landscape. On one slope of the Pin is Castle Stead, the site of an Iron Age fort. In the 19th century there was a flourishing mining industry on the moors above Caldbergh, and the population was much larger than it is today. Now consisting of 15 houses of varying sizes, it has 24 people in permanent residence, with a sprinkling of visitors through the summer months, occupying the three holiday cottages. Being so small it has neither shop, school, church nor public house.

In the past it supported five farms, but these have now been incorporated into two – Ings and Manor Farm. The latter, bearing the date 1686 over its back door, is reputed to have been the birthplace of Dr Miles Coverdale, Bishop of Exeter, who translated the Bible into English in 1535 – so it is obvious that the present farmhouse stands on the site of one much older.

The rambler, turning up the lane from the main road, will find himself through the village in a matter of minutes, and at the top of the hill facing the gate which leads to Caldbergh pasture and the open moorland beyond. Just inside the gate, looking to the right, are several small tombstones, each marking the grave of a pet cat or dog.

Behind Caldbergh, Uffas Gill runs down from the moor, and falls in a deep sided bed to the river Cover. It passes under a modern bridge, built in 1933, making redundant the old pack bridge which went out of use when the road was straightened.

Camblesforth & Drax

Camblesforth is on the A1041 trunk road, five miles south of Selby, and is in the ecclesiastical parish of Drax. Both villages are mentioned in the Domesday Book.

Camblesforth Hall, built in the early 1700s, replaced a former Elizabethan house. A great deal of lead taken from the previous house shows the outline of varying types of footwear and several hands traced out by a sharp instrument. The footwear is of different types, one being of the 15th century with a long pointed toe whilst another is of Puritan shape – mid 17th century.

The Comus inn is thought to be the only one in the British Isles with that name. The name Comus is derived from the son of Bacchus, the Greek god of wine.

From being little more than a hamlet of 30 years ago, Camblesforth has grown up into quite a large village including four shops and a post office. The Methodist chapel built in the 19th century is still used today. Situated on land which was formerly Camblesforth Grange, there is one of the largest glasshouse complexes in the United Kingdom, growing a variety of salad crops, which also provides employment for local people.

Drax is situated near the river Ouse. Its old name was Ealdedrege, meaning a portage, a place where boats were dragged overland or pulled out of the water.

The parish church of St Peter and St Paul dates back before 1086. It has a Saxon christening font and 15th century bench ends. The Augustinian priory of St Nicholas Drax was founded between 1130 and 1139. Slight remains are still in evidence today.

The famous Read grammar school is also part of Drax history, founded by Charles Read in 1667. The Charles Read Foundation Trust built schools in Camblesforth and Drax in the 19th century.

Drax castle was destroyed in the 12th century and all that remains is a wooded mound; a farm bears the name Castle Hill Farm.

In 1973 a new primary school was built in Camblesforth when the village started to grow due to the building of Drax power station, the largest coal fired station in Europe. It has a chimney of 860 ft which overshadows both villages.

Carleton in Craven

Carleton lies at the foot of Pinhaw, with Ramshaw, Sharpshaw and Rombalds Moor around it – Pennine hills with ancient names. The beck comes down from Pinhaw, the oldest houses and traces of past industry at its edge, winding through the village to join the river Aire a quarter mile away. The Aire prevents Skipton's encroachment, it floods easily.

The church of St Mary stands on a slight rise, hallowed ground since the 12th century. This latest building, dated 1858, has many attractive features, one of which is the unique clock made by a village workman, Billy Cryer. It has only seven pieces; a 30 ft long pendulum hangs inside the tower, swinging softly and eerily in the gloom of the belfry, but it keeps good time. With a good congregation and a sense of community, no longer is there intense rivalry between church and chapel.

A dominant feature of Carleton is the large Victorian building which the Slingsby family put up, where raw cotton was carded and spun. Across the road was an older mill where weavers and winders worked when handloom weaving ended. Now, a new modern housing estate covers the foundations of the older mill and expensive carpeting is woven in the remaining building. Once the beck provided three dams for the steam-powered machinery and the road rang beneath the clogs of the large proportion of the population who worked there.

Opposite the Swan is the tithe barn, destroyed by marauding Scots in the 14th century but rebuilt more than once. It has passed from its original use to an infants school and now to village hall, modernised inside but with wide mullioned windows facing the street.

The village is lucky to have a post office with grocery and greengrocery, a corner shop with an off-licence, a butcher and a newsagent. Elizabeth Wilkinson first endowed the Church of England school in 1709, and Ferrand Spence of London founded almshouses for twelve old ladies in 1698. Now, eight persons inhabit Spence's Court, plus a warden, and the peaceful old courtyard makes a perfect background for carols by candlelight at Christmas.

Carlton Towers, family home of the Duke of Norfolk

Carlton 🐦

The village of Carlton lies six miles south of Selby on the A1041 and is the southernmost point of North Yorkshire, being separated from the town of Snaith by the river Aire.

Carlton Towers is the family home of the present Duke of Norfolk, and seat of the Stapleton and Beaumont families. The Towers and grounds are open to the public, and it is a noted example of a Victorian family home.

The Stapleton family have always been Roman Catholic, and the Duke of Norfolk is the country's premier Catholic Duke, so the influence of the family and Catholicism is evident throughout the village. Carlton's Roman Catholic church was built using money from the Stapleton family and completed in 1842, and nearby was a convent school run by nuns.

A noteworthy house in the village is Chestnut Croft. Thwarted in his desire to buy Carlton Towers when it was briefly offered for sale, George Stubley, a wealthy mill owner, commissioned the building of this house, intending as near as possible to emulate the landed gentry. Chestnut Croft is positioned in such a way that it commands views in both directions along the main road and has a lodge, stables and a sweeping front drive.

Until the late 18th century Carlton was a very small village surrounded by marshes. In the 1770s Thomas Stapleton built up the banks of the river Aire so as to replace the existing ferry service by a toll bridge: for this he used land from his own estate, thus building himself an ornamental pond at little expense. The village was then able to develop in areas which had previously been subject to regular flooding. The growth stabilised until the late 1960s when Eggborough and Drax power stations were built, and later the Selby coalfield was developed. Carlton then became the home for many of the workers there. Once an exclusively agricultural area, farmworkers now live side by side with industrial workers.

Carlton-in-Cleveland 🎕

You will find Carlton-in-Cleveland tucked away beneath the Cleveland Hills, south of the market town of Stokesley, just off the A172.

Its houses in the main straddle Alum Beck which meanders down through the village over cobbled ford and under bridges of stone.

Sandstone and hand made brick have been the dominant house building materials with roofs of pantile, some of slate. Barely two dwellings are alike and though time and style have wrought many changes, the facades, roof lines, windows, doors and ubiquitous extensions knit well together to form a pleasing hamlet. Over the years the character of Carlton, whether by chance, good design or hidden boundary impositions of the 'conservation area', has mellowed and matured and appears comfortable within its unchanged landscape.

Though the elegant Busby Hall, home of the Marwoods since its building in the mid 1700s, lies in its sloping parkland on the perimeter of Carlton, the village's own 'big house' is the Manor House. Built by John Prissick the owner of the local alum works in 1707, it is a solid looking residence in the Queen Anne style and is reputed to have its very own wandering ghost. Falling into disrepair, the manor became a sorry sight until reprieved by new owners in 1987. After substantial restoration work it now stands, as in its former glory, lived in and just a bit aloof from the rest of the village.

The Methodist Chapel is near one end, St Botolphs Church of England at the other, both with active congregations. Canon Kyle, the colourful clergyman in Carlton's history, helped to fund the village school which today resounds with the energies of over 50 children.

There is a village blacksmith opposite the post office cum shop, where agricultural and decorative material glows and clanks in the cluttered workshop. Behind the primary shcool is the Outdoor Centre which invariably has upwards of 75 children in residence from the County of Cleveland. These children in orange cagoules, like some curious caterpillar, weave around the village stopping now and then to savour some rural tit-bit.

The Blackwell Ox pub, named after a weighty shorthorn bull bred near Darlington, stands overlooking the green. The Watson Scout Centre lies on the west side of the village in what used to be the original Manor House.

Much has changed in most villages with many becoming dormant museums or musing dormitories, but not Carlton; not yet anyway. Carlton is still a working village with its constituent parts meshing well together. Church Farm has witnessed village transitions first hand and amongst other things has produced and delivered milk to the village folk for about 75 years.

Carlton is a regular start and finish point for ramblers with many clearly signed footpaths criss-crossing the parish. The popular long distance walks of the Cleveland Way and the Lyke Wake Walk skirt the hills above Carlton Bank. Some visitors will notice that two benches were acquired when Carlton-in-Cleveland was adjudged the 'best kept village in forest and vale' in 1981 and 1990.

Carlton in Coverdale 🌿

On a slope of Penhill about 900 ft above sea level, the houses of Carlton line either side of a mile long street. It is the largest village in the dale. The oldest building in the village is the barn of Old Hall Farm, with a dated door-head inscribed 'WFS 1659'.

Three Bronze Age barrows are to be found off the village street, the largest behind the Forester's Arms, the second in the garden of Manor House Farm, and the third in a field at Town Head on the left as the road turns to leave the village. At one time elm trees were planted on them and under the tree in the garden at Manor House people used to sit and smoke their pipes on summer evenings, but they are very much decayed now.

One of the old families in the village is the Constantine family and one residence had been occupied by a Constantine without a break for over 300 years. One of the best known was Harry Constantine who was a poet, known as The Coverdale Bard. He founded the Constantine Charity and the benefits from funds set aside for this charity are still distributed.

The biennial walk of the Coverdale Foresters' Friendly Society takes place in the second week of June on a Wednesday. This society was originally formed in 1816 as the Banks of the Cover Branch of the Ancient Order of Foresters. Later the branch broke away, but some Foresters in the procession still wear the traditional green coats and peaked hats and black belts, and the rest wear green sashes, while some carry staves.

There are people living in Carlton who can remember when the village had a cobbler's shop, a blacksmith and tailor, a butcher, barber, two petrol pumps, two joiners and two general stores, as well as the village post office and general store which has been run by the same family since 1901!

Carlton Miniott 🌿

Carlton Miniott is situated on the A61 Thirsk–Ripon road and stretches for two miles from Thirsk station to Busby Stoop.

The remaining pump is outside Pump House. Most houses owned a pump until water from Boltby was piped to the village about 80 years ago. Then there were four roadside taps and you paid rent for a key.

The Wesleyan Methodists built their chapel in 1838 and when the old stalwarts departed it became the Hambleton Evangelical church in 1976. The parish church of St Lawrence is of red brick and replaced the original church in 1896. Two mice can be found, carved into the oak lychgate, erected by Robert Thompson of Kilburn. The original village school and adjoining schoolmaster's house, both with latticed windows, were built in 1849. They are now the church rooms. The Dog and Gun, now modernised, stands opposite in Church Square. The village shop used to be next door.

When war looked imminent in 1938, farmland to the south side of the village was sold to build Topcliffe Aerodrome. This brought different employment and an influx of airmen. Villagers became accustomed to the drone of Whitley and Halifax bombers taking off for their night time raids on the Continent. In 1973 Topcliffe Aerodrome became Allanbrooke Barracks, and now helicopters cross the roof tops.

In 1848 a line from Thirsk to Leeds was opened, and it became known as Thirsk Junction. There was an impressive station with 380 people on the pay roll. Either side of the railway were the Old Red House and the Railway inn, built for workmen and rail travellers. Now the latter is the Vale of York, both are modernised and specialise in catering. Malt kilns next to the station, where farmers brought their grain to be roasted, were closed down. A creditable coversion to a furniture factory was made, and is now known as Treske – the ancient name for Thirsk.

Carperby 🐾

Carperby is a linear village halfway between Hawes and Leyburn, north of the river Ure.

At the west end is the green with a Jubilee Tree and plaque dated 1897; also a market cross with a tapered shaft set on seven square steps dated 1674. Records show that a 14th century market fell into disuse when the Askrigg market took over in 1587 though it appears that a market restarted in the 17th century.

It is said that in the days when cows calved only in spring, the villagers collectively owned three bulls. To this day the parish land is called Bull Lands and Bull Tussocks. Rather than keep all three bulls over winter, the eldest was killed in November and roasted for the whole village to share – the only red meat some had the chance to eat.

There are two wells in the village. At the east end, St James' runs continually. Near the green, St Matthew's Well, with elaborate stone surround dated 1867, gave water until 1975.

Stone and flags were quarried from hills to the north, and peat cut for use by villagers. Traditionally any person 'who put up a smoke in Carperby village' had sporting rights in Freeholders' Wood to the south, as well as the right to collect wood from October to March.

Many present residents attended the village school, which finally closed its doors in July 1962, after serving the village for 100 years. Unlike some villages, community spirit remains. The annual children's sports and village tea is still held; carols and Christmas readings are popular events; badminton, darts, billiards, snooker and carpet bowls are well supported and the football team flourishes. Despite no shop, limited transport and restricted post office service a thriving happy community remains.

Carthorpe ✍

Carthorpe lies approximately four miles south-east of Bedale and three quarters of a mile from the A1 as the crow flies. It is a linear village, mainly of brick-built cottages with one or two stone-built ones.

Just out of the village is an area known as Howe Hill. This is said to have been a Celtic settlement and three skeletons were found here, a man woman and child, as well as pottery and some jewellery, now in the Victoria & Albert museum.

To the south-east of the village is Camp Hill, which was a large estate with a number of farms in former times. It belonged to the Serjentson family, who built in the village and supported a public school; this is now a private residence but the school motto is still on the end of the schoolroom.

There have been a number of chapels in the village. At the east end, which is known as Hall Garth, there was a Saxon chapel but when last recorded in 1888 there was only a shell remaining and it was being used as a cattle shed. At the west end there was the Primitive Methodist chapel; this was sold and later used as a pig sty but the foundation stone for this chapel is now set into a garden wall. The school room was built as a chapel in 1805 and extended in 1808, and this building is used for all village activities. In 1895 a piece of land was purchased and yet another chapel built. This was extended in 1958, services are held here every Sunday and it is also used for weddings and funerals.

To the north-west of the village is Carthorpe Mires. This is a rather wet area and is now all farm land. There was once a thriving brick and tile works at Brickyard Farm but now there is only a very large lake which is used by a private fishing club. Some of the last tiles made there were used to pipe in a drain from Burneston churchyard. There was another brickmaker's at the other side of the village and it also has a lake.

The village show was re-formed in 1979 and has flourished ever since. It was originally called The Cottage Garden Improvement Society and many years ago they had classes for garden produce, dairy produce, the best turned out harness, the most butterflies in a jar and, one which went on all the year round, the most rat tails!

Castle Bolton 🖾

Castle Bolton stands higher on the hillside, in mid Wensleydale, than its neighbour Redmire, a short distance below. The castle has dominated the scene for 600 years. Now floodlit in the evenings, it dominates the darkness, too.

It was in 1379 that Sir Richard Scrope gained permission to fortify his manor house at Bolton. Stone could be quarried nearby, but timber for the great oak beams was not available here and most of it was carried from the Lake District. Eighteen years later the castle was complete. It was a siege by Cromwell's army that made the castle uninhabitable as it is today, but it is being partly restored with the help of English Heritage.

To the west of the castle there is a wide expanse of land which clearly shows, in a number of fields, the well preserved strips of medieval farming. These are particularly well seen between Redmire and Carperby.

In the 19th century, and later, there were still numerous people in the village with tiny holdings of land, who called themselves cowkeepers, but gradually these holdings were amalgamated, until, in the actual village, there are only two farms.

In Victorian times there was a woman coal merchant in the village, one Bella Jackson, who travelled regularly, with donkey and cart, to the pits of the North-East to bring the village's coal supplies. Then the population was over 300; today's population numbers only about 45 people.

The church is dedicated to St Oswald and dates from about 1250. Simplicity is its keynote. That the church was built before the castle is clear from the little sundial in the south wall, where the noonday sun can never reach it.

The village has never been busier than it is today, but when the tourists have gone home it is very quiet. The children, few in number, go to schools in Leyburn, and most of the older people are retired.

Castleton, Danby, Westerdale & Commondale 🖾

Castleton stands on a ridge dominating the valley with various high dales radiating from it. The oldest part of the village is built of stout stone and still retains its charm. Originally it was the key village of the area, being the commercial and trading centre for the surrounding settlements. It still retains this position, having a number of shops.

Every October from the late 1800s the village hosted an annual cheese fair when the whole of the High Street was lined with cheese wagons. The fair indicated the importance of cheese production in the area, most of the local farmers producing an average of two tons a year.

Hawthorne Cottage in the High Street which presently houses the local bank was where the 'Hand of Glory' was found. This is a human hand said to be taken from the right arm of someone who died on the gibbet. It would have been cured in saltpetre and pepper for a few weeks and then dried. A special candle would be made to sit inside the hand which would then be ready for use by whichever burglar happened to own it. Such a hand was thought to have magical powers, in that upon entering a house with the lighted candle the burglar would ensure that any people in the dwelling remained asleep and could not awaken due to the hand's magic spell. To break the spell the candle had to be extinguished with either blood or skimmed milk. The hand is now on display in the Whitby Museum.

The ancient village of Danby was built by Danish settlers. Danby old parish church stands in the middle of the dale close to where it is thought the original wooden village stood. It is believed the church is built of stone from the old fortress at Castleton.

The watermill in Danby has recently been restored by the present owners and stoneground flour is once more for sale. In the early 1900s Mr Petlar charged one penny a stone for grinding! Danby also has two inns, the Duke of Wellington and the Fox and Hounds which is the oldest in the area dating back to 1555.

High on Westerdale Moor are the remains of an Iron Age settlement with a circular enclosure on the summit. Folk lore abounds about battles fought in this area, known locally as Crown End, some 2,000 years ago between the Romans and Ancient Britons. Westerdale used to be a more thriving community than it is at present and there were two inns, the Horse Shoe and the Crown, both now gone.

On the northern margin of the village is the imposing Westerdale Hall built in the Scottish country-house style in the 1840s, and used during the shooting season by the Feversham estate.

Commondale is a small hamlet connected by rail and road to Castleton and Danby. It is a quiet place now with very few facilities but that was not always the case.

A bleach mill was built in 1753 and situated on the Commondale beck. Weaving from the parishes of Danby, Westerdale and Commondale were sent to be bleached there until 1850. During the building of the railway in 1861 the building on the mill site was used as a public house and called the Diving Duck. The railway linked the village to Cleveland and helped the rapid development of the local brickworks founded by John Pratt. It became the Commondale Pottery until it closed in 1947. The domestic pottery has now become very collectable. The site is now a scout camp under the name of Ravensgill after the beck which runs through down to the village.

Commondale still retains its ancient pannier tracks leading up the steep bank to the moor towards White Cross, passing the school which is no longer used. Smugglers conveyed their contraband from the coast along this path to Gin Garth where it was stored before being distributed.

Catterick ✒

Mention Catterick to most people and immediately they think of Catterick Garrison, the large army camp which lies some four miles from the village. Since the Romans built the fortified town of Cataractonium, right to modern times when, in 1911, the area was recommended by Baden-Powell as the site of a military camp, the village of Catterick has had a history very much tied to the military.

Situated on the old Great North Road, the picturesque village boasts three village greens – Low Green surrounded by houses and two pubs and through which flows Sour beck, High Green above the village on a level with the parish church, and High Street Green (now much reduced) still showing the site of one of the many village water pumps.

The beautiful 15th century parish church of St Anne sits on a high knoll in the village. Usually churches of this size were financed by Royalty but in the case of St Anne's, the funds were provided by Catherine de Burgh and her son, William. The family had risen from peasants to great landowners in just three generations and after building the nearby Brough Hall, financed the building of the church in the village.

The school is housed in a modern building behind the High Street and it is named after the man who first provided for a free school in the village. He also provided from his will six almshouses for deserving widows from the locality. This was Michael Syddall, only one of many well known vicars in Catterick. In fact, through one other vicar, Catterick has a connection with the Navy. The man in whose arms Nelson died at Trafalgar was Dr Scott who, 14 years later, was appointed Vicar of Catterick.

Cawood ✒

Cawood nestles by the Yorkshire Ouse close to its junction with the Wharfe. Early in its history Cawood belonged to the Archbishops of York, being the site of one of their palaces.

In some ways Cawood gives the impression that it ought to be by the sea, with inn names like the Jolly Sailor, the Anchor and the Ferry, but these reflect Cawood's past importance as a port on the Ouse. Boat building was once a feature, but this is now confined to nearby Selby. The ferry played an important part in village life until a bridge was built at the end of the 19th century.

From early in its history Cawood seems to have had a wealth of inns. At one time in the 19th century there were in the region of a dozen! There are still at least eight, which for a population of under 2,000 is generous to say the least. There are still tangible links with the past in that the gatehouse of the palace (usually referred to as Cawood Castle) and a

15th century building, known locally as the banqueting hall, can be seen. The Castle Garth is preserved as an ancient monument, providing a large open space in the centre of the village. Cawood also contains some outstanding examples of buildings with Dutch gables, which are unique to this area. They date from the end of the 1600s.

The Ouse provides a sometimes dramatic backdrop to the church of All Saints. Despite being on the bank of the river, it is built on the highest point in the village, just over 29 ft above sea level.

Originally the area was mainly given to agriculture, particularly market gardening and although this continues, the Selby coalfield and the power stations at Drax and Eggborough are now major employers.

Cayton 🦡

Cayton village lies midway between the seaside towns of Scarborough and Filey and is half a mile off the coast road, the A165, at Cayton Bay.

In the late 1930s Cayton had a closely-knit community of just under 800 people, with houses and cottages built mainly on each side of the main street. Scarborough was four miles away and as there was only a very infrequent bus service the two butchers, the fish and chip shop, the two small general stores and Gerry Agar's shop and post office did very good business, especially the latter as he sold everything from a gobstopper to a pair of wellingtons, and if he did not have what you wanted he would get it for you.

The beautiful little Norman church of St John the Baptist, built in the 12th century, is just off the main street and next to the Blacksmith's Arms public house; the tower and chancel were added in the 15th century. The church is also the parish church of Osgodby.

The trains do not stop at Cayton now, but at the beginning of the century Farmer Stubbs would regularly leave his farm on his horse to go to the station on the first stage of his journey to Ireland to buy cattle. Everyone seeing his horse walking on its own through the village knew where its master had gone. The cattle would be brought back to his farm and eventually end up in his butcher's shop.

The village has trebled in size since the late 1950s as people have come from the West Riding of Yorkshire to retire by the seaside. A new industrial estate has been built nearby bringing much needed employment, so young couples have bought houses on the new estates to be near their employment. This has given a good mixed community. On the outskirts of the village are a number of holiday caravan camps which have been established due to the beautiful golden sands at Cayton Bay.

Church Fenton
with Little Fenton 🍃

As the name suggests this flat, fertile area in the Vale of York was once fenland, later enclosed, and is consequently laced by man-made dykes and drains. A Neolithic axe dated about 2000 BC was found at Church Fenton but earliest references to a settlement are 10th century. The Domesday survey of 1086 records that Fenton was part of the land of Ilbert de Lasey, a Norman knight. The remains of a medieval moat can be seen at the Manor Farm.

One of the smallest cruciform churches in the country, St Mary the Virgin is originally 13th century, mainly late Perpendicular in style, with a 15th century tower. Parish records commenced in 1627.

The village was mainly agricultural until the arrival of the railway in 1839. Industry was then attracted to the village – the brick and tile works down Sandwich Lane, and then in the early 1920s, Firth-Blakely's gasholder and tankworks which employed approximately 500 men. Chicory used in bottled coffee preservation was grown and seasonal work was done by Irish workers who picked and boiled the chicory (c1853). A small row of terrace houses bears the name of Chicory Row. Farm produce, especially rhubarb, and live animals were sent to market by rail.

The Royal Air Force Church Fenton, actually in the parish of Ulleskelf, was constructed in 1936 and, during the Second World War was involved in the defence of the east coast and inland towns. A set of traffic lights on Busk Lane are intermittently used by the RAF as planes are taking off and landing. Drivers resist the impulse to 'duck' as aircraft approach! The tower of St Mary's church is fitted with red warning lights to assist trainee pilots during night flying exercises.

The village stores closed in 1990 after being in use for about 100 years. This leaves only the post office cum newsagents. While many villagers commute to work, Church Fenton provides work in agriculture (particularly arable and pigs), horticulture, chipboard manufacture and the recycling of aluminium waste. The three public houses also provide employment and some civilians are employed by the RAF.

Clapham 🍃

The largest building in Clapham is Ingleborough Hall, the home of the Farrer family for almost 150 years, and in latter years an outdoor education centre. Reginald Farrer, the internationally renowned botanist, introduced many new plants to Britain, some of which remain in the older gardens of the village and in the grounds of Ingleborough Hall. The

Reginald Farrer Nature Trail leads from the village to Ingleborough Cave.

Clapham was an Anglo-Saxon village, the early church thought to have been destroyed by the Scots during their 1318–19 invasion. A new church was built, of which the tower still remains as part of the present church building. Clapham lies on the flank of Ingleborough, one of the famous Three Peaks, from where the village stream gathers, flowing into Gaping Gill – a huge pot hole, the main shaft of which is 340 ft deep. Ingleborough Cave is linked to this system. A show cave, it is dry and well lit to show the many fantastic and beautiful formations, giving an insight into the underground world which exists beneath the mountains. Since the Cave Rescue Organisation was formed in 1935, the unit based in the village has been able to claim credit for more than a thousand rescues.

Seven acres of land are covered by the lake, which holds over 48 million gallons of water and was created by the Farrer family between 1828–32. The waterfall near the church is the overflow from the lake. At the bottom of the fall is a turbine which provided power for the village at one time, and indeed Clapham is the first village to have had street lighting. The lake provided water for the village and for outlying farms for many years. Michael Faraday, the distinguished 19th century scientist, was the son of the village blacksmith.

The National Park Information Centre is situated in the old manor house, which was built in 1701 and converted into a Reading Room in 1790.

Many houses have pigeon holes set in the gable ends, a reminder of an important source of food in years gone by.

Claxton ❧

Claxton is situated just off the main York to Scarborough road, about eight miles north of York, and has a population of about 200. The main street is an old Roman road leading to a crossing over the river Derwent.

Claxton Hall was sold in the 1980s and while empty it was destroyed by fire. The site now houses a factory and some very large modern houses. Claxton Grange which was the home farm for the Hall, was sold by the Church Commissioners and is now a complex of holiday cottages built to blend in with the old farm and buildings.

The village shop once had six assistants, and sold a wide range of goods – groceries, clothes, household goods, farm feeds and paraffin to mention just a few. These were delivered around the villages and isolated farms. The shop closed in 1987 and is now a cafe which opens during the summer months.

The estate had its own brickyard, which at the turn of the century was using a small hand plant, with one down draught kiln, and using local clay. In 1920 the Walker estate leased the brickyard. The new tenant put in modern plant and an 18-chamber Hoffman kiln which could produce over 100,000 bricks a week to supply the demand for new houses. About 35 men worked there until the plant stopped production in 1931 when the bricks were condemned because of the high content of lime in the clay.

The ponds which remained where the clay had been dug out are now used by anglers, and because the ponds are some way from the nearest habitation, they and the surrounding mature and young trees are a haven for a variety of birds. The village pond in the centre of the village was filled in during the 1940s and a small village green created. Plants and trees have been planted there.

There are scattered working farms, but none actually in the village now; and only two men from the village now work on the land.

Cliffe-cum-Lund 🙝

The village of Cliffe, situated four miles east of Selby, is bisected by the A63. It encompasses the village of South Duffield and the hamlet of Lund. It is of Norse origin (Klief), being a small settlement on the banks of the Ouse.

Turnham Hall occupies the site of a moated house dating from Richard I. The listed building Top End House, now a home and a business, used to be the Plough & Ship inn.

The last public hanging in England was carried out at York on Frederick Parker. He was travelling home after his release from Beverley Gaol in the company of Daniel Driscol of Tottenham. When he reached Cliffe he murdered Driscol for his silver watch. He was a Hemingbrough man and his victim is buried in the churchyard. An 85 year old Cliffe resident can remember an eye-witness account of the hanging related to him by someone who had been a young man of 20 and had walked to York to see the hanging.

There is evidence that there was some form of education in Cliffe as early as 1619, and later a school and schoolhouse was built for the benefit of the poor children of Cliffe as a result of the Mary Waud bequest of 1708.

Around 1883 the first Cliffe Cricket Club was formed. In 1922 Jennings Tune took all ten wickets for no runs. A few years ago his achievement was entered into the Guinness Book of Records at the instigation of Mr 'Sandy' Jacques. Mr Jacques is now in his eighties and is the oldest owner of a Yorkshire Cap. It is mainly due to the cricket club's struggles to find a field that a village eventually purchased land for a playing field for cricket and football with swings for the children.

In the past the village supported two splendid Methodist chapels and a wooden mission hut, an off-shoot of St Mary's, Hemingbrough. The mission is now an attractive brick building, built a few years ago after the wooden hut eventually succumbed to severe gales. The chapels alas are now put to other uses.

Cloughton 🦊

Cloughton, or Clotune as it once was called when in the manor of Walsgrave, lies on the junction of the Ravenscar and Whitby roads. It is on the edge of the moors and follows Burniston on the road to Whitby. After Cloughton there are the Duchy of Lancaster forests, the heather clad moors and the sea. Sometimes deer can be seen running across the road and badgers have their setts alongside.

High above the village is the old sandstone quarry which produced stone for Scarborough Castle and no doubt for the small Victorian church of St Mary. There is a delightful lychgate donated after the death of Sir Frank Lockwood, who lived at Cober Hill, a big red brick mansion diagonally opposite the post office that is now a guest house. He was a Solicitor General and a contributor to *Punch*. He must have enjoyed the walk to the sea from his back door through the fields edged with drystone walls.

In the church there is a tablet to Mr and Mrs Bower. It says, 'Near this place the bodys of Mr W. Bower of Clowton and Priscilla his wife, lye interred, They lived together in wedlock lovingly and comfortably seventy and three years. They hospitably entertained friends and neighbours at their house, did much good whilst living and dyed much lamented by the neighbourhood. He died in August 1698 in his 96th year of his age and she lived until Oct. 1699 in her 91st year. They live well who love well and they dye well who live well.'

Cloughton railway station must have been a picture, winning many prizes for being the best kept station. Even now the roses are abundant and the hedgerows along the side of the track to Ravenscar are full of berries and wild flowers. It isn't until one lives in Cloughton that appreciation for it grows and there comes a time when no one wants to leave it.

Coneythorpe with Clareton 🦊

Clareton, mentioned in the Domesday Book, has only two houses left; both are inhabited, one a farmhouse, the other a farm worker's cottage.

Coneythorpe, its population under 100, sleeps just down the hill, five minutes walk away. It lies at the side of the A1, 15 miles from York and five miles from Knaresborough. Some 25 years ago there were five farms and a few farm workers' cottages fringing the green. The Tiger inn is still there and the old pump, now restored, which was once the only source of water for the village people. Many new houses have been built and are mostly owned by commuters, while all the farm cottages are now beautifully restored and sold. The farms have been swallowed up and now only two remain.

In 1283, the Mowbray and Stourtons owned the mansion house of Allerton Mauleverer, known as Allerton Park just over the A1. It stands in a huge deer park that once teemed with game; now there are just a few, but their hoof marks can be seen in the cold snows of winter.

Lord Mowbray and Stourton owned the two villages, all the farms, the Tiger too and all of the surrounding lands until everything was sold in the 1960s to pay death duties. The amount realised was no more than £120,000, then a fortune. The mansion house, a beautiful wood panelled house, had been left to fall into a bad state of repair, but now it has been lovingly restored to its former glory.

Coniston Cold 🦢

Coniston Cold is a small village roughly mid-way between the market towns of Skipton-in-Craven and Settle. It is situated on the busy A65 road which is the old road to the Lake District.

The Garforth family came to Coniston in the early 19th century and built the present church, dedicated to St Peter, in 1846. It has a three tier pulpit and a very high steeple, on the top of which is a weathercock and a very precious clock made by James Harrison of Hull in 1845, only four of which remain out of 14 known to have existed.

Unfortunately, owing to neglect, the old Hall had to be demolished in 1969 and a new one was built. This is an outstanding feature of the village set in beautiful wooded grounds and overlooks a 24 acre lake, an ideal haven for swans, geese, ducks and other wild fowl.

The church of St Peter is now a united benefice with the church at Kirkby Malham and the old vicarage has been converted into two houses. A flight of stone steps on the outside of one of these can be seen from the road and it is said that John Wesley preached from the top of these when he was travelling around the country.

Coniston Cold does not possess a shop or post office now. The latter, which had been in the occupation of one family since its inauguration, closed in 1979. This building used to be a coaching inn, as was Church Close Farm which is across the road. One interesting feature of the old post office, which was named 'The Punch Bowl (or Ball) Inn' is a circular indentation in the front outside wall. Patrons would stand a few yards away and kick a ball to try to hit this. Most of the older houses are listed buildings.

Conistone-with-Kilnsey 🐚

The parish is made up of two distinct hamlets, either side of the river Wharfe.

Conistone clusters round the maypole and village green, a collection of pretty limestone cottages and barns. The school, post office and chapel have all closed, but the church of St Mary is still here, and although altered in the mid 19th century, still boasts two Norman arches and an ancient font. On the hill behind the village is the Pie – a rocky outcrop on the Dalesway long distance footpath. This faces across the valley to the overhanging rock face of Kilnsey Crag, much loved by climbers.

Kilnsey houses the local pub, the Tennant Arms, home of the Kilnsey Angling Club, whose members flyfish for trout in the Wharfe. Fish in abundance can be seen and purchased at Kilnsey Park visitor centre which also has an indoor freshwater aquarium.

Overlooking the village is the Old Hall which is now uninhabited but was once a grange for the monks of Fountains Abbey whilst tending their flocks of sheep in the dale. The lane past the Hall leads to a limestone quarry and beyond to Mastiles Lane, an old droving road to Malham, now much used by walkers.

Alongside the pub is a house, until recent times the Anglers' Arms Hotel, a hostelry of ill-repute. From here the doctor set out to ride home to Grassington through Grass Woods and was there murdered by Tom Lee, with whom he had earlier that evening had an argument. It is said that the ghost of his white horse still haunts the woods at night. There are nowadays horses to be seen on the local roads but these are very much alive and from the trekking centre at Conistone!

Cononley 🐚

Cononley is a small village surrounded by hills, with a stream running alongside the main street, situated about a mile from the Keighley to Kendal road, which leads to the Lakes and the North. Buses serve the village every hour and the railway station was reopened in 1988, after being closed since 1965, so that transport for people without cars is relatively easy. The population is around 800, which increases in summertime due to the fact that several cottages have been bought to serve as holiday homes, and others are let as furnished cottages.

Employment is provided by various industrial firms. Miners used to travel from afar, long ago, to work at the lead mines situated on the outskirts of the village, which are no longer in use.

Farming is also a means of livelihood, with cows being brought through the streets in summertime twice daily for milking, from farms to meadows where sheep and lambs also graze. The Village Care Society plant bulbs in autumn to bloom in spring and have recently planted 60 trees around the village. Six small shops have long since disappeared, leaving only the Cooperative Society, post office, butcher's and a garage for shopping, with the New Inn and Railway Inn being the last of the public houses, the others having been made into private houses.

Over the last 60 years or so, the new estates of Meadow Croft and Meadow Close and other new houses have been built, bringing families to reside here. Time moves on, and it is a long cry from the days when lime carts used to bring lime down to the station from Lothersdale, and Alf Teal's horse knew to stop at the New Inn for his master to have his pint of beer before returning to Lothersdale, laden with coal. 'Toffee David' made wonderful toffee in his small cottage, and Fred Cherry collected timber from the station to transport by horse and cart to the local joiner's shop, Messrs James Laycock & Sons Ltd, which is sadly no longer with us. Sadly, a lot of the colourful characters who were residents have long since passed on, but Cononley is still a very pleasant and quiet place in which to live.

Constable Burton

The small village of Constable Burton stands four miles east of the market town of Leyburn. It has approximately 55 dwellings within its boundary and a population of about 160. The history of Constable Burton goes back to Saxon times when Studdah Farm was mentioned as having its own chapel and burial ground; a Norman doorway is still to be found at the present farmhouse.

Constable Burton Hall, dating back to the 14th century and rebuilt in the 18th century, is the outstanding feature of the village. Set in walled and wooded parkland, its notable gardens are open to the public for much of the year.

The mill was built originally in the 14th century as a fulling mill, its purpose being to wash, shrink and thicken cloth. Rebuilt as a corn mill about 1780 it did good service for the community for almost two centuries and closed in 1951. It is still in reasonable repair. On the western outskirts of the village was the bobbin mill, where a variety of wooden articles were made, including sledges for bringing peat from the moors of Coverdale.

In 1909 the then estate mason found a hoard of hidden treasure in a nearby wood, it consisted of 244 coins of Elizabeth I, James I and Charles I. At the inquest the finder received a token of money for those kept by the authorities and the rest were returned to him. A farmstead built in 1927 was altered into a public house by the owner of Constable Burton estate, Mr Wyvill. This was opened in 1982 and named the Wyvill Arms.

Copmanthorpe

Copmanthorpe lies four and a half miles south-west of York, off the A64. The population in 1951 was 736, but a rise to about 4,500 in 1991 shows that it is increasingly a dormitory village for York and Leeds.

From the A64, Top Lane follows a Roman road, along which the legions once marched from York to Tadcaster. At the Colton crossroads, cattle being driven to the Roman port of Acaster on a north–south route would have met the soldiers. The village lies in the angle between these ancient routes.

The Ginger Beer House was the predecessor of the Fox and Hounds, on the A64. Even when this was a turnpike road, in the mid 18th century, a Copmanthorpe man was fined for careless driving. He drove his wagon without anyone to guide the horses.

In the 13th century, the Knights Templar held the manor and the village was known as Temple Copmanthorpe. The site of their preceptory has not been identified, although stone heads have been recovered.

The conservation area covers Main Street and the streets around the church. St Giles' church dates from 1180. It was a chapel of ease until it was made the parish church in 1866. Until a churchyard was permitted in 1750, people had to go to York for burials. It is said that they drank too much in the alehouses and could not walk home again, so the churchyard was granted to avoid further disgrace! In it is the tomb of Stephen Foster, who died in 1808 aged 94, while still a serving seaman.

Opposite one of the two greens, the post office thrives in a 300 year old house. The Royal Oak has been an inn for 260 years. It is supposed to have an underground passage to a nearby building – the nearest building to the rear is the church!

In the First World War, there was an aerodrome south of the bridge, where 57 Squadron was based, commemorated by a plaque in the church. The first pilots to leave for France were all killed within a few weeks. Although the area is referred to as the 'Drome', there are no remains.

Fifteen or so shops, with friendly staff, cater for most needs. The car park gets crowded at busy times and 1990 saw the first double yellow lines. A working farmhouse and a dairy in the main street are reminders of an agricultural past, now fading.

Coverham, Agglethorpe & Melmerby ❧

Coverham lies in a sheltered site by the river Cover (pronounced to rhyme with 'hover'), two miles south-west of Middleham. It is well known for the remains of a 13th century Premonstratensian abbey, of which only some decorated arches and a Norman gateway remain. Nearby stand a 17th century manor house, outbuildings, a farm and a gatehouse, to whose construction stones from the abbey, including a few effigies, contributed.

At the present time, four families live here, one engaged in farming and one running a nursery.

At a higher level stands Holy Trinity church, presumed to be of 12th century origin. It was restored in 1878. In one corner of the churchyard the ground falls steeply to a small plot close to a waterfall and although there are a few graves there it is said that the church cannot be seen or the church bells heard from them.

A mile further up Coverdale is the hamlet of Agglethorpe (formerly Aclethorpe). The front of Agglethorpe Hall was rebuilt in Victorian times, following a great fire, but the northern part is very old. The Coverham Abbey monks used its cellars for wine making; to the east of the house was a vinery and the monks took the grape harvest through an archway (still extant) down to the cellars. Nowadays the Hall is the home of a farmer and his family.

Another mile up the dale lies Melmerby, a small settlement of 24 dwellings. At 800 ft on the north scarp of the valley it enjoys a wonderful view. Behind the village a grouse moor rises to Penhill, whose dominant position earned its long history as a beacon site in the olden days.

Nowadays Melmerby has but three farmers. The Topham Arms ceased to be a public house long ago and the small Methodist chapel is now the only place where people can gather. Inside it has a quiet charm which belies its traditional plain exterior.

Cowling ❧

Cowling is a moorland parish, situated in the Aire valley, approximately six miles from Skipton. Generations have found enjoyment in the beautiful countryside which frames the village.

The 12th August is the start of the grouse shooting season, known locally as 'the Quack'. Quite often men will sleep in wooden huts on the moors the night before, ready to rise at dawn to shoot as the birds rise from the heather. In good years, juicy bilberries can be had from the moors in July. They freeze well, so there's usually a bilberry pie or crumble on a cold winter's day, with memories of a day spent up on the

Cowling Pinnack and Earl's Crag from Nan Scar

moors, bent nearly double, picking away with the hot sun burning your back.

In the old days most farms had their spinning wheel and one or two handlooms. A lot of houses in the village also had handlooms, with the family all working at them. A handloom weaver would have to walk to Piece Hall, Halifax, if he wanted to get a good price for his pieces of work. Whereas Cowling had been mainly agricultural, with the Industrial Revolution and the power loom it prospered and became a 'Mill Village'.

Cowling was renowned for the beginning of commercial poultry keeping in the early 1900s. Up to 1935 all chicks were sold as hatched, then sexing was introduced. Three Japanese chick sexers, Goshide, Hattori and Tanigushir came to the village, and they could detect the sex of chicks at the speed of 1,200 per hour. As the Second World War threatened, these three popular men had to return to their homeland.

The first bus in Yorkshire, a Milnes-Daimler single-decker, made a triumphal arrival in the village early in 1905, driven from London by Ezra Laycock. Mr and Mrs Laycock and a party of 18 others travelled to London where they collected the bus; then these hardy travellers embarked upon what was to become the longest journey made by motorbus in England up to that date. When it finally arrived in Cowling all the villagers turned out to catch a first glimpse of this 'new fangled thing' and to cheer Ezra whose initiative had brought it to this distant Yorkshire village.

71

Coxwold 🦋

Coxwold is one of the most picturesque villages in North Yorkshire. It lies on the edge of the Hambleton Hills, some 20 miles from York and not far from Thirsk and Easingwold. The main street, lined with well tended grassy banks and attractive stone cottages, rises steeply up the hill to the imposing church of St Michael which dominates the village.

Amongst the historic buildings is Colville Hall, the ancient manor house, and the Old Hall, originally built in 1603 as a free grammar school but now a private dwelling. The almshouses further down the village street founded in 1662 as a hospital for 'ten poor and infirm men' today provide five homes essentially for the elderly.

Two other old and interesting buildings which attract many visitors in the summer are Shandy Hall and Newburgh Priory. Shandy Hall, a medieval priest's house, is renowned as the home of the Rev Laurence Sterne who wrote, whilst parson at St Michael's, *Tristram Shandy* and *A Sentimental Journey* – the former becoming so well known that the house was renamed after it. Newburgh Priory, formerly the home of the Fauconbergs, lies close to the village. In the attics lie the headless remains of Oliver Cromwell, rescued and hidden there by his daughter, Mary, and her husband the first Earl, after the Restoration in 1660 when the vengeful mob disinterred her father and cut off his head.

At the present time the village is fortunate in having a post office cum store, a lively inn (the Fauconberg Arms), a doctor's surgery, a coal merchant, a garage and a resident policeman. Attractions for visitors include a popular tea room and guest house, a pottery and a cabinet maker. In times past most of the villagers in some way worked for the Newburgh Priory estate and although many remain today connected with farming, others cater for tourists or commute to nearby towns.

By the crossroads is 'The Well' and the custom of well dressing is continued for special occasions by some members of the WI. The tradition enjoyed by the children of the village on wedding days is the tying-up of the lychgate and the holding of the bride and groom to ransom.

Cracoe 🦋

On the top of the fell standing sentinel over Cracoe and district is the cairn, a structure wide at the base and tapering almost to a point. It was built in memory of the men in the district who fell in the First World War. When building started around 1922–1923, professional masons were engaged to build it but difficulties were encountered. It is very windy on the fell, even on calm days, 1,600 ft above sea level, and several times the work was blown down on wild nights, so eventually a local craftsman came to the rescue. He had a tent taken up to the fell top along with provisions and lived up on the fell until he had built the cairn.

At the bottom of the hill, near the junction to Hetton village, are a number of houses recently converted from a farmhouse and buildings. Originally they were known as 'Town End' but up to 1917 it was the Bull inn.

There is an old inn, the Devonshire Arms Hotel, and nearby the Cracoe Cafe. The lane running past the cafe between the main road and Back Lane used to be known was 'T'Woggon' but this name is no longer used.

There is a bungalow on Back Lane with two ornamental privet chairs on the lawn. This bungalow used to be an old chapel and was converted in 1923. Idrick House, now the village post office and guest house, also used to be a chapel. After being disused for some time it was converted into a house in 1965.

Seventeenth century houses are in evidence in the village. Typical of the traditional houses of that date, they are known as longhouses. The stone for these houses was quarried locally on Cracoe and Rylstone Fell. The cavity of the walls, which are up to 3 ft thick, was filled with rubble. One wonders if houses built by modern methods will last 300 years.

Crakehall ✣

Crakehall is a pleasant and peaceful village. It lies two miles west of Bedale on the main road up Wensleydale, with its two halves Great and Little being on either side of the beck.

Crakehall is recorded in Domesday Book as having a mill and a small population engaged in working the land. Until recent times Crakehall remained almost entirely an agriculturally based village, with its way of life ordered and dependent upon the seasons and its produce. The passing years have witnessed the changing pattern of farming with today a mix of mechanised farms, some owned, some tenanted. Crakehall had at one time three mills and until quite recently two of those remained in use. Now only one is still in working order and its position by the mill pond and beck make it a most attractive interest point for the many who visit the village. This mill still grinds and sells flour, whilst one of the former mills was concerned with the preparation of linen from flax which for hundreds of years was widely grown in the area.

The green is the heart of the village and it is a delight to the eye with its well kept grass and its large old trees. Around the green are found the essentials of village life with a church, St Gregory's, and chapel, the school, an inn and the village shop. The green is also the scene of play for the village cricket team which has been in existence for 140 years, whilst outside the inn the quoits team play in season.

The mill pond and the beck are separated by a further area of common land known as the Batts, believed to be a corruption of 'butts' when in times past the villagers practised archery. Today the Batts are a pleasant area of grass and trees where children play, dogs run, and older villagers fish.

The village has recently had some new building, but it has been absorbed into the existing surroundings without substantially altering the attraction of the village. Many of the residents have lived in the village and area all their lives; some are newcomers. All blend together to make this not only an attractive village but a friendly one. A walk across the green to the shop will almost always mean a chat with someone.

Crayke ✺

There have been many versions of the village name, ranging from Creca in the 7th century, to Crayke or Craike in the 13th century. The village remained for many years in the Bishopric of Durham, hence the name of the pub, the Durham Ox.

Crayke's most distinguished inhabitant was Dean Inge, who was born in Crayke Cottage in 1860 and became the Dean of St Paul's Cathedral.

The village also has its share of ghosts. Probably the best known of these are Fred who walks the road near the Oulston crossroads and a lady in grey who walks the upper chamber of Crayke Castle. There is also said to be a body entombed in the walls of Crayke Castle, which has its own ghost.

The church at Crayke, St Cuthbert's, has a very long history, the present building dating from about 1436. The rood screen in the church is 15th century, the pulpit dates from 1634 and the pews from 1660.

The manor and castle belonged to the Bishops of Durham until sold by Bishop van Mildreth in 1828. The first castle was probably a motte and bailey Saxon stronghold. The present building is 15th century and was ordered to be demolished in February 1647.

Cropton ✺

Cropton is a quiet village lying on the limestone upland, east of lower Rosedale. At the south-west end of the village is a triangular green at the junction of roads to Wrelton, Rosedale and Newton-on-Rawcliffe. Here there is a magnificent view towards the moors west of Rosedale, a favourite stopping place for photographers.

The village consists of one unusually broad street, once partly common grazing, together with an unpaved back lane to the east and a by-road. The houses are mainly stone with red pantiles. Many were rebuilt in the 18th and 19th centuries from earlier cruck houses and longhouses; two still have medieval crucks. Within the village stand several farmhouses with scattered holdings; two or three are still active farms but in the last 20 years several have become private residences. They have long gardens and crofts at the rear.

Cropton (population about 230) fortunately still has a village shop/ post office. Within living memory there were three shops plus a butcher; now travelling vans bring bread, milk, meat and fish. The church of St Gregory, west of the main street, is a Victorian building on the site of an earlier church. It contains a 12th century font and medieval window. In the churchyard, where once stood village stocks, is part of an ancient cross.

At the bottom of the village stands the New Inn, greatly extended within the last few years. Once there were three alehouses in Cropton. Now the pub brews its own beer; Cropton beers are becoming known to Real Ale enthusiasts.

A feature of the southern end of the village are deep hollows either side of the roads, the remains of disused limestone quarries, an industry for which Cropton was noted. For centuries limestone was kiln-burned and carried north over the moors for agricultural use.

The history of Cropton goes back a long way. There are prehistoric barrows within the parish and Roman camps at Cawthorne. Behind the church lie the mound and ditch of the Norman castle, on a fine site overlooking Rosedale. The tradition of Easter egg-rolling on the steep mound continues. Bumps in the same field reveal the structure of a Tudor hall, later demolished.

Dacre & Dacre Banks ⚜

Dacre is an ancient word meaning 'trickling stream' and the village is mentioned in the Domesday Book as being 'waste'. Bounded by the river Nidd on its northern edge, the development straddles the B6451 between Darley and Summerbridge, being about ten miles from Harrogate and four and a half from Pateley Bridge. In the Middle Ages Dacre was the site of one of the monastic granges of Fountains Abbey which is some ten miles to the north-west.

In addition to farming, the quarrying industry developed in the area, while flax spinning, both at home and in a small factory, provided the yarn for the hand-loom weaving of both linen and harden. A former corn mill is now the centre of a large thriving business dealing in timber; the saw mill is adjacent to the bridge over the Nidd. One of the most interesting reminders of former times is the old Quaker burial ground at Heckler's Hill, first used in 1682 when these early dissenters flourished in Nidderdale.

The nucleus of modern Dacre is a well-kept village green on which a fund raising fete is held on August Bank Holiday Monday. Adjacent to the green is a well equipped village hall, and nearby is the local hostelry, the Royal Oak. Many of the houses are old, but modern development started in the 1960s has blended well. There is a village shop, a large garage and two health centres run by rival group practices serving an extensive area of Nidderdale. The Anglican church, dedicated to the Holy Trinity, was built in 1837 and has a modern vicarage, its large Victorian predecessor now a nursing home. The United Reformed church stands at the top of the hill on the road to Darley; it was built as a Congregational church in 1827.

Dalton, near Thirsk 🦋

There are many places in Yorkshire called Dalton and the name means a village or homestead in a valley. This Dalton is recorded in the Domesday Book as Deltune and is situated on a tributary of the Cod beck five miles south of Thirsk. The population is just over 400.

For centuries the occupation of most of the inhabitants was farming but the years after the Second World War brought great change, when various industries became established in and around Dalton, including a turkey processing factory. The frozen poultry industry began in buildings erected for Dalton airfield. This airfield opened in 1941 and was occupied mainly by the Royal Canadian Air Force. It closed in 1945. However, still scattered throughout the village are a great variety of buildings which were constructed to serve the airfield.

The parish church of St John the Evangelist is a very interesting building and was part of a building programme instigated by the 7th Viscount Downe, whose Dawnay Estates at that time owned many of the farms in the village. The architect was William Butterfield and the church has stained glass windows designed by the pre-Raphaelite artists, William Morris, Edward Burne-Jones and Ford Madox Brown. The church was opened in 1868.

The Rev Sabine Baring-Gould author and hymn writer, married a Yorkshire mill-girl half his age who bore him five sons and nine daughters. His best known hymn is *Onward, Christian Soldiers*, written in 1864. He came to Dalton in 1867 before the church was completed and when the congregation met for worship in a barn.

There were two Methodist chapels in the village, both now closed, but the Methodist congregation continues to meet for worship in the village hall. The Primitive Methodist chapel is now the post office and general stores, being the only shop in the village. There are two pubs – the Jolly Farmer and the Moor and Pheasant (formerly the Railway Inn). The London–Edinburgh railway line runs near the village but the local station has been closed. As well as being responsible for the building of the church, the Dawnay family also built the school, which was opened in 1873 to accommodate 70 pupils. It closed in 1966.

Dalton-on-Tees Village Hall, formerly the School House

Dalton-on-Tees 🪶

Dalton-on-Tees lies about five miles south-east of Darlington just off the A167 Darlington to Northallerton road. The village greens are registered as common land and the children play football, cricket and other games there. There used to be a number of pumps round the village but only the one standing on the green remains, unused for many years.

In 1856 the majority of the houses were labourers' cottages and those belonging to John Backhouse, who also built the school, were whitewashed. Rawlings cottage was adjoined by the old village Reading Room, which was last used over 60 years ago and is now part of the cottage.

Dick Preston, the mole catcher, used to live in one of the old cottages next to the blacksmith's shop, which has sadly been recently demolished and a new house built on the site. The blacksmith's shop was on the corner directly in front of the Chequers inn. The latter was formerly the Crown and Anchor, but the name was changed when the disused local airfield was turned into a motor racing circuit after the Second World War.

The aerodrome was built at the beginning of the Second World War and was used by the RAF as a bomber base. Two Canadian squadrons, the 431 Iroquois and 435 Blue-hose were based there. There is a bronze statue of an airman looking to the sky at the south end of the village, a smaller copy of one in front of the Municipal Building in Winnipeg.

In the field across the road from the village hall are some earthworks, still visible, which were excavated in 1973. A mound approximately 40 ft × 50 ft is surrounded by a ditch 30 ft wide, but during the excavations no evidence of a structure was found. Sherds of buff pottery suggested a 13th century date for the construction. Connected to the ditch by small channels are three rectangular depressions, two shallow, now dry, and one deeper still holding water. The site appears to have been a group of fishponds, the shallow depressions suggesting breeding tanks, and is probably of 13th century date and most likely connected with the Old Manor House across the main road.

There has been a substantial amount of new housing built in the last 30 years and the majority of inhabitants travel to work in local towns, but there are still two working farms in the village.

Danby Wiske

Danby Wiske is a small village situated between the North Yorkshire Moors and the Yorkshire Dales. It consists of approximately 60 houses and a pub surrounding a small village green beside the river Wiske, some five miles from the market town of Northallerton.

The original village was sited close to the church, but at the time of the great plague, new houses were built further away from the river in an attempt to escape from this dreadful disease.

The church is interesting in that its dedication appears to be unknown. Above the Norman doorway there is a carving in the stone which is thought to date from 1090 to 1120, and the font is also Norman in origin. Below the church is the old rectory, now converted into two houses. This itself is very rare, being only one of three moated rectories in the country.

Across the river is Lazenby Hall. The present Hall, which is now a farmhouse, was built in the 1620s by Richard Peirse who was given the land by Charles I and it is reputed that there is a tunnel running from the hall to Danby Wiske church, but the whereabouts of this tunnel remain unknown. To the east of the present Lazenby Hall are the remains of the village of Leisenchi, which is Anglo-Saxon in origin and is mentioned in the Domesday Book.

Years ago the village could boast many tradesmen including a blacksmith, a fishmonger, two tailors, two carpenters and two shoemakers, but sadly none remain. Originally, there were three pubs in the village, but there is now only one, the others having been converted to private houses. The White Swan, which was originally called the Grey Swan and is itself over 350 years old, is a popular overnight stopping place for people attempting the famous Coast to Coast walk, created by A. W. Wainwright, which runs from Ravenglass in Cumbria to Robin Hood's Bay on the Yorkshire coast and passes through Danby Wiske.

Darley ♔

This beautiful village is set between Birstwith and Dacre, on the banks of the river Nidd, some nine miles from Harrogate.

There are quite a few interesting old buildings, including The Holme, a thatched house dating back to 1677. The Pullan family lived there for more than four generations, and ran a laundry business next to their home for many years. Highfold Cottage also dates back to the 1600s and is situated on the main street, next to Claremont. Originally it was two cottages with a living area below and hayloft above, and was used as a wood store and garage for many years. The old Quaker meeting house and burial ground is situated at the top of the lane, opposite the entrance to Daleside Park. A stone tablet on the wall gives details. The local band currently practises here. Wyngarth on Stocks Green dates back to 1674.

Fringhill Mill, once a twine mill, was owned by the Skaife family. The Verity family now run an animal fodder business here. A water-wheel worked the mill, originally, and the three dams feeding it can be seen on the right of Fringhill Lane.

Darley Mill, from the 1600s, was a corn mill, which was idle for many years. Around 1920/21 it was purchased by Fred Skaife. Renovations took place and corn was again processed, but after several years the mill fell idle again. In the 1970s a market garden was opened here and later a plant hire business and at one time there was a tea shop. In the 1980s the mill was purchased by PondenMill and after tasteful renovations, it opened as a mill shop and restaurant which attracts many visitors.

The paint mill was in use until the early 1950s. It is now a private house and stands alongside Darley Beck, beyond the bridge opposite Darley Mill.

Dick Turpin reputedly lived here in the 1700s; his abode remains 'Turpin Lair'. The junction known as 'Catch'em Corner' supposedly refers to the times when Turpin held up and robbed the stage coaches at this point.

Deighton near Northallerton ♔

The name Deighton means 'ditch town', after the moat which surrounds a four acre field behind the village. Very little is known about this ancient monument, but it is believed that a fortified manor house once stood there. A drawbridge was removed at the end of the 18th century.

The present manor house was built in the 19th century and occupies a site overlooking the village and surrounding farmland, dotted with plantations and coverts. The whole village once belonged to the lord of the manor, but the estate was split up and sold early in the 20th century.

Not far from the village, the course of a Roman road runs in a north–south direction. Part of it is still in use today where the public road joins it. Most of it is hidden beneath fields and is only used by horseriders and walkers. The Roman road marks one side of Deighton parish boundary.

Apart from the more modern buildings in the village, the cottages, Three Horseshoes inn (closed in the early 1950s) and surrounding farmhouses were all built with the narrow red bricks made out of local clay at the now tumbledown village brickworks.

In summer, the chestnut trees lining the road provide a shady green archway leading to the church at the northern end of the village. All Saints' church was a chapel of ease. The present building dates from 1715 but part of it is believed to be much older. The stone font is from the 12th century and one of the two bells is described as being 'of decidedly early shape' and thought to originate from nearby Mount Grace Priory. The whereabouts of the original altar is something of a mystery, as beneath the richly embroidered frontal there is nothing more than a shabby old chest of drawers with the drawers taken out. Perhaps during the restorations of 1901 someone took a fancy to it!

Denton 🦢

Denton is situated in beautiful Wharfedale, two miles east of Ilkley. Denton Park estate covers 2500 acres of agricultural land and moorland. At the centre of the estate Denton Hall faces south with superb views of the River Wharfe and Ilkley moor beyond.

Perhaps the most famous of the families who have made their home at Denton Hall were the Fairfaxes one of whom, Thomas, Lord Fairfax was General to Oliver Cromwell during the Civil war.

The present Hall was completed in 1778. It was commissioned by Sir James Ibbotson and designed by John Carr of York, an associate of the renowned architect, Robert Adam.

The estate now belongs to N. G. Bailey and Company Ltd., Electrical contractors, and is their management training centre. The Hall was extensively renovated whilst preserving the appearance and character of the original building. The internal layout remains unchanged with the magnificent staircase and highly decorative ceilings and the furnishings reflecting the period in which the Hall was built.

The farms on the estate are run as a profitable concern by the N. G. Bailey company with a large dairy herd, bull beef unit and various flocks of sheep.

St Helens Church, Denton contains memorials to the Ibbotson family. The painted glass dated 1699 is the work of Henry Gyles of York. It bears the arms of Thomas, fourth Lord Fairfax and also depicts David playing a harp.

Dishforth

Anyone visiting Dishforth today sees it as a quiet oasis away from the busy A1 and A168. Houses of character hiding behind old stone walls line what is now Main Street, but was once called the green lane. One or two of these houses date back to the 1600s, albeit with a little updating. One house it is said had furniture that moved around. No, not a poltergeist, only such undulating walls and floors that furniture had to be fastened into place.

The newest Wesleyan chapel was built in 1892. An isolated cottage near the entrance to the village was the old chapel. Behind the church in The Green is the old Baptist chapel, now used as a garage. Christ church, 200 years old in 1991, was once a chapel of ease, reputed to be built over an earlier site, which is perhaps the reason why it stands on a slight mound.

Farming has always been the main occupation. There were at least eleven farms, but now only four remain. Land ownership was surprisingly scattered, fields not always being adjacent to the farmhouse, but

Christ Church on Main Street, Dishforth

stretching away down nearby roads. Nearly every house boasted a field or garth.

Topcliffe Road is part of the old coach road leading from the ford, turning left down Main Street. When carts and carriages clattered over the cobbles or setts, the noise could be heard many miles away. The road goes on past the church and Crown Farm. A plaque on the wall of this house depicts a crown and the date 1856 which shows this was Crown property until bought in 1969. This also applies to the Crown inn opposite and the land whereon stands the village hall. Next to the Crown is the Black Swan inn.

The old road continues on past Lingham Lane and Back Lane, past the old Poste House and bears left on its way to Boroughbridge, or did. Now it only goes as far as the airfield and the village sports complex, officially opened in 1990, after a lot of hard work put into the scheme by the villagers.

Draughton ✣

Draughton, pronounced 'Drafton' with a short 'a', is listed in the Domesday Book as Dractone.

It has its manor house, last rebuilt in 1669, with the ghost of a man murdered by his brother; remnants of stocks on the village green; the site of a pinfold; ridge and furrow remnants of a medieval open field system, and evidence of earlier enclosed barley fields; 17th century hedges and ditches and mid 19th century dry stone walls; a tithe barn, now a house; and a water mill, later a cotton mill. The post office was once a smithy where coins were forged as well as iron. In the early 19th century a Methodist chapel was built, now a house; a school, now the village hall, opened in 1851 and closed in 1932; and in 1897 an Anglican church was built.

The southern boundary of the township tops the moor at 1,000 ft above sea level, and the eastern boundary runs along the river Wharfe at 300 ft. Most of the area is steep with just a few level fields. On the moor-top prehistoric man passed along an ancient trackway which the Romans paved. This remained the King's Highway between Ilkley and Skipton until the mid 18th century when General Wade built his military road between York and Lancaster at a lower level touching the village. It is now the A65.

Draughton is situated on the Craven fault, where the rock reaches the surface in a gigantic inverted V. The limestone was quarried for stone for building and lime for burning in the 18th and 19th century. The last of four public houses, the Matchless, closed long ago.

Besides the ghost in the manor house, each of the many gills has its elf or boggart. Witches were commonly feared, the only defence against them being horseshoes nailed to house and stable doors. Only recently at least one house always had witch stones (river pebbles with holes worn through) hanging by the front door.

Dunnington

Dunnington was formerly known as Dodintone or Doniton. It was mentioned in the Domesday Book, and coins minted during the reign of Constantine were discovered in the village in the 1820s when excavations were being dug. Situated four miles from York, it lies between two former Roman roads.

In the centre of the village stands a stone cross. This has a stone shaft with a ball finial, put up in 1840 and restored in 1900. Remains of the early medieval cross can be seen in the rectory garden. It is said that money and food was left at the site of the cross during the plague of the 14th century.

The church of St Nicholas dates back to Norman times. A large extension was built in the 1980s to meet the needs of modern day life. In 1801 the population of the village was 481, by 1961 the numbers more than doubled. In 1990 the numbers were in excess of 3,000. The Wesleyan Methodists built a chapel in 1805 in York Street, replacing it in 1868 with a larger building in Common Lane. Today like the church, the chapel is a focal point for many organisations.

The village was well known for the manufacture of farm implements, and many can be found in nearby museums. Agriculture was the mainstay of everyday life.

Much of the country's home-grown chicory was grown in Dunnington; up to twelve kilns were used to dry the roots. Many itinerant labourers were used during the harvest, the Irish labourers from York amongst them. For most of the year around 400 people were permanently employed. The industry declined when the government imposed high taxes. Three kilns stood in 1972; the largest in Common Lane was a long two storey building with a half-hipped roof and flight of stone steps leading to the first floor. Kiln Cottage is still there, whilst modern houses stand on the old kiln site.

Football and cricket were the two sports played in Dunnington before the Second World War. It was well known that mothers and grandmothers of players would threaten the referees with Scauder's Pond if the decisions went against the local teams. After the war a sports and playing field was bought. Community efforts by the villagers provided a superb sports complex long before they became the norm.

Easby ✿

A couple of miles from Great Ayton is the hamlet of Easby, nestling at the foot of Easby Moor on which stands the monument to Captain James Cook, the famous navigator and explorer.

The present population is about 75 and people are mainly occupied in agriculture or in the shops and offices of Stokesley and Great Ayton. Others commute to Teesside for their employment.

Most of the farms and cottages were part of an estate but in the early 1980s this was sold, some to tenants whose families had been there for many years.

There are no shops but there is a Methodist chapel. There is also a private chapel in the grounds of Easby Hall, a Georgian gentleman's residence, once the home of the Emerson family. The Hall itself was closed as a residence in 1934 and until the late 1980s was used in various ways. Then it was sold to the present owners who are renovating the house to its former glory to be lived in once again. The private chapel was closed for worship as recently as 1986 and it is hoped that it will be opened again in the future.

Easingwold ✿

Easingwold lies on the busy A19 between York and Thirsk.

The New Rose and Crown, a coaching inn, was an important staging place for the Royal Mail between York and Edinburgh. It later became a convent and school, and was finally converted into flats. The New Inn was also a staging post and is still in use today as a public house.

Easingwold once boasted a railway station, linked with Alne. It opened in 1891. The earliest train was known as the Coffee Pot because of the shape of its engine. Sadly all that remains now is the Station Hotel, another public house.

At the northern end of Easingwold stands the parish church of St John the Baptist, which contains the parish coffin, one of only two left in England and soon to be lent to the Victoria and Albert museum. It was used by the poor of the parish who could not afford to buy a coffin for their dead. Although there was a church and priest at the time of the Domesday survey, the present building dates mainly from around 1400.

The cobbled market place houses several shops, pubs, banks, the post office and public conveniences. A market is still held every Friday. The centrepiece is the town hall which, in its time has housed the fire station, a cinema, a dance hall and is now a printing works. The old tollbooth stands to the back of it, but is now in poor condition.

Uppleby is a Danish name and may not have been occupied before the Viking invasion in the 9th century. A Tudor House still stands along this street and a Tudor public house, the Blue Bell, now demolished, was run by Anne Harrison, better known as Nana Randan. She was permitted to use the 'chief seat' in the parish church. Her grave is near to the church door and it is said that if you run round it three times and spit on it at midnight she will come out.

Not long ago most of the residents were involved either in farming, the trailer works or the cloth mending factories. Although the factories have all closed down, farms still surround the whole of Easingwold. As it has grown with the building of new houses, more and more residents are commuting to York or even further afield.

East & West Ayton

The joint villages of East and West Ayton are situated four miles west of Scarborough on the banks of the river Derwent, at the entrance to the Vale of Pickering.

The castle, which is now in ruins, commands a view over Forge Valley. It took the form of a fortified dwelling and dates from the reign of King John.

The church building is of traditional Norman design and dates from the 12th century, being founded as a chantry chapel of St John the Baptist. The doorway arch and font are both Norman and of considerable interest.

A bridge over the river Derwent separating the two parts of the village existed before 1492, but the present four-arched stone bridge dates back to 1752. In 1961 this proved inadequate, and in order to carry all westbound traffic, a new level bridge was constructed beside the old one.

Forge Valley Woods is a portion of the National Park, mostly within the East Ayton boundary and well known to both walkers and motorists. It is now owned by Scarborough Corporation. In 1950 the Forge Valley cottages were demolished, and thus was severed the last link with the ancient iron working industry from which the valley took its name.

As the village could now be classed almost as a dormitory suburb of Scarborough, local occupations now cover all aspects of modern life. There are still several active farms in the village, but now a large proportion of the working population need to travel beyond the village boundaries. When the WI was founded in 1919 there existed in the village a miller, a saddler, a blacksmith, a clogger, two tailors, two shoemakers and a haberdasher, also two grocers and three public houses. Coal was delivered by horse and cart from a depot at the station.

In recent times, residing in the village for over 90 years was a celebrated watercolour artist, Nathan Brown. He was a founder member of Ayton Art Club and his work is now owned by admirers worldwide.

East Scrafton 🌿

Half a mile along the road from Caldbergh, travelling west, is the small community of East Scrafton, consisting as it does of only a farm and one large house. From East Scrafton a footpath leads down to the river, passing the foundations of St Simon's chapel, a small building once used by the monks of Jervaulx. On over the narrow timber footbridge the path eventually emerges on the road leading to Carlton. This was the route once used by the children of Caldbergh and East Scrafton to reach the schoolhouse at Carlton.

East Witton 🌿

East Witton is situated at the entrance to Wensleydale, two miles south-east of Middleham and one and a half miles west of Jervaulx Abbey, in sight of the confluence of the rivers Cover and Ure. It nestles under Witton Fell, a typical Pennine plateau, 1,100 ft above sea level.

The houses are set round a broad village green and a tiny stream flows through the back gardens of all the houses on the south side of the village. This is known as Flesh Beck. The only water supply was from three taps which are placed on the green. The tap which stands at the bottom end of the village is a large glacial boulder and was brought from a field down Cover Bridge road by 20 farm horses in 1859.

There was a coal mine behind Witton Fell known as Farmery Mines. In 1820 disaster struck, 20 miners were killed and all are buried in one grave in the new churchyard.

The present village was rebuilt in the early 19th century following a disastrous fire in 1796. A new church dedicated to St John the Evangelist replaced St Martin's church. There are some very interesting gravestones still to be seen in the old churchyard.

A pub named the Blue Lion was run by the same family from 1856 to 1989. The Fox and Hounds was also a pub until the mid-19th century when it became known as the Temperance Hotel on relinquishing its licence. Later it was renamed the Holly Tree inn. It is thought to be one of the oldest buildings in East Witton and the site of the stud farm for horse rearing by the monks of Jervaulx.

Before the First World War the village employed stonemasons, joiners, a tailor, seedmerchant, flour miller and butcher, foresters, farmers, farm labourers, a blacksmith and gamekeepers, plus two shops and a post office. Most of the people were employed by the estate. In 1969 Mr H. L. Christie died and the estate was sold to Mr R. Hill of Clifton Castle.

Ebberston ✺

Ebberston is a small village (population 400) situated on the eastern boundary of Ryedale and in the fertile Vale of Pickering. The Main Street runs directly north to south and largely consists of stone-built properties with red pantiled roofs. There are some brick-built and slate-roof properties which appeared when planning laws were less rigid.

The parish church is St Mary's, situated some distance from the village at the foot of Kirkdale (site of the former village). The church is most attractive – it has many beautiful stained glass windows and is of Norman origin with Norman pillars and font.

Close to the church is Ebberston Hall, built by a member of the Hotham family in the style of a Palladian villa, reputedly for the owner's mistress, although apparently the lady in question was not sufficiently impressed to live there. The present owner is Michael West de Wend Fenton and the property, known as the 'smallest stately home in the country' is open to the public. A former owner was the colourful Squire George Osbaldeston, known for his sporting activities as the 'Hunting Squire of England'.

To the north of the village is an area known to local people as 'The Dale' but now renamed 'Chafer Wood' and leased to the Yorkshire Wildlife Fund. Within the area of Chafer Wood is the remains of the pinfold where the pinder enclosed stray animals, to return them to the careless owners only on payment of a fine.

Also within the wood, at a high point with a fine view of the village and across the Vale of Pickering to the Wolds, is a stone-built cairn built to mark the site of a cave in the hillside where in AD 704 Alchfrid, a King of Northumbria, rested after being wounded in a battle fought in a field opposite St Mary's church and known as the Bloody Field. Alchfrid was taken to Little Driffield where he died and is buried. The stream through the Bloody Field is known as the Bloody Beck and was reputed to 'run red with the blood of long-dead warriors'. The more prosaic would say that the colour arose from traces of iron found in bore-hole planting!

The Grapes inn is the only surviving public house, and has been owned by the Thorpe family for many years, though not now run by them. There is also a small hotel, the Foxholme, and several holiday cottages and caravan sites. The local cricket team flourishes and there is a golf driving range within the parish.

Elslack ✺

Elslack is a small rural parish with old stone buildings and lovely countryside. It is situated in the heart of the Pennines and the Pennine Way passes through part of the parish. There are buried remains of a Roman fort and a Roman road runs through the village.

Elslack Village

At 1,274 ft, Pinhaw Beacon stands on the heather-covered moor above the village, from where there is a wonderful panoramic view of hills, dales and mountains stretching for many miles. At the time of the Napoleonic Wars Pinhaw Beacon was manned continually, ready to complete the chain of communication in the event of invasion. During a raging blizzard in January 1805 one of the beacon guards, Robert Wilkinson, perished and was buried on the moor, later to be exhumed and laid to rest in Broughton with Elslack churchyard; a stone suitably inscribed marks the spot where his body was found.

The beautiful old church which covers the combined parishes of Broughton and Elslack stands on the north-east side of Elslack. The parish boundary with Broughton actually runs through the churchyard.

The population today is only half that of the early part of the 19th century, and there is no village shop or post office. The local occupation is farming, with the exception of a small firm dealing in agricultural machinery recently started on the site of the old railway station.

During the 19th century the Moorhouse family occupied and farmed White House Farm, which included part of the church glebe lands. To diversify from farming they started making and selling lemon cheese, this being the start of the famous Moorhouse jam making industry of Leeds. Some of the ancestors are buried in Broughton with Elslack churchyard.

Exelby 🌿

The village of Exelby lies two miles from Leeming and two miles from the market town of Bedale. Its older houses were made from the local brickworks, and in the old days it also had a sand and gravel quarry.

Agricultural land has vanished as more houses were built. There were 25 houses in Exelby in 1938, while a present day count comes to around 50.

In the past it had two blacksmiths, three public houses, a molecatcher and a shoemaker. Today there is one public house called the Green Dragon, two joiners, one builder and a poultry farm. The chapel was lost recently, when it was made into a private house.

Fadmoor 🌿

Fadmoor is a little village situated on the edge of the North Yorkshire Moors. It has limestone-built farmhouses and buildings and various cottages and smallholdings surrounding a village green, which at one time many years ago had a water race running through it.

The village shop and post office closed down in the 1970s and these premises are now incorporated into the Plough inn which is sited next door. Opposite the pub was a cobbler's shop and the District Nurse lived on the other side of the green. In 1836 on the Boon Hill road to the north of the village a chapel was built. In 1969 it was converted into a dwelling house. Two bungalows were built on the opposite side of this road in the early 1970s, one on the site of an old limestone quarry where there are caves of archaeological interest.

The beautiful valley of Sleightholmedale, with the river Hodge flowing through it, is in the parish of Fadmoor, and some years ago field lime was produced there. Electricity was brought to Fadmoor village in 1948/9 and it is one of the few villages not to have street lighting. In 1737 water was brought down from Ousegill springs a few miles north of here by means of an open rill, and at that time Jersey wool was produced, giving rise to the saying 'as strong as Fadmoor Jersey – three threads an armful'.

It is mostly a farming community and covers an area of 1,910 acres. There are two sheep sales held in the autumn of each year, and another annual event is a produce and handicraft show, a combined effort with the neighbouring village of Gillamoor.

Farndale ✤

Farndale is a scattered farming community in the heart of the North Yorkshire Moors National Park, consisting of two hamlets: Low Mills derives its name from having had two cornmills, and Church Houses, which is near the church. The picturesque cottages and farmhouses are built of local sandstone.

The dale's greatest claim to fame is that of the wild daffodils which grow along the banks of the river Dove. These were reputedly planted by the monks from the nearby abbeys many hundreds of years ago. They are now protected by the Nature Conservancy Council, as years ago people visiting from towns would pick them to sell in the markets. Now, anyone found picking them is fined.

Farndale originally had a parish church and mission room and two Methodist chapels, but now has only one chapel in High Farndale and St Mary's parish church. There also used to be two schools but these are now long gone. In years past, there were also four shops, including a post office which is the only surviving facility.

After the daffodils, comes the summer. In the long summer evenings, the local men enjoy a game of cricket, followed by a pint in the local pub. Perhaps the highlight of the year is Farndale's Agricultural Show, when old aquaintances and families return from near and far to renew friendships.

There has been a revival of the old game of 'Merrils' and Farndale, at present, boasts the World Champion Merrils player. This game has been played for generations by farmers and farm lads during the long winter nights. They would play in the stable on a board carved into the inside of a corn-bin lid.

Farnham ✤

Farnham is an ancient and beautiful village some two miles from Knaresborough. The Domesday record of 1086 notes that Farnham had a church and a priest at that time and part of the present church dates from about 1180.

It is thought the shape of the village has changed little over the centuries, the same track from Scotton crossing the mires, passing the church on the higher ground, winding through the cottages and on to Knaresborough. Another track from the north joins at the village green; it was a packhorse road and remains today as a bridleway.

Farnham has probably always lived from agriculture but it has in its time housed weavers, and in 1757 a copper mine was opened but it failed – said to be due to poor management. Some of the houses date from the 17th century although the house which was formerly the smithy was built in 1727 and a number of other houses seem to be of the same period.

In 1990 the population was around 140 and there were some 55 houses. The quarry has been worked out and has become a rather beautiful lake, now the home of the very successful Ripon Sailing Club.

The church is still beautiful and stands high over the main street with the village green to one side. It houses a colony of rare bats.

Perhaps the most remarkable thing about Farnham is how little the village has changed over the centuries, the only amenities being the church and a public house. There is no street lighting, garage, shop or post office, in fact little evidence of the impact of the 20th century. Long may it remain so.

Farnley

Farnley is situated one mile north-east of Otley and forms part of the picturesque Washburn valley, separated from the town by Otley Plantation. Farnley Hall is one of the most famous places in Yorkshire, especially to those who are interested in art. It was here that the great J. M. W. Turner returned time and again to paint the beautiful countryside.

The Hall has been associated with the Fawkes family for seven centuries and it was Walter Ramsden Fawkes who was Turner's friend and one of his kindest patrons. Turner visited Farnley annually over a period of 17 years from 1803–1820 and it was where he did some his best work. His paintings of the house and the surroundings formed the beginning of the great Turner collection. These paintings have since furnished the local historian with much information. Turner also designed the imposing East Lodge gates which still stand overlooking Leathley.

All Saints' church is situated on the edge of the village and was used jointly with the Palmes family, before Lindley was taken into the Farnley estate by Thomas Fawkes in 1686. The original structure was erected in 1250 but in 1851 the church was restored by Francis Fawkes and is a reconstruction of a building dating from the 12th and 13th centuries. The interior contains a stall by Thompson of Kilburn (the 'Mouseman').

Today there is no shop, no post office and no pub in the village. This in no way deters the walkers and tourists who come for the sheer enjoyment of the countryside.

The local farms consist mainly of grassland for cattle and sheep. There used to be many small fields with hedges. During the 19th century some hedges were replaced with stone walls and larger, squarer fields were made. Low lying fields were flooded at that time and made into a lake and some small arable fields were made into a woodland plantation.

Fearby ✎

Fearby's large village green is an attractive feature today but years ago the residents held gaits for horses and geese on the green, and Fearby was known for its considerable numbers of geese. The Grange at the east end of the village is the oldest building, a barn of three bays divided by cruck trusses and thought to have once been a dwelling.

In the 1850s there were eleven farmers and 23 labourers, three carpenters, six dressmakers, three innkeepers, three grocers, two black-smiths and two straw bonnet-makers! Fearby was a busy place again at the beginning of the 20th century, especially when Harrogate Corpora-tion Railway opened in 1905 for the building of Roundhill Reservoir. That was completed in 1910 and Leeds Corporation took over the line to build Leighton Reservoir. That started in 1908 and was completed in 1926; the line skirted Fearby on the south side.

As late as the 1920s Fearby had several shops including a butcher's, a cobbler, a joiner and a blacksmith's. Local people remember as many as 50 horses waiting to be shod. The village had its own policeman and district nurse. The Wesleyan chapel was rebuilt in 1849 and the adjoining schoolroom added in 1927 for the Sunday school.

Sixty years ago, Fearby Gala was quite an event and Fearby Horse Sports, held behind the village institute, had trotting races. This event almost led to divorce amongst members of the Sports Committee when the men retired to the Black Swan afterwards.

Although nowadays there are only four farms in the village, there were 14 all producing milk only 50 years ago, most of them disappearing in the 1980s.

Fearby Village Green

Felixkirk 🦎

Felixkirk is approximately four miles from Thirsk. It is a pretty village, with public house, church and the old school house now the village hall.

Opposite the Carpenter's Arms public house is a motte, which was probably the site of a timber castle. The old vicarage stands at the top of this mound, now private property. The old school stands on the tiny green, and just across from it is the very beautiful old church of St Felix.

Felixkirk's place in history is assured as one of the local headquarters of the Knights Hospitallers of St John of Jerusalem, from the 12th century until its dissolution in 1530. The Knights were the patrons of the church and appointed the priest. When one enters the church through the Norman door, the thought of the proud knights that came this way centuries ago to worship cannot be far from one's mind.

The road past the church climbs up to Mount St John, which was founded by William De Perci. The De Roos gave the manor in which the community settled, and many other local dignitaries gave other land. Only a fragment of the original house remains, but the place still has the feel of reverence of age and sanctity. It is privately owned, but the gardens are opened to the public once or twice a year for charity.

Felliscliffe 🦎

Felliscliffe is a country parish, including the village of Kettlesing. Three streams meet in the village in the Tang Beck, which travels on to join the river Nidd at Hampsthwaite.

In the centre of the village is a large triangular area of land, within which is the primary school, two houses made of brick and one stone house converted from a barn which has one of the becks flowing underneath. There are three bridges within this small area.

The old chapel is now a house, but memories remain of the organist, who had a hat with tall feathered plumes which waved about above the screen as she played. The new Methodist chapel just up the hill was built in 1930/31, the woodwork being done by a local man. Felliscliffe chapel of ease was built in 1897 by the Kezmathalch family, who also built five church cottages.

Until comparatively recently there were two shops in the village – the post office, a popular place for children to buy sweets, and a corn merchant's who provided everything for humans and animals alike, now sadly gone. The blacksmith no longer plys his trade and the old malt kiln is now a house. The cornmerchant's warehouse, once a centre for both shopping and news, is now divided into cottages.

The area has changed over the years and the knee-breeched men of the past, with their twist for chewing, their pipes and their snuff who used to gather in the Queen's Head for a drink and companionship, would scarcely recognise it, but the spirit, friendship and companionship of this close-knit country community remains the same.

Fencote 🦋

Little Fencote is a tiny hamlet of 20 houses, a quarter of a mile south of Great Fencote, and for this reason was also known as South Fencote in earlier times. Most of the houses, a mixture of old and modern, are clustered around the village green at the eastern and with Fencote Hall at its head. It is a quiet attractive hamlet surrounded by farmland growing all the usual arable crops and grazing sheep and cattle, and the village green in springtime is a carpet of daffodils planted some years ago by a thoughtful villager.

One of the owners of the Hall in the mid 19th century was a Mr Plews. He and his family were great benefactors of the parish, every week buying a beast from the local butchery from which soup would be made and distributed to the poorer people twice a week. They are also credited with helping to finance the building of St Andrew's church at Great Fencote. The road leading from Little Fencote to the church was known as 'Corkscrew Lane' because of the number of bends in it, but some of these have been eliminated in recent years.

'Old Salutation' is the oldest building in the village, the first recorded date being 1673, and is situated at the far western end at the corner of Low Street. It was a coaching inn on the route of the Great North Road and became well known for its 'cockings' when the periodic cock fights would regularly attract crowds of noisy spectators. It was later a pub when coaching days were over, then a joinery and later a farm in about 1944.

There is still a blacksmith's forge in the village, which was run by three generations of the Dodsworth family. Mr Eddie Dodsworth, the last Dodsworth blacksmith, still lived in the village until a couple of years before his death in his nineties in 1987.

A house known as 'The Stud Farm', which stands a short way south of 'Old Salutation' on Low Street, was built about 1857 and a number of famous racehorses of the time were bred there. It was sold in 1884 and became the home of the Bedale hounds until the present kennels were built a little further north along Low Street by the Duke of Leeds in 1920.

Flaxby 🦢

Situated about a mile to the north-east of Goldsborough, and part of the parish, is the hamlet of Flaxby.

Once a mainly farming community, today the new houses and bungalows outnumber the older cottages, and in the last few years the remaining farm in the village has been sold and the buildings converted into desirable homes.

During the 19th century it had its own public house – the New Inn, a shop, a toll bar and school. The school started as a free school in the reign of Charles I and still remains, being used as a village meeting room. Just outside the village is the site of a medieval village called Newton – now only recalled by a field name.

Like Goldsborough village, the people of Flaxby are very concerned about the encroaching industry in the area – particularly as the old railway station now has several firms sited there including a rapidly expanding potato packing factory and wholesale frozen food storage depot.

Follifoot 🦢

The charming village of Follifoot lies in a rural situation about four miles south of Harrogate and has won awards in the Best Kept Village competition.

Although not mentioned in the Domesday Book there are signs of early settlement in the area. Along Pannal Road are the remains of a prehistoric mound at Alexander Hill, and Saxon remains have been found in Rudding Park. A tiny green at the top of Main Street supports a 7th/8th century Saxon cross found in the park and given to the village in 1967 by Sir Everard Radcliffe in memory of his grandparents.

Nearby is the oldest cottage in Follifoot (1631 is carved on the door lintel), the old stocks, the shop/post office and the Lascelles Arms – a hostelry for over 250 years. Opposite is the war memorial bus shelter. Walking down Main Street with its pleasant old Yorkshire stone cottages and their pretty gardens, you reach Horse Pond Beck – its name reflecting a long association with horses. Indeed, the name 'Follifoot' is thought to derive from the Old Norse meaning 'place of the horse fight'.

Dominating the top of Main Street is the fine 19th century Regency-style gatehouse (Rudding Gates) which leads into the estate and Rudding Park, a splendid Grade I listed Regency-style building standing in lovely grounds. Now restored it is used as a conference centre, with caravans and holiday chalets occupying a small area of the gardens. A superbly situated cricket field within the park is well used by the village throughout the summer.

A quite rare 17th century stone pound located along Knaresborough Road was restored by the WI in 1975 to commemorate European Architectural Heritage Year. Nearby is the church of St Joseph & St James (1848).

The village has changed dramatically over the past 30 years. Where once there were various trades plied – a corn miller, tanner, shoemaker, tailor, wheelwright, flax spinner, butcher and blacksmith, Follifoot now has only an agricultural engineering business and a well known joinery and undertaking business run by three generations of Townsends. A blacksmith's forge operated from Sycamore House for over a century which is thought to have produced the wrought iron work in Rudding Gates. Of the nine local farms, now all 'desirable residences', only some of the farmland exists and is run by the Rudding Park Estate.

A major development in Follifoot was the erection of Hillside, one of the first model council estates, although many of the houses are now privately owned. Other small housing developments, viewed with some alarm at the time, have in fact injected new life and enthusiasm into the village.

Fryup Dales

Fryup is not a village but rather a community scattered across the two dells of Great and Little Fryupdale, which between them cover an area of about six square miles. The land in Fryup lies between 450 and 1,000 ft above sea level and is bounded on three sides by Danby and Glaisdale High Moors and, to the north, by the valley of the Esk. Steep sided valley walls sweep down to narrow valley bottoms where flat fields are scarce and two becks empty into the river Esk. In this large area lives a small population thinly spread amongst isolated farmsteads and cottages.

For several centuries Fryup was used by the lord of the manor at Danby Castle to graze his own stock and as a source of income by leasing grazing rights. Apart from this ranching the only other activity we have record of was quite extensive iron smelting in the 13th century and these operations are celebrated by names, still existing, such as Furnace Farm, Mine Pit and Cinder Hill. By the middle of the 17th century the Danby estate, then owned by the Danvers family, was sold to meet debts and that part of it containing Fryup was bought by the Dawnay family, later the Lords Downe. It was from this date, 1655, that the dale started to take on its present form with the former pasture land being enclosed and divided up into a number of tenant farms.

'What a peculiar name' is the reaction of many people on first hearing the name Fryup but it simply derives from Freya, a Norse Goddess and 'hop' being an enclosed valley.

The two dales of Fryup meet at Fairy Cross Plain and it was here that a public house and smithy stood. Its liquid offering must have been quite potent for, as the name implies, here dwelt fairies and trolls and the sound of their nocturnal buttermaking filled the night air. Although the pub has long been closed Fryup was, in living memory, a self-sufficient community having a school, a church, two chapels, two shops and with the services of a blacksmith, a tailor, a joiner and a stonesman all resident in the dale. But, as with many other rural communities, all have now been lost, with the Methodist chapel, one of the earliest in the area, being the last to close a few short years ago.

Fulford 🦢

The village of Fulford lies two miles south of York on the A19 (Selby) road. There were originally two villages, Water Fulford and Gate Fulford, but in the early 19th century they became one.

Some traces of Roman occupation were found in a quarry near the old church, but Fulford really entered the history books with the battle of Fulford, on 20th September 1066. Tostig, the dispossessed Earl of Northumberland, with Hardrada from Norway, overcame a force from York under Earl Morcar. They were themselves defeated five days later at Stamford Bridge by Harold Godwinson.

In 1763 the manor of Water Fulford came into the possession of the Key family. Ten years later, John Key bought the manor of Gate Fulford and so became lord of the manor of both Fulfords. The Key family held the lordship until 1930, being great benefactors to the community. In 1771 John Key built a schoolhouse and endowed a school for '20 poor children'. It is now a private house next to the chapel.

The old church, St Oswald's, is believed to have been built about 1150, with the chancel added 30 years later. It was used regularly until 1866, when the new church was built and until about 20 years ago services were held once a month. It was eventually sold and renovated as a dwelling.

Methodism came to Fulford in the second half of the 18th century. Before the first chapel was built in 1820 the people met in various houses. On one occasion they had to leave because their singing upset the owner's pigeons.

The Fulford Show dates back to the middle of the 19th century. It is held on the playing fields, which is also the venue for cricket and football clubs, a thriving tennis club and a children's playground. Along Heslington Lane is the Fulford Golf Club, used for international competitions.

A laundry was founded early in this century, and existed until the 1970s. Now the main employer of labour in the village is Britton's Dairies.

Gargrave ❧

In upper Airedale, Gargrave is a picturesque stone-built village. South of the village, at Kirk Sink, is a Roman villa site, excavated and then re-covered in the 1970s. Artefacts from the dig may be seen at Skipton and Cliffe Castle museums.

St Andrew's parish church contains fragments of Celtic crosses. In 1318 a Scots raid destroyed the original building. Apart from the 16th century Perpendicular tower, the present church dates from 1852 and has French stained glass windows.

An ancient church dole, known as the Poor Lands Charity, is still distributed to older residents in December. Within living memory, one family was refused payment because they owned half a pig! Times have changed.

Once a thriving market town, Gargrave became a bustling transport centre after the canal was built in the 19th century. Lead from the dales mines was loaded onto barges at one of five Gargrave wharves and the barges returned with coal, corn, glass and other merchandise. Gargrave now plays host to the canal pleasure boats, which tie up between the many locks, used to lower the water from the upper levels.

The cotton industry also thrived in the village until 1932. Two mills are now in residential use. When Airebank (Low) Mill also closed Gargrave fell into a depression in the early 1930s. Then Johnson and Johnson took over the building and to this day the production of medical supplies is carried on there. Gargrave once had a saw mill driven by a water wheel, now restored but not actually in use. Near the site of this mill is an aqueduct – the canal goes over the river, the road goes over the canal and the railway goes over the road.

The ancient summerseat by the river has recently been restored by the parish council. Opposite the summerseat there used to be a watering trough – now marked by a tall lamp-post. Amongst others, the trough was used for watering the horses of the gipsies travelling to Appelby Fair.

Three pubs remain in Gargrave – the Swan, the Mason's Arms and the Anchor inn. The Swan was once a main coaching inn, with blacksmith, saddler, post office, shoemaker and tailor conveniently to hand.

Gayle ❧

Just a mile from the market town of Hawes lies the village of Gayle. Like so many villages in the dales, Gayle is best approached from above. After driving or walking from Wharfdale over the fells for some miles, a steep hill and sharp twist brings you suddenly into the centre of Gayle.

In summer the old stone bridge that links the two halves of the village, 850 ft above sea level, is a favourite meeting place for many of its residents. Beneath the bridge runs Gayle beck over a series of broad-stepped cascades on towards Hawes.

Gayle was originally a farming settlement and the oldest dated building in the village is inscribed 1611, but in some places foundations of earlier buildings are visible.

Gayle had, at one time, a breakaway Methodist sect associated with the Sandemanians in Scotland. They were based at what later became the village institute but now only their graveyard remains. The Methodist chapel built in 1833 is still a strong influence in the village.

In pre-Victorian times Gayle's population numbered about 350 and apart from farming there was employment in the local quarries, coal mining in Sleddale and the imposing cotton mill built some 200 years ago. This later changed to a water-driven saw mill but is now, although in good working order, only used occasionally. It is the oldest textile mill in the country.

Nowadays, although the farming industry continues, the emphasis is on tourism. The population is now only approximately 130 with some houses becoming second or holiday homes and others showing bed and breakfast signs.

Giggleswick

The derivation as far as one can ascertain, comes from 'Gigel', a personal name found in early tax rolls, and 'wic' meaning a village. Giggleswick lies below the limestone scar, part of the Craven fault. The quaintly named Tems beck flows through the village and sturdy picturesque cottages line the main street, where can be found the village post office.

A notable feature of some of the older properties in Giggleswick is the date stones which can be found over doorways. These, together with those in nearby Settle, are some of the most distinctive to be found in the dales.

The population of approximately 764 people is centred round the church, which is dedicated to St Alkelda; she is believed to have been a Saxon saint who was strangled for her faith. The market cross still stands close by the church gate.

Giggleswick school, originally started as a chantry by James Carr, was granted a Royal Charter in 1553 by Edward VI.

To commemorate the Diamond Jubilee of Queen Victoria, Mr Walter Morrison, a governor of the school who lived at Malham Tarn House, had the chapel built. The copper dome is a well known landmark and dominates the skyline. Many of the village houses are owned by the school and are used to accommodate the girls who have recently joined the school.

The site of the old corn mill is near the gate of Catteral Hall, now the prep school for Giggleswick school. The old workhouse, known as

Castleberg Hospital since the 1930s, has been fully modernised in recent years.

The famous Ebbing and Flowing well lies on the A65 north of the village.

The hamlet of Stackhouse lies within the parish of Giggleswick under the eastern side of Giggleswick Scar. The name is derived from an Anglo-Ssxon family and is mentioned in the Domesday Book. It was an appendage of Furness Abbey.

Gillamoor 🌿

Gillamoor is a pleasant working village containing six farms, situated at the edge of an escarpment overlooking the moors and guarding the entrance to Farndale.

In 1737 Joseph Foord, a surveyor from Kirkbymoorside, constructed an aqueduct and watercourse to bring water from a moorland spring to Gillamoor, Fadmoor and Kirkbymoorside using various sizes of outlet to ensure that each area received its correct share. Today, water of excellent quality is supplied from a local reservoir still filled by the moorland spring.

The Royal Oak pub, formerly thatched, retains many attractive features. In the 1960s to 1970s Friday night was kipper night with Whitby oak-smoked kippers cooked over an open fire, to the delight of the local cats!

The Methodist chapel was built in 1867 to commemorate the centenary of the departure to America on a mission of two local men, Joseph Pilmoor and Richard Boardman. St Aidan's church, originally a Norman foundation, was rebuilt in 1802 by James Smith of Farndale.

The glorious 'surprise' view from the top of the escarpment was a favourite vantage point for watching the trail hounds, some of which were kennelled in the village. Today it is the Sinnington foxhounds which provide the spectacle. From the viewpoint one looks down on the Gillamoor mill mentioned in King John's charter of 1206. It ceased working in 1895.

There is a very rare four-faced sundial dated 1800 in the centre of the village, a great attraction for visitors, and opposite are the remains of the village pinfold or pound.

Gillamoor once had a shop, famous all over the region for its hams and bacon, and there is still a 'limited opening' post office. However the blacksmith's forge, the two joiner's shops, two stonemasons, the garage, reading room and billiard room have all gone.

Gilling East 🌿

Gilling East lies in a beautiful wooded area on the edge of the Howardian Hills, watered by the Holbeck stream. The small hamlets of Cawton, Coulton and Grimstone are also included in the parish.

Cockpit Farm, Cawton was once a public house, where cockfights took place in an adjoining field, and nearby Spring Farm derives its name from a holy spring dedicated to St Wilfred. Today the place is a quiet haven for tourists, and the villagers are fighting local plans for a proposed large gravel extraction plant.

Grimstone Manor, in the 13th century, was once exchanged by its owner for ten pounds per year for life, a silk robe, furs, and two weeks hospitality at Martinmas and Christmas, quite a bargain! Today there is still a manor, but the parish is better known for rose growing.

Gilling church of the Holy Cross dates back in part to the 11th century. It contains a rare 14th century slab tomb of an unknown knight. There is also a small Roman Catholic church, dedicated to Our Lady and Holy Angels, originally being the reading room and school house.

On a hill above the village stands Gilling Castle, built as a fortified manor house in 1349 by Thomas de Etton, eventually becoming the home of the Catholic Fairfax family. The castle is now a boys preparatory school for Ampleforth College, but is open to the public in summer, along with lakes, gardens and a nine-hole golf course.

The old primary school serves as the village hall, and a model railway engineering club has built a small gauge line, circling the village hall and old playground. They hold regular open days, when all ages can ride on the model coaches.

Girsby & Over Dinsdale 🌿

These quiet rural adjoined parishes lie almost encircled by a loop of the river Tees, on the northernmost boundaries of North Yorkshire with County Durham.

This is essentially private estate land; though some of the farms and many of the houses are independently owned. The present estate owners do not reside within the parishes.

The two Anglican churches are situated across the borders into Durham, St John the Baptist being in Low Dinsdale and what is known as Girsby church lies just inside Sockburn parish. Such are the complexities of the boundaries, making administration difficult. There is evidence to show that Girsby was once a much more extensive village. Now it is a tiny hamlet with four houses and a church. The tiny church perches high on the edge of the river valley. A metal footbridge spans the river; replacing a former swing bridge – now in disrepair.

The river Tees here was once renowned for its salmon fisheries and the site of the fish locks and salmon ladder is still identifiable. A red sandstone seam is exposed along its course and this warm colour is evident in many older local buildings. Along the tree-lined river banks the giant hogweed is prolific and grows to spectacular heights.

The gamekeeper at Over Dinsdale, a well known figure, was a fine forthright conscientious gentleman. He tended the game, organised the shoots and kept the rabbit population under control. Unwary poachers quickly responded to the awesome grip of his strong right arm, and would rarely return for a repeat of his vigorous counselling.

Today farming is still the most important industry and source of employment. There is no longer any estate work and the cottages are being bought independently and developed, creating some changes in the community. The development of busy Teesside Airport on the site of the old aerodrome brings noise, but also convenience and to some, employment. Local gentlemen have formed a shooting syndicate; clubs from surrounding towns use the river for coarse fishing.

Ivy Cottages, formerly the Laundry at Over Dinsdale

Glaisdale

Glaisdale is one with the village of Lealholm as a parish on the river Esk near Whitby. Glaisdale is one of the four 'fingers' of dales running up to the Yorkshire Moors. The farming along the dale is good; there are a number of farms, two of which were mentioned in the Domesday Book, and two that still have 'witch posts'. There is a legend of a hob (a fairy, or brownie) at Hart Hall farm who performs chores whilst the farmer sleeps.

In the 12th century there were early iron works and the sandstone cuttings on the hillside are evidence of the quarrying in the 16th and 18th century. Waterloo Bridge was built of this. Later in the 18th century Glaisdale had a small 'South Sea Bubble' when iron ore was discovered. Money was poured in by Victorian businessmen and three furnaces and a 250 ft chimney was built. The population increased from 600 to 2,000 with workers. Houses were built for them and are still there today, along with a handsome Mechanics Institute. The village thrived; sadly although

many shafts were sunk and much ore was removed by the newly-built railway, the project itself also sank quickly, as did the population. It now stands at 1,300. The land used has gone back to farming land.

The village has three pubs spread at convenient stopping points for the many walkers who pass through on the Coast to Coast walk. There is one store/post office, a butcher, two churches, a school and an institute that replaced the earlier Mechanics Institute that disappeared with the old ironworks.

The main attraction for visitors is the Beggars Bridge over the river. It was built in the 17th century by a certain Thomas Ferris, a poor farm worker who loved the daughter of a wealthy Glaisdale farmer, who did not consider him a suitable suitor for his daughter. Thomas decided to go to seek his fortune elsewhere but was prevented from bidding his love farewell by the river Eske being in full spate. He resolved that when he returned rich he would build a bridge over the river, and that is what he did.

Glasshouses

Looking down the hill to Glasshouses from the Pateley Bridge – Ripon road, one sees a collection of grey stone houses, with a sprinkling of modern bungalows. A tall chapel spire completes a village which nestles into the valley beside the river Nidd, overlooked by the woods and tall rock formations of Guyscliffe. The village appears to straggle towards its larger neighbour, Pateley Bridge, one and a half miles away, but remarkably, Glasshouses has managed to retain its own character. Situated off the Harrogate – Pateley Bridge road, it does not attract many tourists, apart from walkers exploring the Nidderdale Way.

The name Glasshouses has a long history. Derived from the Old English 'glaes hus', house where glass was made, it first appeared in 1386. Although no local record of glassmaking exists, legend has it that the glass for Fountains Abbey was made in the area.

The Metcalfe brothers bought the flax mill in 1835, at which time 78 workers were employed. The Metcalfes were regarded as good employers, providing terraced cottages for their workers with piped water, 'foul' drainage and gas lighting in the 1860s.

The Metcalfes also supplied the educational and spiritual needs of the village. They provided a school in 1861, the Wesleyan Methodist chapel in 1866 and in 1872 established a Mechanics Institute, with a reading room and lending library. From 1875 until 1933 there was also a Primitive Methodist chapel. The chapels were the source of most of the social life of the village, with Sunday school outings and prize-givings, chapel anniversaries and bazaars.

The mill was taken over in 1912 by the Atkinson family, who installed more modern machinery and improved rope-making processes. The spinning of flax and hemp went on until 1972 with the large waterwheel, unusually, being used well into the 20th century. The business then closed and the mill was sold to its present owner. It now houses a variety of small businesses.

Glasshouses also has a thriving cricket club, which has fielded men's and ladies' teams since 1871. At one time, the men fielded two teams of such prowess that it was said the mill chimney would fall down in shock if they lost.

Glusburn & Crosshills 🌿

The villages of Glusburn and Cross Hills in South Craven are nowadays practically inseparable and largely interdependent, Glusburn being dominated in many ways by the adjoining and much younger village of Cross Hills.

Situated near the intersection of the main roads from Keighley, Skipton and Colne, Cross Hills provides the area with a wide variety of shops, many of them old-established businesses founded in the late 19th century. It also houses a large comprehensive school drawing pupils from many surrounding villages. Curiously, despite its significant position, Cross Hills is still not named on many road maps.

Cross Hills is, however, predated by some 750 years by the neighbouring village of Glusburn. Stretching along the busy Keighley to Colne road to the west of Cross Hills, Glusburn is still dominated by Hayfield's spinning mill and the Institute. These impressive buildings were both built by Sir John Horsfall in the years 1870–1896, along with the rows of tied terraced houses.

The Institute, a splendid building, housed a reading room, games rooms, swimming bath and slipper baths and a large hall, all for the use of the mill workers. Attached to the building is a Baptist chapel, still in use today. Sir John was a strict abstainer and even today there is no public house in the village itself.

A fire in August 1969 destroyed part of Hayfield's Mill, but it was rebuilt and since its merger with Sirdar Wools in 1972 still provides employment for many local people. The lovely old house where the Horsfalls lived is now a nursing home and the beautiful gardens have made way for luxury bungalows.

Higher up the Colne road was the old smithy and villagers remember Fred Overend, the carter, wearing a sacking apron and chewing 'baccy', driving his horse-drawn cart through the village.

The road through the two villages has now become a 'feeder' road to the new Aire Valley trunk road between Skipton and Keighley and there is a constant stream of traffic from Lancashire and back. A far cry from the days of Fred's horse-drawn cart.

Goldsborough 🌿

This small village is rather special in that it was an estate village from just after the Norman Conquest until 1952 when the farms and cottages were sold by the present Earl of Harewood to help pay enormous death duties on the death of his father Henry Lascelles, husband of HRH Princess Mary, Princess Royal.

On either side of the chancel in St Mary's church there is a tomb bearing the effigy of a knight. Both of them are fine examples of crusader armour of the 14th century. They have been identified as father and son, both Sir Richard de Goldesburgh, 1308 and 1333.

During the 1920s the village was famous because Mary, daughter of George V and Queen Mary, lived at the Hall after her marriage. Her eldest son, George, was christened at the church, the ceremony being attended by the King and Queen.

St Mary's, which dates from the early 12th century, has many interesting features, including a Norman doorhead and columns, and perhaps more unusually it is a 'green man' church. This Celtic god of fertility with his grotesque oak-leaved head is well hidden on one of the Goldsborough family tombs.

During restorations in 1859 a lead casket was unearthed which contained Viking jewellery and coins. The best of the find is in the British Museum and some of the coins were melted down to make the collection plate which is used every Sunday.

Goldsborough, with its old brick and stone cottages and farmhouses and stone entrance pillars, is still what it has been for centuries, a quiet rural backwater that was associated with its distinguished owners over the years. The biggest challenge for the future lies with the increasing urbanisation and industrialization from Knaresborough and the adjacent A1, where already a giant steelworks is in operation.

Grantley 🌿

The village of Grantley is in Skeldale, about 500 ft above sea level in beautiful unspoilt country. It is a community of 26 houses. There are three farms, one at each end of the village and one in the centre. Being grassland farms, dairying and sheep form the main part of this industry.

Although it is quite a small village, it is thriving. There is a Methodist chapel, which has a shared service once a month with the church of Winksley, a nearby village, a large village hall, a well stocked shop-cum post office, the Grantley Arms public house and a splendid new school.

Grantley Hall, once the home of Lord Grantley, then the Furniss shipping family and then the Akeroyds, became a convalescent home for soldiers during the Second World War. It is now an adult College run by the North Yorkshire Education Authority, with courses open to the public and closed courses for teachers and others.

Within half a mile of the village, on the Pateley Bridge road, there is a saw mill. Owned by a family in the village it is a hive of activity, employing about 17 people from the village and round about, supplying farmers, landowners and the National Trust with all manner of fencing and woodwork and doing contract work.

Grassington

Grassington, with a population of approximately 1,200 people, is one of the best loved little 'towns' in the Yorkshire Dales, although the locals prefer to say 'they are going into the village'. It is sheltered on the north-west by Grass Woods, 200 acres of woodland, once part of the estate of the Duke of Devonshire and now owned by the Yorkshire Wildlife Trust.

One day that has been celebrated for many years is Feast Sunday, always the first Sunday after the 11th October – the feast of St Michael associated with St Michael's church, which is situated on the riverside. The Feast Sports takes place on the football field on the Saturday nearest to the 11th October. One of the traditional events was the 'tea cake eating race'; the children had to eat a tea cake, run to the other end of the

Grassington Village

field and the winner was the first one to be able to whistle a tune – no easy feat!

At the end of the 18th century the population reached 3,000 as a result of the leadmining industry, relics of this being still evident at Yarnbury. Many large families occupied the small miners' cottages which still remain today with little alteration to their exteriors. These cottages with their beehive ovens and inglenook fireplaces are much sought after for holiday cottages and people seeking to retire to the area.

The central part of the village is now a conservation area. The church house was built as a farmhouse in 1694, later becoming a temperance hotel until it was purchased by the Church in 1925. The Old Hall dates back to the 13th century. The former smithy, now the flower shop, was the home and blacksmith's workplace of one Tom Lee who in 1766 reputedly killed the local doctor as he rode through Grass Wood. He was executed in York and his body gibbeted near where the murder had taken place.

Great Ayton

Of Anglo-Saxon times little remains at Great Ayton other than the name. The old Norman parish church, All Saints, built early in the 12th century, contains fragments of Anglo-Saxon crosses, ascribed to the late 8th century and found in the vicarage garden adjoining the churchyard a century ago.

From humble origins here came Captain James Cook RN, probably the greatest English explorer and navigator. Captain Cook's mother and five of her children are interred in the churchyard, and as part of the Captain Cook Heritage Trail, the grave is visited by thousands of visitors. The old church became redundant in 1876 when the new parish church was built.

During the 18th century the Quakers were to play an important part in Great Ayton. In 1700 they were establishing a meeting house at the High Green. Among them were the more wealthy members of the community, involved in the local industries of tanning, oil mills, weaving, corn milling and agriculture. One of their interests was education. In 1841 Thomas Richardson endowed the British school (now the village library) and about the same time founded the Friends' school, originally as an agricultural school for children of Quaker parents.

To the east of the High Street is Newton Road, known locally as 'California'. This is a reference to the rapid increase in the community due to the influx of miners and quarrymen during the 19th century, which replaced the rural industries. It has been estimated that more than 800 Ayton men were employed in ironstone mining. All mining had ended in the 1920s and the village is now a dormitory for commuters to the larger industrial centres.

In 1972 when the local government boundaries were being redrawn, Great Ayton seemed bound to become part of the new County of Cleveland. The villagers united as one man in protest and avoided the unthinkable. It is now the most northerly large village in North Yorkshire and the village gala instituted in 1973 to celebrate the victory over the planners is repeated every other year with decorated floats, fancy dress parade and a great fair on the High Green.

Great Barugh ﷽

People have lived in Great Barugh for centuries, the barugh, or hill, keeping most of the village safely above the winter floods of the river Seven, before the flood banks were built. There are remains of prehistoric tumuli and a Roman villa was excavated earlier this century. A Roman road led to York. The lighter coloured crop patterns in fields behind Manor Farm are thought to be foundations of medieval buildings and a fishpond. These are clearly visible from the air.

Agriculture was the main occupation of the villagers over the years, but the rapid mechanization of farming after the First World War reduced the numbers of men and women employed on the land. Most of the cottages which were their homes have gone too. Now most of the inhabitants earn their livings by other means.

One of the oldest building remaining is the Golden Lion inn. The Anglican chapel of ease and the Wesleyan chapel are now houses and the school, which was opened in 1859, has gone.

Fishermen enjoy their sport on the river Seven and during the summer months, the caravan park just outside the village is a popular choice with holidaymakers.

Great Edstone ﷽

Great Edstone is a tiny hamlet situated on a flat-topped hill two miles south of Kirkbymoorside. The parish church of St Michael stands at the west end of the village, an 11th century church with an Anglo–Danish sundial over the doorway, marked with only eight divisions. There is a 12th century font and the wooden bell tower houses a pair of unusual bells cast in 1350. From the doorway there is an impressive panoramic view of Ryedale looking southwestwards towards the Vale of York.

Between the churchyard and village street stands the ancient pinfold, used years ago to impound stray livestock until claimed by the owner. The tiny Wesleyan chapel standing at the east end of the village was built in 1823. It resembles a tea-caddy, just waiting to have the lid lifted off. The one-roomed school complete with bell tower, minus the bell these days, has now been extended and is the village hall. The Grey Horse public house stands in the centre of the village on Wapping Lane. There is a manor house, complete with gargoyles.

There used to be four working farms in the village itself, but now only two remain. There is now a fine village green, in the centre of the village, which was once a rather dirty pond.

Great Langton 🦢

Great Langton is a delightful hamlet situated close to the river Swale. There is a beautiful parish church approximately one mile from the village, built in the 12th century. Mother Shipton, the famous witch and prophetess of Knaresborough in the 15th century, is said to have prophesied that Langton church would one day sink into the ground and be washed away by the river. It is true that the church is gradually sinking, the floor has at sometime been raised 15 inches from its original level and even the present floor is two feet below the ground outside, but the structure stands firm.

The Wishing Well, once named Langton Hotel, is in the centre of the village with some of the older houses to one side and new properties beyond, including the Methodist church – now a private house. The church of the Good Shepherd and the village school are no longer in use, the school closed in 1978.

Grewelthorpe 🦢

The small village of Grewelthorpe, population 383, lies six miles north-west of Ripon and three miles south of Masham. It is a leafy, pleasant, village with houses clustering around a spacious village green and large village pond.

There is good reason to believe that the Romans knew the area and had a camp at the northern end of the village. Early in the 20th century a complete skeleton of a Roman soldier was uncovered on Grewelthorpe Moor. The skeleton was reburied in Kirkby Malzeard, though his sandals can still be seen in the York Museum.

Like most villages, in bygone days Grewelthorpe had a variety of businesses necessary for a rural area. There were several shops, two blacksmiths, tailors, a shoemaker, a tannery and a wool warehouse, a bakery, a cream cheese producer and, in one cottage, straw was plaited to make hats.

There are two public houses, one, the Crown, was an old coaching house and built in 1624. The Methodist chapel, with its distinctive steeply sloping roof was rebuilt in 1866. The church, dedicated to St James, was built in 1846 and is surrounded by a beautifully cared for churchyard. In the main street is the school, built in 1876. From here and the school playing fields, there are beautiful views across the neighbouring countryside to the Hambleton Hills.

Near the village are the Hackfall Woods, where the river Ure flows through woods of great beauty. During the 19th century these were developed, waterfalls created and the follies, which date back to the 18th century, were transformed into vantage points. In 1930 the Hackfall was sold to a timber merchant, the gates were closed, trees felled and the follies left to collapse. Now the Woodland Trust are caring for and restoring the woods.

Gristhorpe & Lebberston 🌿

Two small villages, they share an adult population of approximately 500 and are about five miles from Scarborough and two miles from Filey.

Lebberston, the smaller of the two, has a Hall and a public house. Gristhorpe has a Hall, a manor, a public house and a small church that is owned by the Beswick family who live in the manor. Some of the cottages are 300 years old.

In 1834, the skeleton of a man was found on Gristhorpe Cliffs, and was presented to Scarborough Museum (where it still is). Experts say he would have been a chief from the Bronze Age, 1500 BC. He was buried in a coffin that had been hewn from a log of oak, thus being well preserved.

In 1915 the *Mekong*, a Japanese gun-boat, was wrecked on the cliffs. Members of the crew were able to scramble ashore and were given hospitality by local people.

Gunnerside 🌿

Gunnerside is situated 17 miles from Richmond in the heart of Swaledale in the Yorkshire Dales National Park. It still retains much of the charm of the typical dales village.

This was once a thriving lead mining village, but as the mines closed in the late 19th century, so the population dwindled. About 100 people now live here, with 46 houses lived in and about the same number as holiday homes. The population trebles in summer.

When the lead mines began to close many people left to find work in the Durham coalfields, the cotton mills of Lancashire and some to emigrate to America and Spain. One of the most important days in Gunnerside's calendar was Midsummer Sunday (the first in July) when many of the people who had left returned to reunite with friends and family and to hold a service of thanksgiving in the chapel, which would be full to overflowing. John Wesley preached here and the village has had strong Methodist traditions ever since. Another event which still takes place is the 'Shortest Day Festival' in December, believed to be derived from a pagan custom.

On the third Friday in October Gunnerside still celebrates Gunnerside Fair. This was originally a market, where people came from the surrounding area to sell their sheep and cattle, to browse around the market stalls and meet friends. Local people still have fairings bought at the market. This was always followed by a local concert supper and dance, one of the highlights of the year. The date is still celebrated although the market no longer exists.

Most functions take place in the village hall, built, as was the chapel, by local people. The village has a pub and a cafe, both run by local families.

Halton West 🌿

Halton West is situated two miles from Hellifield and separated from it by the river Ribble. It was purchased by Thomas Yorke of Gouthwaite in 1737, who realised the potential of 2,123 acres of good farming land. His son built Halton Place, a Georgian house overlooking the river, and the estate has been passed from father to son ever since.

The farms were improved, more cottages built and by 1877 a school was needed. One was built and a schoolmistress employed. This was followed by a church to replace the churchroom in one of the cottages and a village institute for the use of the village population.

Halton West Bridge, spanning the Ribble, is a vital link for the community and when it had to be repaired during the winter of 1987 it caused great inconvenience to those who live on the eleven farms and in the twelve cottages.

Hampsthwaite 🌿

Hampsthwaite is an attractive village with a population of about 1,000, in a lovely setting on the river Nidd. The ancient narrow bridge and nearby church are on the site of a way used by the Romans travelling between Ilkley and Aldborough. Traces of the Roman tin-mining industry, when Hampsthwaite was part of the route for the transport of minerals, can still be seen in upper Niddersdale.

The church of St Thomas à Becket has remnants of Saxon building in the tower. Celtic crosses found in the area are set into the porch.

The family of the writer William Makepeace Thackeray lived here, as did the family of Amy Woodforde-Finden, the composer of the *Indian love lyrics*; her effigy in white marble is in the church, and the graves of the men in her family, all soldiers, are in the churchyard. A more macabre memory of the past is at Cruet Farm, where a murder took place. It is said that an upstairs door mysteriously opens and closes of its own accord and an ineradicable stain still exists on the flagged floor.

Some modern housing has been built since the Second World War, but the centre of the village, in the conservation area, retains the charm of older times. With Harrogate only five miles away, Hampsthwaite could be just another commuter village, but this is not so. The well-attended church, chapel and school; the post office, shops (some mobile), medical facilities, garages and small businesses supply most of the needs of residents. The Joiner's Arms and a restaurant are noted for comfort and good food. The mobile library makes a regular visit. All these services give the village a great deal of independence.

Farming has remained the important local activity, with sheep grazing the hillsides, some cattle, and arable fields along the more level valley bottom. The river Nidd winds through the open fields with trees edging its banks, and provides trout and grayling for the local anglers.

Harmby ✍️

Harmby is a fairly large village one and a half miles from the market town of Leyburn.

The former manor house, modernised in the 19th century, is now a private dwelling, not a farmhouse as it was till the 1960s. A chapel adjacent to the house was nearly all pulled down in the 19th century and the stone was used for the farm buildings. A part of the chapel is incorporated into the present house and there is a priest hole, now bricked up. There is also reputed to be a monk's grave in the house beneath a black slab – but no ghosts as far as we know.

New housing estates have sprung up over more recent times at the top and bottom of the village, while the old part is formed by a very steep hill, or Harmby Bank as it is known. Like many villages there are no shops and Harmby has never had a post office. Butchers, bakers and travelling shops are a thing of the past. The Methodist chapel is sited at the bottom of the hill and was built in 1855 on land given by the Storey family who lived nearby.

A limestone quarry ran here for a number of years supplying stone to builders and grit and gravel for the roads. The quarry is now landscaped and run as two separate caravan sites. The Express Dairy ran a thriving milk-collecting station in Leyburn for approximately 30 years, again providing employment for locals.

There is only one public house, the Pheasant inn at the top of the hill on the main Bedale road. This was formerly the Railway Tavern; the railway line runs approximately 200 yards to the north of the pub. This stretch of line is used each day by a mineral train collecting stone from Redmire quarry, the deadend for this line at the moment being Redmire station but there are ideas for opening the line again further up the dale.

Harton ❧

The entrance to Harton from York-Malton road is through the 'Griffon Gates'. There is still evidence of these gates but the cottage once incorporated is now derelict. The piers, topped by the sculptured 'griffons', were demolished by the heavy traffic in the Second World War. The occupants of the cottage used to have to cross the road to their bedroom.

Unfortunately none of the thatch of old remains, as many of the houses are now tiled or slated and modernised inside. The chapel is now a pleasant cottage. The school closed too due to a lack of pupils but the building is now a village hall, well supported by the small community and the church at Bossall.

The village is dominated by the manor house, a lovely farmhouse dating back to the 17th century. It contains many original features including a very fine oak staircase, moulded and beamed ceilings. Of special interest is the sulphur stone of which the front hall is paved. This is one of the few examples of this stone in the north of England.

Harton forms part of the Chomley Estates and has been owned by the Strickland family since 1865. Some land has been sold for new houses and bungalows have been built on the foundations of old cottages and on other sites. The District Council built four houses. The village has changed from a farming community to a mainly residential one. The number of inhabitants is about 60 with a wide range of ages and occupations. There are now three farms, the land having been amalgamated to form larger units. Family run agriculture is still the main occupation in the village as other residents travel away to work.

In 1807 a leaden vessel was uncovered by a plough and found to contain about 300 Saxon silver coins, some silver rings and pieces of spurs.

Hawes ❧

Hawes is situated in Upper Wensleydale on the river Ure, and is the main centre in the northern part of the Yorkshire Dales National Park. Wensleydale is a wider dale than the neighbouring dales of Swaledale and Wharfdale. Its scenery is perhaps less dramatic but pleasant and open.

The hill country of the dales is traditionally sheep country and the Swaledale is the most common sheep in the dales. The Swaledale, with its black face and grey nose, is a very active sheep and can scratch a living on poor land.

The founding on an auction mart in 1887 in Hawes changed the way local farmers disposed of their stock. For nearly 200 years stock had been sold in the cattle market in the centre of the town and in adjacent garths. There has been extensive development and the Gimmer lamb sales in

September and Swaledale tup sales in October are the highlights of the farming year. Newly calved cows and calves are sold every week and other cattle are sold at regular sales.

St Margaret's church was built around 1850 after a faculty was granted for the demolition of the 'old chapel'. It was built in local stone and some local men worked on it.

Several organisations are still surviving in Hawes after many years. The Hawes and Abbotside Angling Association began to regularise fishing and issue licences from 1844 and is still in business. They issue licences to increasing numbers of visitors. Hawes Brass Band was formed around 1865 and the famous Brass Band Contest at Hardraw Scar was first held in 1881. The band and the contest continue to flourish today.

The famous Wensleydale cheese is made locally at the dairy which is owned by the Milk Marketing Board. The dairy is the largest single employer of labour in the upper dale. The rope works was started during the 19th century and the business has been extended and taken on extra workers.

The natural beauty and character of the area attracts many visitors and tourism has become a main industry in the town. This brings with it some prosperity but also the attendant disadvantages and pressures associated with the influx of people and traffic.

Hawsker cum Stainsacre

Hawsker cum Stainsacre is a joint township in the parish of Whitby, comprising about 3,790 acres and a population of about 825. Mr Constable Strickland is the lord of the manor.

The village of Hawsker consists of two parts, High and Low Hawsker. It stands south by east, four miles from Whitby. One of the oldest buildings is Hawsker Hall, built in about 1867. The shaft of a headless cross stands in a small enclosure that belongs to the Hall. It is said to be the only relic left of the chapel founded by Aschetine (or Aschetil) de Hawskesgarth in the reign of King Stephen. In 1877, the present church was erected and dedicated to All Saints, as the old church had been.

Principal landowners at the turn of the 19th century included Captain Turton of Upsall Castle who owned Larpool Hall, an elegant dressed stone mansion in the classic style situated on the side of the Esk, overlooking Whitby. Today, it is a country house hotel and restaurant.

Stainsacre is united with Hawsker for fiscal purposes. The Hall today is owned by Cleveland Education Authority and is used as a residential centre for youth work and outdoor pursuits.

Cock Mill, a secluded place in the woods, was used for gambling and cock fighting in the old days, as well as a hide-out for home-coming sailors eluding the press gangs. Strange, ghostly tales were told of 'The Gentleman in Black' who frequently took his seat at the gambling tables.

On the cliff, known as Ling Hill, two lighthouses were erected in 1858 by Trinity House, as a guide to mariners approaching Whitby. When both lights were seen, all was well but, should the two lights appear as one, the vessel must change course or be dashed on the rocks. Many ships have been wrecked along this coast.

Until the 1950s, the water supplies were the village pumps. Hawsker had a cobbler and a tailor. Both villages had blacksmiths and a local shop with a post office. Stainsacre's has been closed for a few years now but Hawsker's is still going strong. There is still a windmill (without sails) at Hawsker, but the village pond has unfortunately been filled in.

A favourite game in both villages was quoits. There was friendly rivalry among the men of all the neighbouring villages. It is still played today at Hawsker. Of course the pub is usually in close proximity because it is thirsty work!

Haxby 🦢

In the 9th century, in the ancient forest of Galtres, Haac the Dane settled with his family on the low ground beside the river Foss, some four miles north of the city of Jorvik (later to become York). Now, more than a thousand years later, the forest has been reduced to a few isolated groups of trees, but the Domesday township of Haxebi has flourished to become the present day village of Haxby, with a population at the 1981 census of over 9,000, when it was still growing.

Situated in the Vale of York, only about 50 ft above sea level, the land around Haxby was ideal for agriculture and, over the centuries, as the forest was cleared, more land became available for farming. By the early 18th century, the village comprised a wide street with a row of farms and dwellings on each side, with each row serviced by a back lane, situated in the centre of four large open fields farmed by the strip method. In 1769, following the Act of Enclosure, the land was divided into farms, with 65 proprietors receiving allotments of land.

The village grew at a steady rate until the mid 1950s, and by then the smallholdings had been amalgamated into much larger farms. With the increased demand for home ownership since the Second World War, large housing estates have covered most of the medieval fields and the farms have gone from the village centre, with the old farmhouses that survive being either private houses or commercial premises.

Although most of the working residents of Haxby go out of the village for employment either in York or its surrounding industrial estates, the village itself is well serviced, with amenities including three supermarkets, three banks, three pubs, two restaurants and an hotel. A large playing field, managed by a voluntary body, provides a variety of sports and recreation on what was part of the grounds of the manor house. The latter was demolished in the 1950s, and on its site is a local authority residential home for the elderly.

Healey Village with St Paul's Church

Healey

The name Healey is derived from 'heil' meaning holy or sacred and 'ley' meaning pasture or meadow. A barn at Firs Farm is the oldest existing building, and is thought to have been a Catholic chapel a long time ago.

Another interesting building is Healey corn mill. It was built in 1756 and was powered by water from Healey Pasture, near Gollinglith Foot, and the remains of the mill race can still be traced near the road. It was converted to diesel power in the 1940s and was last used for grinding corn in 1980. Now it is used as a Christian holiday centre for young people.

The church of St Paul was built in 1848 by Admiral Vernon Harcourt, lord of the manor, with stone from Healey quarry. The view from the porch must be one of the finest in Yorkshire.

Moor View was at one time the village shop and there was a public house, the Black Horse, until 1956. There was another mill down by the river Burn. First built for grinding corn and then changed to a cotton mill, it later became the Swinton estate sawmill and is now Swinton trout farm.

An interesting feature in the area is the Druids' Temple, not far from the trout farm, towards Ilton. It is like a miniature Stonehenge, built around 1800 by William Danby, after he saw a similar temple on his tour of the continent.

A day's fly-fishing can be enjoyed at Leighton Reservoir, which is stocked from the estate trout farm. This is Leeds City water supply, Harrogate's comes from Roundhill Reservoir. The siting tower on the moor is one of a series of three, marking the pipeline to Harrogate where the water gravitates.

Gollinglith Foot (pronounced locally as 'Gownley' Foot) is the entrance to Colsterdale. Now just a few houses, it was once a thriving mining community. Iron, lead and coal have all been mined from the area. Typical of the surrounding areas, several of the buildings were once thatched with heather. It had its own school for many years, founded in 1787.

Hellifield 🦪

The village came into being in the late 19th century with the advent of the railways. The Lancashire and Yorkshire, the London and Midland and Scottish Railways joined at the junction of Hellifield. They later became known as the LMS. Up to this time it was a small farming community, then terraces of houses were built, the first two being Lancashire and Yorkshire Terrace and Midland after the railways. Then followed rapid development until the 1930s.

This was followed by an auction mart with cattle coming in from all over Britain. There was a large cattle dock adjacent to the railway marshalling yard and a private road to the auction mart. Most of the land around and a number of the farms belong to the auction.

The majority of families were connected to the railways. For some families it was the second and third generation employed there. Most boys wanted to be engine drivers, that was considered high up the ladder. The engine shed closed in the 1960s, but today there are still transport connections, this time road haulage. A large number of men are employed this way; mainly owner drivers. August 1990 saw another change, when the auction mart closed for sales – this is now being carried on in Skipton.

The church was built in 1906. Prior to this the village was part of Long Preston parish and church services were held in the schoolroom, which is known as the Institute. The population had grown so that in 1914 a new school was built on the outskirts of the village, still very much in use.

There are plans afoot to restore the station as it is the entry to the

Settle–Carlisle line. There is a good selection of shops in the village, as well as a high-class gents and ladies outfitters and the Black Horse, where a pleasant drink and a meal can be enjoyed.

Helperby & Brafferton

Brafferton is a Saxon development dating from at least the 7th century AD, and possibly earlier. Helperby was built a little later by the Vikings. It was a busy agricultural and trading centre, being the furthest navigable point on the river Swale and where the river could be crossed. The area produced excellent malting barley and there was a brewery in the village until comparatively recent times.

Helperby/Brafferton today is an unusual twin village with houses clustered together along a main street, cobbled on either side and with the gardens behind. It is a thriving community with a growing population of around 800. Amenities include two grocery shops, petrol pump, butcher, hairdresser, post office, doctor's surgery, fish and chip shop, four inns and a coach hire company. There is an excellent Church of England primary school, at present catering for about 60 pupils. There are several new housing developments for commuters working in York, Leeds and Teesside but the main street boasts some fine old houses. Sadly, most of the original village was destroyed in a great fire in the 17th century.

It was built largely for the farming community and corresponding trades and craftsmen. Helperby Hall estates have been in the Milnes Coates family for many generations; Lady Celia died in 1985 aged 100 years, and the Queen Anne residence has been restored by Sir Anthony, her grandson. The Coates family also built the almshouses in 1873 and the fountain commemorating Queen Victoria's Diamond Jubilee in 1897. This water was carried daily in buckets by the residents until mains water was installed in the 1930s.

St Peter's church dates back to early Christianity. In AD 626 St Paulinus, later the first Bishop of York, baptised many people here in the river Swale. The oldest parts of the present church date from the 15th century – the tower and chancel.

Hemingbrough

The village of Hemingbrough is situated on the A63 between the towns of Selby and Howden. It also banks the river Ouse, with its busy river traffic. The river was the only access to the village from the west until the building of Selby toll bridge in 1792, and Landing Road was the way into the village from the river.

Surrounded by flat, open farmland, the spire of St Mary's church dominates the village. Part of the church's nave dates back to the 12th century. White stone, quarried at Tadcaster, was used to extend the church in the 13th and 15th centuries, when it became a collegiate church under the jurisdiction of the Prior of Durham (until the suppression by Henry VIII in 1534) and trainee priests lived in a house still standing opposite the church, which is reputed to be haunted. An upstairs room in the house is said to be chillingly cold even on the hottest day in summer.

The church is well known for its bench-end carving, showing figures of dragons, a monkey and a jester. A misericord – a hinged projection on the underside of a choir seat – dates from about 1200 and is possibly the oldest in England.

Whilst agriculture was the main occupation in the 18th century, the 19th century saw a decline in the importance of Hemingbrough as industries developed in nearby Selby. The more recent population explosion has been as a result of the construction of Drax power station and particularly of the opening of the Selby coalfield, with several housing estates covering farmland.

Still the most interesting houses in the village are those in Main Street, north and south of the church, built of dark red bricks, burned and of uneven size and shape made from the clay of the local brickyard.

There was, in the past, a working mill and a bakehouse; these have disappeared but corn merchants, crop sprayers (by helicopter) and agricultural engineers still function.

Heslington

In the 1940s and 1950s Heslington was a quiet place built on a crossroads. There were a few farms scattered round the surrounding countryside, but Main Street just consisted of several cottages, a couple of pubs, two shops, a chapel and the manor house. The church stood opposite the Hall at the top of the village.

In the 1950s, 30 or so council houses were built at the end of School Lane, but by far the biggest change in the history of the village came in the 1960s, when Heslington was chosen as the site for York University.

At about this time the whole estate was put up for sale, and bought by Lord Halifax. Suddenly, houses began to spring up in the shape of Hall Park, Badger Hill and Holmfield estates. Any cottages which became vacant were quickly snapped up and house prices rocketed. Almost overnight, four banks appeared in Main Street and the village school – Lord Deramore's, was enlarged ready to take on extra pupils of many different nationalities. Even the church had to be extended, and became multi-denominational to accommodate the students.

Heslington Hall became the administration centre for the university and a new road, with colleges on either side, was built as a way in to York. The boating lake, which had once been a feature of the garden at the Hall, was now extended to become a large lake, around which most of the university buildings lay.

From a sleepy little backwater, Heslington was now as full of hustle and bustle as a city street. Although this has its drawbacks, there are certain advantages of living in and around Heslington. Some of the university sports facilities are available to the public, and it is very pleasant on a sunny afternoon to stroll through the immaculately kept campus to feed the ducks and wild fowl.

Hetton & Fleets

Hetton stands on a small hill overlooking the Aire valley with the rolling Pennines beyond. The old green lane leading out of Hetton wends its way over the hills to Gordale Scar and Malham. Half way up the lane is the site of the old fever hospital pulled down in the 1920s.

Hetton possesses an old inn, the Angel, with a wide reputation for good food. Many years ago a market was held on the cobbled area in front of the inn.

The Methodist church, built in 1859, stands near the fork of the roads to Gargrave and Winterburn and the old wall by the signpost is known as Smithy Wall as it stands opposite the site of the old smithy. The triangle of land between the two roads was once the village green.

Straight Lane, known locally as 'Fairy Lane', winds its way onto the road in Rylstone and is a short cut to church. Halfway along the lane there is the narrow Kirk Bridge. The stone slab forming the bridge is eleven ft long, three ft wide and eleven inches deep and the centre is worn away by the many feet which have crossed it.

There are many old buildings in Hetton. One which used to be the old post office is believed to be 13th or 14th century and is of historical and architectural interest.

Fleets, with a population of 17, is surrounded by becks and trees and extends for just over a mile. The scenery is most picturesque as the hills rise up the Fleets side to Boss Moor, 1,000 ft above sea level, and on the other to Rylstone Fell. The houses at one time were closely connected with the big house as they were either built for workers or tenants to farm on the estate.

Heworth

The leafy village of Heworth, now a suburb one and a half miles to the north-east of its grand neighbour York, can trace its origins back to at least Roman times. Remains of a Roman villa and Roman coffins have been found not far from the site of a Roman road which skirts the village.

The village evolved on slightly higher ground than its immediate environs which were mostly boggy wastes. It is as Huuorde, 'chief enclosure', that it is recorded in the Domesday Book of 1086 and almost 500 years later in 1568 the manor of Heworth consisted of only eight houses, six cottages and a water mill.

During the 16th century when York suffered severely from the plague and almost a third of its citizens died, drastic measures were undertaken. Plague lodges were erected towards the southern boundary of Heworth and victims of the disease were taken there from the city, most probably to die.

It was not until the 1800s that Heworth began to assume a little of its present day appearance when many of the large Victorian houses were built, to be followed in the present century by smaller villas.

The two main centres of worship are comparatively modern, the present Holy Trinity church was built in 1869 and the old Methodist chapel erected in 1825 was replaced in 1890.

Heworth today is a far cry from the hamlet of 1586 but it still has a great deal of village charm with its tree-lined roads and varied housing, with just a hint of its interesting past in some of the old cottages and quiet lanes.

Heyshaw

'We arrived in November 1945 at Heyshaw Farm, Heyshaw, in the parish of Dacre', remembers one resident. 'It was the oldest farm in the hamlet of six farms and two derelict cottages. The date over the door and on the beams in the bedroom, shaped just as they had been cut down, was 1662. It had water from the spring from the moor, paraffin lamps and primus stoves, and an outside lavatory with two holes. The fireplace was made by Todd of Summerbridge, the oven having a large hole in the bottom which had to be filled with salt to stop the smoke coming through.

'The grassland at Heyshaw is 800 ft above sea level and 1,100 ft on the moorland. The view was the only good thing about the house – York Minster, the White Horse and Harrogate.

'The great snowstorms of 1947 cut Heyshaw off from everything from January to April. The milk had to be got down to Dacre village by farmers digging out and a sledge was the only means of getting out or to obtain food for all the cattle and people.'

In 1884 Heyshaw Moor had a quarry called Guys Cliff Quarry. The remains still stand, a large iron 'three legs' (used for lifting stones) and foundations of buildings, and tons of stone lay cut to large sizes. Wagons pulled by six horses went down the overgrown road to Dacre station, opened in 1862. Many horses and men were killed as the road was very steep and dangerous. The last stone from the quarry was taken to make the docks at Hull.

Now all the farms and cottages have mains water, electricity, telephones and a very good road, and the population is 24.

Hillam ❧

Hillam is a small village (population 381) some nine miles west of Selby.

Hillam Hall, built in 1827, is a listed building of considerable character. It stands surrounded by the Dower House, Hall Farm, Home Farm, Orchard Farm and the Coach House. The gardener and the coachman lived in nearby cottages. On adjoining land, the Hillam Cricket Club, a thriving organisation, have their well kept ground and pavilion, the land given to the club in perpetuity by the Lyons family.

In Hillam Square opposite the Cross Keys inn is the village pump, together with a mounting block and an old stone water trough. The existing pump is one of two that were put on this site in the first half of the 20th century, necessary when Hillam had no piped water supply, although some properties were lucky enough to have their own wells. It is said that in times of plague the stone trough was filled with vinegar and before coins changed hands, they were first thrown into the trough in order to disinfect them and so prevent the spread of disease.

At Hilltop, a piece of land known locally as 'The Burying Garth' and owned at the turn of the century by the Society of Friends, is thought to have once been a Quaker burial ground.

The Brick Pond off Betteras Hill is a stretch of water now owned by a local fishing club, but on a map circa 1880 the site is shown as a brickworks with a light railway to the siding at Monk Fryston. It is said that whilst quarrying for clay, workmen struck a spring, the site flooded and the brickyard pond was formed.

The butcher, shoemaker, grocer and post office have now all gone and their services are to be found in the adjoining village of Monk Fryston, as are the parish church, primary school and community centre. The village, once a working community based on the seasons and farming calendar is now less so, with some very pleasant residential areas for people working in neighbouring towns and cities.

Hinderwell ❧

The village of Hinderwell was known in the Domesday Book as Hindrevvelle, the name being derived from Hilda. St Hilda is reputed to have rested here on her journey from Guisborough to Whitby Abbey and refreshed herself at the well in the churchyard, there to this day. The well was restored in 1912 and local schoolchildren hold a well-dressing ceremony every year.

Hinderwell is situated about three quarters of a mile inland from the coast and lies between Staithes and Runswick Bay. Whilst lacking the charm of its neighbours, it is nevertheless an attractive village. It is comprised largely of one long street with buildings of mixed architecture, including several listed properties. The parish church of St Hilda standing at the northern end of the village dates from about 1234.

During the latter half of the 19th century, until his death in 1907, Sir Charles Mark Palmer played a very influential role in the community. In the early 1850s he commenced extensive mining operations working the large beds of ironstone found along the coast between Staithes and Runswick Bay. He then formed the harbour at Port Mulgrave close to the mines and the ironstone was shipped to his furnaces at Jarrow.

In 1865 Palmer bought the nearby Grinkle Park estate and took up residence. Four years later he purchased the adjoining Seaton estate from the Marquis of Normanby. Hinderwell was one of the principal villages on this estate and benefited much from his expert management of the land.

Life in the village changed considerably after the Second World War. Gone are the railway and cinema. A new housing estate was built, and more recently, a new school adjoining the estate. The chief occupation of the district is agricultural and the area is famous for its Cleveland Bay horses. There are very few dairy herds to be seen these days and more land is being cultivated for cereal cropping. A small percentage of the population is constantly changing, but the village still retains its community spirit.

Hirst Courtney

Hirst Courtney is a small village situated six miles from Selby and 17 miles from Doncaster. The main landowners used to be the De Courtneys, Stapletons and Weddells but the land has gradually been sold to private ownership.

There were two large flax ponds, one at either side of Marsh Lane. Boats used to bring flax up the river Aire to Landing Lane where it was unloaded then washed and dried. The ponds have recently been filled in, planted with trees and it is now a conservation area.

There is a public house in the village, which is enlarged by each new landlord. The village has a school, a cricket team and a children's playground but the shop and post office has recently closed down.

Hornby & Hackforth 🌿

The twin villages of Hornby and Hackforth are situated in a pleasantly rural area, near the market town of Bedale and only a few miles from Catterick. Historically the villages are inextricably bound together, and formerly belonged to the same estate.

The St Quintins built a castle at Hornby of which only the tower named after them survives. The castle stands on a small hill in wooded parkland, and is surrounded by lakes and streams. For most of its life it was never a strongly fortified building but a castellated mansion, which even today, as it rises out of the morning mist, could have come straight out of a book of fairy tales.

The small but ancient church of St Mary nearby was first erected in the Norman period, but again, through the ages there have been substantial alterations and additions – even discoveries. Indeed, it was during restoration work carried out by the Duchess of Leeds in the mid 1880s that hitherto uncovered Norman carvings came to light.

Hackforth is just over a mile from Hornby, and comprises a few cottages and farms, with a total population approximating 120 souls. Hornby shares the same post office, school and inn.

A small brook runs across the bottom of Hackforth from the old mill near the Greyhound inn, so called because greyhound racing used to take place on the green in front. A few houses and bungalows have been built since the Second World War, including five council houses and two flats, but none in recent years.

The Dukes of Leeds took good care of their tenants and workers, and when the estates were broken up in 1930, they ensured that each cottage was sold with an allotment so that villagers could grow their own fruit and vegetables. This they still do, and some produce deliciously flavoured strawberries.

Horsehouse in Coverdale 🌿

This is the only village in the parish of Carlton Highdale, steeped in history and surrounded by many scattered farmsteads and hamlets stretching from Coverhead in the west to Gammersgill and Fleensop in the east and across to Swineside.

Horsehouse, as the name implies, was once a staging post on the axial drove roads linking markets in Wensleydale, Wharfedale and Nidderdale and latterly, on the main coach road from London to Richmond. It was once a busy place with a school, two public houses, one church, two chapels and a local post office/shop which opened from 7.00 am to 8.00 pm.

A local charity known as Forsters Charity, dating back to 1897, is used to purchase coal and logs for the welfare of the older members of the parish. Then there is the Constantine Trust. This was first mentioned in 1904, having connections with a former pupil – the Coverdale Bard, Henry Constantine. This money is used for the educational needs of the children, providing a book at Christmas time. The school closed in the early 1940s and the building is now used as the village hall.

Neither of the two chapels remain; one was converted into a house in the mid 1960s and the other closed in 1983. St Botolph's is the parish church of Coverdale, which today is part of the united parish with Middleham and East Witton. Originally built in 1530 as a chapel of ease, it was rebuilt in 1869.

The Thwaite Arms is the only remaining public house. There remains one shop which is the post office and general store, which during the tourist season provides tea and refreshments and also bed and breakfast.

This is still sheep country with many people involved within the farming industry, but the community has changed. The area is attracting more and more visitors who come to enjoy the peace and tranquillity.

Horton-in-Ribblesdale ✤

Horton is an upland parish at the source of the Ribble and the Wharfe, lying between the three peaks of Whernside (2,414 ft), Ingleborough (2,373 ft) and Pen-y-ghent (2,273 ft). The hamlets within the parish are Newhouses, Cam Houses, Selside, Brackenbottom, Studfold and Helwith Bridge. The course of a Roman road crosses the northern edge of the parish from Chapel-le-dale to Cam Fell.

There are three quarries; two at Helwith Bridge and one in Horton quarrying limestone, slate and granite. Limestone is used as building stone and fine examples of dales buildings, long and low with small windows and slate roofs, are seen everywhere. Dry stone walling is characteristic within all the dales area.

In bygone days, Horton had a general store, a dress shop, a butcher's, wheelwright, cobbler and blacksmith and garage. The post office was run from a private house. Now there is the post office and general store and cafe, offering a unique service. Walkers clock in as they set out on the 25 miles over the three peaks, and clock out on their return. By using this system a check can be kept on their safety.

St Oswald's was built in 1120 and has been restored but still retains many primitive Norman features. A grammar school was in existence in 1725. The first building stood in the churchyard, but is now used as a private dwelling.

Many of the houses in the district are listed buildings and steeped in history, one being Lodge Hall formerly known as Ingman Lodge. It is said years ago a judge used to travel the area on horseback and try cases.

woodland. Halfway down is a path leading to an old lime kiln with quite well preserved twin arches. Going further down the steps through the woods is situated King Arthur's Oven, an oven-like crack in the limestone which is supposed to be connected to Richmond Castle where King Arthur and his Knights lie sleeping.

Hunton & Arrathorne 🌿

Hunton was mentioned in the Domesday Book. Together with the nearby hamlet of Arrathorne, the village nestles in its own little 'dale' in a triangular area formed by the towns of Richmond (north), Leyburn (west) and Bedale (east). The oldest standing buildings occupied to this day are Manor House, Low Hall (both with priest holes) and Old Hall (a latterday coaching inn), all circa 16th century; many cottages are nearly as old. A small castle once stood at the top of Church Bank near where St John's church (built 1793–4) stands today. Every generation is told of a secret tunnel (never verified) leading to Old Hall at the other end of the village.

Once the main employment was farming together with the services needed to keep the community thriving, which included two butchers, three shops, three forges, a cobbler, a tailor, five public houses, a candle-making factory, a glove-making factory and a milk bottling factory for local deliveries.

Although there have never been any almshouses, there is a small group of bungalows especially for the elderly, also a small number of council houses. Nowadays, the village is very much 'on the up'. Blending with original properties, gaps between have been built on, and two small estates have been built.

Hunton is very proud, and quite rightly so, of its yearly Steam Engine Rally with many exhibitors from near and far. The two public houses are well-known throughout the area and the village shop-cum-post-office is well stocked by the owners. Milk deliveries come from the local dairy yard, and a small designer knitwear business, giving work to several out-workers, is well established. Also using local labour, a purpose-built factory for the design and manufacture of fire surrounds has been discreetly built on a sheltered spot.

Lambs still gambol in fields right in its heart. Two streams still babble merrily through and join up to the east, where lies Hunton Mill built in the 13th century but no longer operating, now a private dwelling.

Husthwaite ❧

Husthwaite, at the western edge of the Howardian Hills, is a blend of old stone dwellings, mellow Victorian and Edwardian brick houses, and a variety of 20th century maturing properties.

The green, where three lanes meet, is beautifully cared for. Not so long ago there stood at its east end a quaint brick house with a verge of marigolds, a garden and an orchard. In the middle of the green was an elm planted to commemorate the Diamond Jubilee of Queen Victoria. Every October, games were suspended in expectation of the arrival of the travelling fair. It came on the Coxwold road and as the caravans settled on the green there were roundabouts, swing boats, a hoop-la stall, a coconut shy, and a lady selling brandy snap. On the lane outside the White House were more stalls. Refreshments were prepared in the Black Bull public house (now a charming brick, wood and plaster cottage), where early customers would find, amongst other goodies, a clothes basket piled high with jam tarts.

The old house had to go when the lane was too narrow for the motorcar. These days a lime tree is the feature of the green and under its branches children from the village school have recently planted bulbs to flower in spring.

To the north of the green is the church of St Nicholas, a symbol of continuing Christian worship since Norman times. The porch, rebuilt in 1878, protects the original Norman archway which frames an oak door of obvious antiquity.

Until fairly recently Husthwaite was known as the Orchard Village. Apple, pear and plum trees still produce a bountiful harvest, though not so great as when carried by horse and waggon to the Beeching-axed Husthwaite Gate railway station close by Elphin beck, or collected by wholesalers to be taken by road to markets as far away as the Durham coast.

The highest point in the village is Beacon Banks, from where the Armada was signalled in 1588. In the Second World War the Home Guard kept watch there for a possible invader, whilst a searchlight and Lewis gun team manned a station on the slopes of the same bank.

Hutton Bonville ❧

Hutton Bonville is a scattered parish with a population of under 70, including the tiny parish of Lovesome Hill.

The parish church of St Lawrence stands amid the fields a mile from the village, close to a once magnificent Hall, demolished in 1964 after standing empty for 40 years. It was the home of the Hildyard family who built the school at Lovesome Hill in 1878.

Lovesome Hill in the 17th and 18th centuries was called 'Lowsy Hill'. The community, whose buildings stand on a hill, still uses the original narrow coach road and the main A167 runs parallel to it.

The village has not altered much over the last few years but two new properties were built in 1967, bringing the total of homes to nine. Just out of the village on the road to Palms Hall, originally Palmers Hall, a property of some note, six more houses have been built, including an animal sanctuary, bringing the total number of properties in the parish to 29. Included in this total are nine farms with two cottages.

Lovesome Hill toll bar was at the south end of the village and an old building still stands which was used by the toll keeper. Across a field east of the village was Cuckoo Well, and the village pump was close to the school.

There is a good sized caravan site at Hutton Bonville, sheltered behind a wood, with views over to the Pennines. Open air services are held here during the summer.

Hutton-le-Hole 🐑

Hutton-le-Hole is a beautiful village in the North Yorkshire Moors National Park. It lies in the small valley of Hutton beck, which flows down from the heather covered moorlands. The traditional stone cottages, with pantiled roofs, are built around a large green, with white wooden fences and divided by the beck. Moorland sheep keep every corner of the green closely cropped throughout the year. Late summer sees the moors turn purple as the heather flowers.

The area has been continuously occupied since prehistoric times. The history of Hutton and the surrounding area is well presented in the buildings and displays in the Ryedale Folk Museum situated in the village.

The common rights are administered by the Court Leet of the Manor of Spaunton, which to this day remains responsible for the management of the moorland and Hutton Common. This little piece of history still affects village life, eg a small 'fine' or rent to a maximum of £2 is levied for private enclosure of commonland, such as a fenced garden in front of a house. Courts Leet date from the Middle Ages and only a handful now survive in England. Recently, a new lord of the manor inherited his title and, following ancient custom, he and numerous common rights holders 'walked the bounds' around his lands, through knee-high heather and even waist-deep streams, taking two days to complete the circuit.

The village school, shop and post office have become shops and cafes mainly serving visitors, although locals do use them and of course work in them. One might wonder just how many ice-creams are sold on a typical holiday afternoon! Farming in the village has almost been taken over by tourism. However the sheep are still gathered twice each day and taken up to the moor by members of the Farrow family and their dogs.

In October, after the harvest, the Mell supper is served to villagers and friends. The church, St Chad's, has a small but devoted congregation. Hutton's pub, the Crown, is popular with locals and visitors alike. The village also boasts a very active bowling club and a tennis court. Quite a lot of villagers give regular voluntary help to the museum, which also organises various special events such as the World Merrills Championships.

Hutton Rudby 🌿

The picturesque village of Hutton Rudby, with about 1,300 inhabitants, lies midway between Stokesley and Yarm on the banks of the river Leven. Alongside the river stands the very fine 600 year old church of All Saints, with Rudby on the hill above.

The green, with its very fine trees, two of which were planted to mark WI anniversaries, and wonderful show of daffodils and crocuses in springtime, adds to the great charm of the village. Delightful cottages and houses abound, with lovely views of the Cleveland Hills.

The Reverend Robert Barlow, vicar from 1831 for 47 years, said on his arrival in the village, that the church was more like a cowhouse. He, along with Lord Falkland, the patron, made great improvements. It was the Reverend Barlow who built the present vicarage, over a mile from the church but halfway between Middleton and Rounton churches for which he was also responsible. During the cholera epidemic of 1832 the vicar endeared himself to the villagers by caring for the many sick and dying – sometimes six a day – when all others of means had fled.

People have been living in Hutton Rudby for a very long time. A Stone Age barrow was excavated in the 19th century, showing evidence of a prehistoric settlement at Folly Hill.

During the 17th century weaving as a cottage industry was started in the village, as indicated in the parish register; 23 weavers were mentioned in 1722. Later a linen mill was established, flax being grown on the area near the river, which was also used for bleaching and drying the cloth. Due to cheap imports the linen industry declined and was replaced by sailcloth making, some of which was supplied to the Russian navy in 1870. The mill closed in 1908 bringing to an end 200 years of industry in the village, which also included paper-making.

Huttons Ambo 🌿

Huttons Ambo is two villages – High Hutton and Low Hutton – lying approximately one mile apart: this division goes back to Conquest days, or even earlier, when two manors were held in High Hutton and a third in Low Hutton. Their names, Bardolf, Mynchon and Colswayn, are remembered in the names of three modern houses.

High Hutton consists mainly of stone-built houses and farm and estate buildings adjacent to the drive of Hutton Hall, a large Georgian house which is now divided into flats. St Margaret's church, built in 1856, stands near the Hall.

Low Hutton, the larger village, is bounded on the east and south sides by the railway and the river Derwent. Its main street is flanked on one side by a wide green overlooked by some pleasant 19th century houses and a variety of later buildings. Until 1912 the Shepherds' Feast, which lasted two days, was an annual event with a marquee, roundabouts and swings on the green and a beer tent which had to be guarded overnight! There was a free dinner for members and races were run with silk handkerchiefs as prizes. On the second day there was a cricket match. Four terrace cottages in Low Hutton were owned by the Shepherds' Club and let to retired farm workers. They are still known as Club Cottages.

In a field called Gateskew (ancient name Gaytskogh or Gaytescowe) on a commanding position overlooking the Derwent, a flat grassy mound shows the site of the medieval Hall of Hutton Colswayn and probably a much earlier Roman camp. Excavations in 1953–4 revealed traces of both a timber and a stone building. In the centre of the village one wall of the Manor Farm built on an 11th century monastic site forms part of the village pound.

There are several working farms, so generally there is work going on in or close to the village and tractors going to and fro. As both villages are situated on a loop road off the A64, traffic is mostly local. There is an excellent village shop and post office in Low Hutton, which is not only a great asset but a fount of information on all that goes on!

Ingleby Arncliffe 🌿

Ingleby Arncliffe is in the Domesday Book as two distinct manors held by the King: Englebi and Ernclive. In 1890 the estate was sold to Sir Lothian Bell, ironmaster, and the Bells are resident today.

Below the wooded hills of Arncliffe stands Mount Grace Priory, the largest and best preserved of all English Carthusian houses and the only one in Yorkshire, founded at the end of the 14th century. Above the priory on the route of the Cleveland Way is the chapel of Our Lady of Mount Grace, a popular pilgrimage for Roman Catholics. There was a church in Ingleby Arncliffe in AD 830. It was replaced by a Norman building attached to the manor and surrounded by a moat. This fell into disrepair and was rebuilt in 1821 under the patronage of Bryan Cooper Abbs using some of the old stone. In 1952 the Queen Mother visited the church and honoured the village with the presentation of a coat of arms of George VI, the only one presented in his reign.

The Tontine, now a restaurant, standing at the junction of the A19 and the A172, was built as a coaching house in 1804 to serve the new turnpike road from Thirsk to Yarm. It was later used as a posting house for the Royal Mail. When the Thirsk to Picton railway opened it was redundant and became a farmhouse.

At Ingleby Cross around 1914 a village hall and a new inn were built by the Bell family and in Ingleby Arncliffe a water tower to provide water to standpipes for the villagers' use. Today an ancient bier and an antique fire engine are housed there.

The Monks House is the oldest building in the village and is of architectural interest, dating back to the 16th century.

There is an international coach company based in the village, started in 1922 by a butcher who took his meat to the shambles in Stockton and decided to run a bus for the benefit of the locals. It was later taken over by his son-in-law Harry Atkinson. One can catch a bus to Paris from the village!

Ingleby Greenhow 🎋

Ingleby Greenhow is an isolated village, recorded in the Domesday Book as Englebi. It is tucked away in a valley below the Cleveland Hills, far from any sizeable neighbour.

It was the property of the Baron De L'Isle & Dudley until just after the Second World War. The manor house, 350 years old and now converted to luxury flats, is just outside the village to the south, with a fine lime avenue which follows the line of Ingleby beck. North of it is the partly Norman church of St Andrew.

Also outside the village itself, and nearly half a mile to the north, is the old station, and near to it, a little west, is the water mill, now a residence but still working in the 1950s.

The parish became much larger with the advent of the railway, with cottages built for the workers. The ironstone from Rosedale was carried by rail to the fast growing town of Middlesbrough. Then the railway was axed by Beeching and the business people who now live in the village commute by car. Old houses have been modernised and new ones built. There is also a new school and village hall and an inn with a restaurant.

Ingleton 🎋

Ingleton, the name meaning Beacon Town, is the gateway to the Three Peaks of Ingleborough, Whernside and Peny-y-ghent.

During the 20th century, the village and surrounding area has seen many changes. At one time, besides farming, employment was divided between coalmining, quarrying, tanning and cotton spinning. There was

Ingleton Village from the railway viaduct

a railway and station, many shops and a cinema. Today, there are still farms and one working quarry outside the village but the principal source of Ingleton's economy is tourism.

Since the latter half of the 18th century, Ingleton has been known for its caves and mountain scenery. However, the famous waterfalls of the Ingleton Glens were hidden in tree-filled, craggy ravines, so difficult of access that even farmers and quarrymen working nearby were unaware of their existence. Joseph Carr had discovered them in his youth before 1865 but it was not until 1885 that the Falls were made accessible to the general public. Thousands arrived on excursion trains run by the Midland Railway company. Now the railway is defunct, visitors continue to arrive by car, coach and on foot.

The rivers Twiss and Doe combine in the village to form the river Greta, which, with its salmon leaps, provides a favourite haunt for anglers and herons.

The parish church of St Mary stands on a hill in the centre, on the site of the original Norman church. The nave has been rebuilt twice due to subsidence, but the tower is original 13th century.

Included in the living of Ingleton, three miles out of the village on the old Roman road, is the little church of St Leonard at Chapel-le-Dale. Re-roofed and beautified in 1876 it is at least 400 years old. Inside there is a plaque to the workmen killed between 1869–1876 when building the Ribblehead viaduct and the famous Settle–Carlisle railway. Over 200 souls are buried in the churchyard, many having died in a smallpox epidemic in 1872. Nearby is the 300 years old Hill inn, once a coaching inn, now a popular venue during the Three Peaks Race.

135

Keasden 🐾

Anyone following the sign to Keasden off the A65 at Clapham will be puzzled when, after driving several miles, they find themselves over the border into Lancashire, having missed Keasden altogether. This is hardly surprising as Keasden is an area rather than a settlement. There is still a church and a telephone box, but the Methodist chapel closed in 1986 and the school has also gone.

The community now consists of isolated farms, houses and weekend retreats. However, this was not always the case. Church records for the 17th century list most of the farmhouses which still exist, but also name many people living in Keasden Lane and on the High Moors. There is now no trace of these dwellings, but perhaps we can conjecture a thriving hamlet, possibly in the area where later the church, chapel and school were built.

Records of the activities of the time list such craftsmen as blacksmiths, cordwainers (shoemakers), carpenters, weavers, and in fact all the other crafts necessary to sustain an isolated community.

'Keasden' is Old English meaning 'cheese valley' and indeed huge stone weights from cheese presses can still be found on some farms, though the recipe for the local cheese has long been lost.

Of more than 40 farms recorded in the 17th and 18th centuries only some 15 remain. Services are still held in St Matthew's church, built in 1873, and the church hall about half a mile away was formerly a bobbin mill.

Kelbrook 🐾

Kelbrook is situated mainly to the east of the A56, a busy main road connecting Colne in Lancashire with Skipton in Yorkshire. Though 'transferred' to Lancashire in 1974, Kelbrook retains its Yorkshire heritage.

In the late 18th and early 19th centuries the village began to grow along Dotcliffe Road and the Colne/Skipton road, now called Main Street. Wool was being spun at Dotcliffe mill, the machinery being powered by a water wheel. In 1851 there were 906 people living in Kelbrook and hand loom weaving took over from farming as the principal form of employment. There were 326 weavers making Delaine or Worsted cloth – in some cases all the family were involved, the parents and the older children weaving and the younger children winding the bobbins to replenish the shuttles.

Then the mill incorporated a weaving shed and villagers were forced to abandon their hand looms and work in the mill. Cotton weaving went on there until 1959 when the mill was forced to close after a disastrous fire.

This was the work of an arsonist who also burnt down a barn at Tunstead Farm and tried to set fire to the house of the local headmistress and the village saw mill.

The church of St Mary the Virgin stands on the old road. It was consecrated in 1839 and so saved Kelbrook worshippers a six mile return journey to Thornton. It has a clock with four faces which is rather unusual for a village and the children of the village carry on the old custom of tying up the gates of the church during a wedding ceremony and only untying them when the groom has thrown a handful of coins over the gate.

Methodists had worshipped at a 'preaching place' – a barn or cottage perhaps – since 1814, then a chapel was built on Waterloo Road in 1826. The chapel was on the first floor with dwellings underneath and it also had a school house. When it became too small it was converted into three cottages, which became known as Faith, Hope and Charity.

Kettlewell ✎

Kettlewell is in Upper Wharfedale, in the Yorkshire Dales National Park, surrounded by drystone walls and the Pennine Hills. It is a great favourite of travellers, tourists and hikers who come at all seasons to enjoy the magnificent scenery and the many footpaths and bridleways.

Cam beck, running through the village to join the Wharfe, powered a watermill in the 13th century, which was later converted to a cotton mill before being demolished in the 19th century. Evidence of 17th century leadmining can be found, with even earlier earthworks visible by the narrow Coverdale road. For many years Kettlewell was a busy market centre, where packhorse routes converged. According to hearsay, there were 13 alehouses to cope with the crowds. Three public houses remain, the Blue Bell dating from 1680, the Race Horses and the King's Head.

The parish church of St Mary was built in the reign of Henry I but the font with the crest of the Percy family is the sole surviving witness; the present structure dates back to 1880. The churchyard and lychgate, surrounded by trees, wild flowers and rosebeds, attract many visitors. The Methodist chapel at the top end of the village has recently been sold for conversion to two houses, and its stained glass windows are now in the parish church.

The fact that this is a conservation area, together with the steep surroundings, has prevented sprawling growth. The post office and village store provides a cheerful welcome service; a second grocery shop, a gift shop which occupies the site of the former smithy, and a dairy, all add to the village amenities, together with a well-established garage and many guest houses and 'B & Bs'. Farming families still make up much of the population and there are many more sheep than people, even in the tourist season.

A link with Kettlewell's lead-mining past is the existence of the Trust Lords, who meet to decide on land and boundary issues. They were originally gentlemen from London with interests in Great Whernside and the area around. The secretary is still called by the old title of Bar Master.

Kilburn

The two Kilburns, known locally as 'high town' and 'low town', are about a quarter of a mile apart. High Kilburn, a circle of houses around a large village green, is situated on a shelf on the hillside. The view from the village green embraces a large part of the Vales of York and Mowbray and can only be described as spectacular. The beck which flows through Low Kilburn becomes the river Kyle as it flows towards Easingwold.

The 'White Horse' cannot pass unnoticed by anyone travelling through the vales of York and Mowbray. The horse, made in 1857, was the brainchild of Thomas Taylor of London, formerly of Kilburn, who donated £1 towards the cost. The remainder of a total subscription of £4 8s 0d was donated by local people. The horse was carved on the hill by 31 men of Kilburn under the direction of the local schoolmaster John Hodgson, who designed the figure. Covering almost three quarters of an acre it is whitened and maintained by a committee of local people.

The late Robert Thompson must be the village's most famous son. His 'mouse' furniture is sold to many parts of the world and his workshop in the village attracts thousands of visitors every year. Specialists in ecclesiastical work, Thompson's pulpits, pews, lecterns and altar screens adorn countless churches throughout Britain and further afield.

The village 'Feast' is still celebrated on the first weekend after 6th July. In addition to an open air service on the Sunday and sports on the Monday, there is the ancient custom of the Lord Mayor's procession on the Tuesday night.

The church of St Mary, founded around 1120, is largely Norman, except the tower, which was built in 1667. Inevitably, Robert Thompson's mice feature in a large part of the interior woodwork of the church. The pulpits, lectern, altar rails and most of the pews are his work, as is the small St Thomas's chapel which was totally refurbished in oak in 1958 as a memorial to Robert Thompson.

In the 13th and 14th centuries Kilburn was the home of the King's Forester and all the land to the west of the village, still known as the parks, was one of the King's hunting grounds.

Kildale ❧

Kildale is a little village on the North Yorkshire Moors, not far from Captain Cook's Monument. Its church of St Cuthbert was rebuilt in 1868 and just to the west is one site of a motte and bailey castle.

On 13th May 1769, twin sons were born to Thomas and Jane Jennett. This was a time when many babies did not survive birth. These two, however, not only lived, but lived to become famous, each in his own sphere.

William became a well-known surgeon, practising in Gerard Street, London. Greatly esteemed, he died at the age of 75 years. Thomas, described as an intelligent and interesting lad, became a printer and publisher in Stockton, first as a partner of R. Christopher, then later alone, publishing well known local poems, plays, sermons etc.

Thomas also took a keen interest in the town of Stockton. His integrity in civic affairs as a member of the Town Council resulted in his being elected mayor of the town on no less than four occasions – 1819, 1838, 1839 and 1840. He died in 1846, greatly mourned by colleagues and friends who published a biography of his achievements.

Considering the lack of schooling and other educational facilities at the time these boys were growing up in Kildale, their achievements in the world of medicine, books and civic affairs are remarkable.

Kildwick ❧

The ancient ecclesiastical parish of Kildwick is centred around the small village of that name which nestles against the hillside on the north side of the Aire valley. The picturesque village lies between Keighley and Skipton, just outside the Yorkshire Dales National Park, and is approached over the river Aire bridge, built by the canons of Bolton Priory in the early 14th century.

The church of St Andrew which dominates the village was rebuilt in the 14th and 15th centuries and the choir was later extended to such an unusual length that it became known as the 'Lang Kirk o' Craven'. Looking to the left after climbing the graceful church steps you will see a headstone in the shape of a church organ in memory of the well-known 19th century organ builder John Laycock from nearby Glusburn.

The Leeds to Liverpool Canal cuts through Kildwick, the road to the neighbouring village of Farnhill actually passing underneath the canal. Until the early 1930s heavy horses could regularly be seen pulling barges laden with wool and silk for the many spinning and weaving mills in the area, as well as domestic supplies for the busy nearby towns.

Sadly, many of the mills have had to close down due to the decline of the textile industry, but most have diversified to provide accommodation for numerous small businesses. At Farnhill, the silk weaving mill now houses a light engineering firm.

The canal is now used by colourful pleasure boats which often moor at Kildwick for the night and find it a pleasant and peaceful haven, especially now that the busy main Skipton to Keighley road has been rerouted so that it no longer cuts through the heart of the village.

Above the village stands Kildwick Hall, a fine Jacobean house which was started in the early 1600s and remained in the Currer family until the turn of the century. It became an hotel soon after the Second World War. In a beautiful and historic setting, it is complete with a resident ghost – the 'Blue Lady'.

Killinghall

Situated two miles north of Harrogate, this ancient settlement grew at the junction of the Leeds to Ripon turnpike (1752) and the Dudley Hill (Bradford) and Ripon turnpike (1753). These roads are now known as the A61 and B6161 and on the latter can be found an old milestone.

The river Nidd divided the townships of Killinghall and Ripley and there has been a bridge here since very early times. There were always two mills at this point on the river. One was a corn mill but the other was put to a variety of uses. In the 15th century it was a fulling mill for felting cloth and in 1871 it was a sawyer's. Shuttles were made there for 400 years and one of the shuttlemakers named Mitchell invented a new type. In 1960 the mill was closed and Mr Yeadon the shuttlemaker departed leaving all his tools, lathes and shuttles.

A house dating from the 17th century is Levens Hall in Lund Lane. It was the home of Capt John Levens, a Parliamentary officer and a member of the Society of Friends or Quakers. He died in 1688 and is buried in the orchard where his children are also interred.

Primarily a farming community, other occupations in the village have included sieve maker, maltster, wheelwright, muffin baker and linen weaver. Weaving was done at Knotty Ash Cottage in Lund Lane. Stone was quarried near Killinghall Bridge and the last building to be constructed of Killinghall stone was Harrogate's Municipal Offices.

The village has experienced considerable housing development since the Second World War. Today there are three public houses, a post office, an antiques shop and a general stores. On the outskirts of the village on Killinghall Moor a large housing estate was started in the 1970s. At Penny Pot Lane there is an army camp for the Army Apprentices College. In spite of all this building and its close proximity to Harrogate, Killinghall is still a separate village and has retained its character.

Kirby Hill

Kirby Hill lies to the north of the small market town of Boroughbridge. Its main claim to fame is that it is exactly halfway between London and Edinburgh on the old Great North Road – a fact marked by the milestone which still stands there today.

Standing on Dere Street, the Roman route from York to the Northern border, the area is steeped in history. Tradition has it that the current church site was used in pre-Christian times and indeed there are portions of a Roman structure built into the church wall. Built on the highest point in the surrounding area, the lovely church of All Saints, chiefly Norman in origin, enjoys commanding views over the Vale of York from the dales in the west to the moors in the east.

By the 17th century the area was agriculturally rich and prosperous and Kirby Hill saw a lot of traffic from Scotland to London and back. Indeed it was common to see cattle being driven through the district, stopping to be shod at the local smithy. For the geese a more imaginative footwear was necessary – their feet being covered for protection with wet tar, by walking them through a local yard.

From the 18th century coaching became a popular form of transport and the Blue Bell inn, which still trades today, became very popular. The rings in the cellar walls still bear witness to the many prisoners who were tethered there overnight when being transported to trial or prison.

In 1967, when the A1 was directed to bypass Kirby Hill and Boroughbridge, the villagers breathed a sigh of relief. Kirby Hill has now regained much of its original character as a picturesque agricultural settlement standing proudly overlooking the rolling North Yorkshire countryside, yet still taking its part in modern life.

Kirby Knowle

Kirby Knowle is a small village a mile down the road from Upsall, having a population of about 20. The majority of the ten or so houses are owned by one family, the Furnesses, who also own the land around the village and employ most of the people in it. The village is shadowed by a small hill known as The Knowle and the land then rises higher to the Hambleton Hills.

The church of St Wilfred was rebuilt in 1872 on the site of a former much smaller church which was said to be one of the oldest in the country. St Wilfred was one of the original founder monks from Lindisfarne so he may have brought Christianity to the area.

The old school still exists although it is now used as a meeting place and for evening classes. It was closed about 30 years ago and originally served the villages of Upsall and Cowesby as well as Kirby Knowle and

The Old School, Kirby Knowle

the outlying farms. Although there have never been any more than ten houses in Kirby Knowle, in 1851 there was recorded a population of 129.

There is a very large Hall commanding imposing views from the top of a hill between the two villages, which is known as 'New Buildings' – however a dwelling has stood on the same place since 1085.

Kirby Sigston

Kirby Sigston is a hamlet three miles from Northallerton and near to the A19. In the old days when farmers used to go to the market town of Northallerton to sell their butter and eggs, traps were the means of transport, very few people having cars in those days. Kirby Sigston consists of farms which have been handed down for generations, some farms still going strong after 100 years.

A lot of the farms used to belong to the Lascelles family, one of whom lived at 16th century Stank Hall. The Hall and Sigston Castle, which belonged to the Sigstons in days gone by, are now both farms. It is said that an underground passage stretched from the church to the castle. At one time Woodend Farm was a public house where the monks from Over Silton and Kepwick way used to stop for refreshments before crossing over the Cod beck to the church.

St Lawrence's is a beautiful church; it was called by one bishop who came on a visit, 'A Cathedral in the Fields'. It has a big oak door with strap hinges and latch. A restored Norman church with a bell tower, the long chancel has a plain parapet with gargoyles on the walls, and a plain Norman arch leads to the chancel. The font has a Norman stem although the font itself has been replaced.

In the few remains of medieval glass are shields and a two-headed eagle, the arms of the Sigstons whose castle stood on a moated site half a mile from the church. In the church an inscription to Thomas Lascelles of 1703 reads 'that with gentle hands he restored sight to the blind'.

Kirby Wiske 🪶

The village of Kirby Wiske is situated half a mile from the A167 and four miles north of Thirsk. The river Wiske encircles the village and meets the fast flowing river Swale.

The parish church of St John the Baptist stands on raised land in the centre of the village. The present church is of Norman origin and contains some beautiful stained glass windows. During the digging of the foundations for the rectory in 1855 about 40 skeletons were found, believed to be casualties from the nearby battle of the Standard, between the Scots and the English in the 14th century.

Overlooking the village is Sion Hill Hall, probably one of the last country houses to be built in England. Designed by Walter Brierley, it was built in 1913 and eventually bought by Mr Herbert W. Mawer, to house his remarkable collection. The Hall is now owned by a charitable trust and is very popular with visitors still wishing to view the collection.

The former Sion Hill Hall was built on land belonging to the Lascelles family in 1760 and designed by the architect John Carr.

Kirby Wiske is also known as the birthplace of Roger Ascham who wrote the famous standard works on archery. He was a brilliant scholar and became Latin tutor and secretary to Mary Tudor, Lady Jane Grey and Queen Elizabeth I.

Kirk Hammerton & Green Hammerton 🪶

Just off the busy A59 about halfway between York and Harrogate lies the village of Kirk Hammerton.

The church, now dedicated to Sir John the Baptist, was for 600 years dedicated to St Quentin, and it is built on a high knoll at the corner of the village street. The exact date of its construction is uncertain, but was probably around AD 950. The Saxons did not normally build in stone but some of the enormous stones used at the base of the tower show signs of Roman tooling and may have been taken from a Roman building somewhere between Aldborough and York.

Kirk Hammerton seems to have had an unremarkable history over the centuries but the village must have been involved in the Civil War battle of Marston Moor which raged only a few miles away across the river

Nidd. Tradition has it that many of the slain were interred in pits in the churchyard and numerous skeletons were unearthed in 1926 when a lamp post was being erected.

The present Kirk Hammerton Hall, a large brick building, stands near the triangular village green, with the war memorial, opposite the church. Built originally in 1768 it has been altered at least twice. The south-facing windows overlook a stretch of parkland where a flock of St Kilda sheep graze.

A mill house stands by the river Nidd but the weir and wheel are broken now. No corn has been ground since 1923. Kirk Hammerton had both a blacksmith and a saddler in those days. Until the mid 1960s there was a bridge across the river to the village of Tockwith and strong efforts are being made to have this rebuilt.

Green Hammerton church was built in 1876 and dedicated to St Thomas. The village school was built behind the church and is still in use today. Green Hammerton is known in the annals of Methodism as for many years the famous Thomas Segmore, otherwise known as 'Alleluia Tommy', lived here.

An old cottage at the north end of the village green is reputed to have given lodging to Dick Turpin on his ride to York. There is an old hollowed oak tree opposite this house and for many years an old man known as Wishy Watson slept there.

In former years both villages had several inns and little shops but now only one public house remains in each village; the Bay Horse at Green Hammerton and the Crown at Kirk Hammerton. Each village also still has a general store with post office.

Kirkby Fleetham

There is mention of a church at Kirkby (Chirchebi) in the Domesday survey, and every possibility of a small settlement being there for many years. The village of Fleetham also existed from this early time and was situated about one mile from Kirkby. Sometime in the 16th or 17th century the houses at Kirkby were demolished. The reason is believed to be that the then lady of the manor did not wish the estate workers to live so close to the manor house! The whole area was landscaped and the people of Kirkby were resettled in Fleetham. The village became known as Kirkby Fleetham.

The original church at Kirkby was probably a wooden structure, as the history of St Mary's at Kirkby goes back to the years long before the Norman Conquest. The church was rebuilt in Norman times, and the round-headed arch of the north door is a relic of that earlier building. Kirkby Hall was completely rebuilt in 1785, and was a family home until the early part of the 1980s, when it was sold and became a country house hotel. The church, Hall and a small row of cottages are now all that remains of Kirkby. The area around is beautifully landscaped and gives the visitor a wonderful feeling of peace and tranquillity.

The village of Kirkby Fleetham is built around a traditional village green. This has been an important factor of the development of the village, in that it has retained the essential character of a small village community, despite new housing developments.

Beside the village school is the Black Horse inn, a very popular place for both villagers and visitors. At the turn of the century the village had another public house – the Three Tuns. This is now the site of the post office and busy village shop.

The village has always been rich in old characters and personalities – but the strangest of all was not a person but a lion! The old grinding mill just outside the village had become a taxidermy business known as The World of Nature – a very famous place in animal circles. They received animals from zoos and circuses all over the country. One day a litter of dead lion cubs was delivered. However, one little cub was found to be still alive, and was hand reared by the family. He grew into a magnificent lion, but still a family pet. His wonderful roar could be heard through the air on a still evening. Quite strange for a small Yorkshire village!

Kirkby Hill ✍

Kirkby Hill is a settlement built tightly round a small village green dominated by the parish church of Kirkby Ravensworth. According to the Domesday Book a church and priest existed here in 1086. The present building dates from the 14th century and is dedicated to St Peter and St Felix. Medieval gravestones and decorated stones have been re-used externally and in the tower steps. The tower houses two bells, one dated 1664 and the clock, circa 1921.

In 1556 Dr John Dakyn, rector of Kirkby Ravensworth, founded a grammar school and almshouses beside the church. This trust is administered by the vicar and six wardens each elected for two years by named scrolls sealed in wax, drawn from a water pitcher. Dakyn House is now converted into six flats. There is a plaque recording rebuilding in 1954.

'A boarding school of some repute' (1923 Baines Directory and Gazetteer) existed at the manor from about 1700 to 1840. Fees were 22 guineas per annum 'no extras and no vacation.' This is one of several London schools in the area immortalised by Dickens.

The trough on the green provided the village water supply until 1965. The Shoulder of Mutton inn is on the north-west corner of the green. There is a fine view of the dale below to Teesdale and beyond. A footpath starts just along the road from the inn, which leads down to Ravensworth.

Kirkby Malham & Hanlith 🦢

Kirkby Malham, or 'the church place in Malhamdale', has a Danish foundation. The name indicates that there has been a church in the village for over a thousand years, though the present church was built by the monks of Deerham Abbey, who owned the land, by 1490. It is of almost cathedral proportion and seems much too big for a village with a population of only 65 people. It was however built to serve a very large area, even today the parish covers 35 square miles. The church, though lovingly restored, is unspoilt and has a peaceful atmosphere.

The village of Kirkby Malham has changed little over the years, the attractive stone cottages and the church hall stand close together in what is known as the Main Street with the Victoria Hotel at one end. Some of the houses have 17th century date stones.

Hanlith lies across the river Aire on the hillside overlooking Kirkby Malham. It is a quiet retreat from busy life where time seems to stand still. Originally it was a farming community, but in recent years the population has changed. The farming families have been joined by families from many other backgrounds, which has enriched the community. The top of Hanlith Hill commands a breathtaking view of Malhamdale and, because the villages have changed little in size, it is possible to imagine the dale as it was centuries ago. Perhaps, it can be said, even life has changed little in the dale. The children still attend a village school and the people support each other in their joys and sorrow.

Kirkby Malzeard 🦢

Situated east of the Pennines and overlooking the Vale of York, this area of rolling farmland lies six miles north-west of the historic city of Ripon. From rough pasture 800 ft in the west, the land drops eastward to 450 ft across grassland drained by becks and gills flowing into the rivers Ure and Laver. This scene of isolated farms, small fields, winding lanes and pockets of woodland focuses on the village of Kirkby Malzeard.

It is a linear village with towered church, market cross and wide main street. The houses and farms are almost entirely built of local stone with slate, stone or Yorkshire roof tiles. The church of St Andrew dates from the 11th century. The church bells have been rung for more than 400 years and in 1591 one of the bells was recast – records show that this was actually done in the church.

The church school was first built in 1640 and at the moment has approximately 57 children aged five to eleven years. The Mechanics Institute which now stands in the main street was first built in 1848 to provide adult education, but went on to become the centre for weekly dances and concerts. Funds are still raised to keep the 'Mechanics' functioning and it is one of the very few surviving.

Few places have a Sword Dance and none more famous than Kirkby Malzeard. It probably originated in prehistoric times as a ritual to make the grass grow tall and to wake the earth from her winter's sleep. It is now only performed by visiting dancers, usually at the buttercross.

Kirkby Malzeard gained a market charter from King Edward I in 1307, granting a market every Monday and a fair on the eve. The market lapsed in the 19th century and villagers are now served by a village shop, post office and butcher.

Many people commute to work as the main local employment is farming with approximately 39 farms, most of which are small units which are unable to support a family. Many farms are dairy farms with milk collected by bulk tanker and delivered to the dairy. Kirkby Malzeard Dairy is the village's largest employer, cheese is produced by traditional methods and much is exported. Coverdale cheese is a speciality and the dairy attracts many visitors.

Kirkbymoorside 🐾

Kirkbymoorside nestles under the heather-clad North Yorkshire Moors. The wide main street, cobble edged, climbs steadily from the A170 to the gold course and the moors. The manor dates back at least to 1086, when it already had ten farms, a mill, a church and a priest.

In the 12th century Robert de Stuteville established nuns at Keldholme priory nearby and built a wooden ditched-enclosure castle on the hill above the town. In the 15th century a stone castle was built by the Neville family on a new site in Manor Vale. Much of the stone was later used to build the old toll booth, now the memorial hall, and only a fragment of castle wall remains.

In 1687 George Villiers, Duke of Buckingham died at 'the best house in Kirkby' after catching a chill hunting on the moors. This house, known thereafter as Buckingham House, still looks much the same and is a familiar landmark in the market place.

A street market is still held every Wednesday, under its original charter, a busy meeting place for local folk and inhabitants of nearby villages. Nowadays it is also a considerable tourist attraction.

All Saints' church, dating back to 1086, has been rebuilt many times, but still contains 12th, 13th and 14th century fragments. There are also Catholic and Methodist churches, and a Friends meeting house dating back to 1652. A 17th century grammar school next the churchyard became later a literary institute and is now a library.

Farming was of course a main occupation. Flax was grown on the south side of the town and many women and children were employed spinning and weaving linen. The part of the town known as Kirkby mills preserves the memory of this industry. There were iron foundries, quarries, cabinet makers and brickworks.

No account of Kirkbymoorside would be complete without a mention of its famous brass band, many times northern champions. Consisting entirely of local talent the band is able to run both junior and senior bands, does much work for local charities, and is in turn hugely supported by the local population.

Kirklington 🌿

Kirklington is situated between Ripon, Bedale, Thirsk and Masham in the Vale of York, about a mile west of the A1 and half a mile off the B6267 road. The 80 houses are placed mainly round the village greens in a designated conservation area.

The oldest buildings of special interest are the church of St Michael the Archangel, the once moated hall, built in 1571 by Sir Christopher Wandesforde, and the old Academy. There is a ghost associated with the Hall known as The Grey Lady. In the front entrance there is an enormous old trunk which once contained all the Wandesforde family papers and deeds. It is said that if it is ever moved from the Hall disaster would befall.

The businesses in the village include a blacksmith, a public house – the Black Horse, a family butcher, a post office, grocer, off licence and newsagent, two builders and Agriparts. The Wandesforde family still own four farms and several cottages in the village rented out to tenants and their families. A poultry farm employs most people in the village.

Langcliffe 🌿

Langcliffe village stands one mile to the north of Settle and is on the direct route to the Three Peaks, Pen-y-Ghent, Ingleborough and Whernside. The road bypasses the village, which lies under the 'long cliff', sheltered from the east winds coming off the Pennines.

The village is clustered around a large, circular green with other small greens interspersed with houses which encroached in the past. Nowadays this would be prohibited but the effect is to add charm to the scene. One of the buildings encroaching onto the green is a former candle-making factory, now converted into houses.

The village is built chiefly of the silver grey carboniferous limestone, although a sandstone called millstone grit is also used in construction. Langcliffe is built on the edge of the Craven Fault where the two stones meet, and this is probably the source for Langcliffe Fountain, as the water percolates down through the soluble limestone to the impermeable millstone grit. The fountain, which had until the end of the First World War an elegant Victorian urn as its termination, now has a stone cross; monument to those who died from the village in the war.

The church, set aside from the village centre and still with its rookery, is Victorian, as is also the Wesleyan chapel with its handsome bell tower. The green roads, bridle paths and footpaths used by travellers and merchants, some who came from as far away as Lombardy to buy fleeces, are now used by the many visitors to the dales. They, as their predecessors, still stop to refresh themselves at the fountain. Langcliffe is now, as then, a sheltered spot for the weary traveller coming down off the 'Tops'. Life would have been hard in the old days, but even so, there must have been time to stop for a few moments and admire the charm of this village in its setting of green and silver grey.

Langthorpe 🦊

Langthorpe lies to the north-west of Boroughbridge along the banks of the river Ure. The origin of the name is Anglo-Saxon, literally meaning 'long village', as indeed it still basically is. Although receiving mention in the Domesday Book there is little detail of the village given other than references to several manors.

There is no church within the parish boundary and just one public house, the Fox and Hounds, a picturesque old coaching inn on what would have been the road to the cathedral town of Ripon.

By the turn of this century an additional terrace was built to house the workers in the brewery by the river, and between the wars, one of the large Georgian houses lining the road was converted into a home for Barnado's children.

There has been quite a bit of additional building but the village still retains its charm, with its grass verges strewn with masses of daffodils every spring.

Lastingham 🦊

Lastingham is a small village situated on the edge of the North Yorkshire Moors, within its National Park boundaries, around 300 ft above sea level and 30 miles north of York. It was chosen by St Cedd as the place to build his monastery in AD 654, a place described by the Venerable Bede at the time as being 'more like a place for lurking robbers and wild beasts than habitations for man'. The present church of St Mary, built in 1078, occupies the site of that Celtic monastery and contains one of the few apsidal crypts in England.

The Blacksmith's Arms, opposite the church, has not changed that much since the late 18th century, when it was kept by the curate's wife in order that she could eke out the stipend of £20 per year and help to keep their 13 children. Rev Jeremiah Carter was hauled before his superiors for playing and dancing in the pub on the Sabbath. He explained that his parishioners had to travel many miles over the moors to attend the services in this very widespread parish and they needed refreshments before returning home. He maintained that in order to direct them from too much liquor and 'bad' conversation, he would play his fiddle and would not refuse the young folk if they wished to dance. It appears that the Archdeacon was well satisfied with this.

Today Lastingham is still quietly nestling in a natural hollow, whilst the moorland-fed stream gently tumbles between the tiny greens and cottages. One side of the village edges onto open moorland, which stretches away to the north. The other side is lush with woodland and arable farmland. Lastingham comes within the medieval manor of Spaunton, still active in its land management through the Court Leet. Several farmers have grazing rights and sheep roam freely on the moors and through the surrounding villages.

The attractive and well kept stone-built cottages, with their pantile roofs, remain much as they were in the early days. The bridge at the top of Low Street has a commemorative tablet to John Jackson RA, a celebrated artist who was born in the cottage opposite in 1778.

There are three holy wells in the village, dedicated to St Chad, St Ovin and St Cedd. They once formed part of the water supply to the village, until more recent times when the mains water was piped from West Ness.

Lealholm ❧

The village of Lealholm lies within the North Yorkshire Moors National Park, beautifully situated on a bend of the river Esk. It owes much of its present charm to the management of the estate by the late Sir Francis Ley under whose guidance, at the turn of the century, much of the development took place and many of the unusual and colourful trees were planted.

The village, the surrounding areas and the many visitors it attracts are well served by the post office, the busy garage, the Board inn and the well-stocked village shop. Lealholm is less well served on the picturesque, but unfortunately threatened, Esk valley railway line.

The Methodist chapel is the oldest place of worship, and celebrated its 150th anniversary in 1989. Approaching the chapel by crossing the river Esk on the stepping stones, one can then marvel at the marks on the outer wall of the building which record the levels to which the river rose on two separate occasions in past years, most seriously in July 1930. The figures on the gable ends are by Eskdale's local poet John Castillo (died 1845) who lived and worked in Lealholm as a stonemason and was also a lay preacher. Not far from the chapel is a long disused Quaker burial ground.

This community is still very much a farming one, as it has been for many centuries. At one time, in the 1920s, the quarrying of ganister above Lealholmside brought extra trade to the village and contributed to the business of the railway station. The ganister was pulverized and made into silica bricks which were used as furnace linings for steel-making.

Lealholm is a sporting village and supports both a cricket and a football team. 1990 saw the opening of the cricket club's new pavilion financed largely by public subscription. There is also a village quoits team which takes part in local league matches and in summer the sound of metal upon metal can often be heard coming from the quoits pitch on the village green.

Leathley 🌿

The village of Leathley follows the river Washburn to the point where it enters the river Wharfe on its southern boundary.

As with the history of most villages, there was a self-contained community until the 20th century, with farming as the main occupation. There was a smithy run by the Forrest family for generations, a cornmill using the Washburn as water power, an inn which was closed by the Fawkes family, a village pound – some of the wall remains, a toll house and bridge, a school and library. Today the church, almshouses, village green, parish hall and many 200 and 300 year old stone houses and large barns add to the typical Yorkshire beauty.

The stocks and water pump, neither still in use, have recently been restored by the parish council. The water pump was installed to ensure drinking water for travellers and their horses, when the inn was closed by the influence of nonconformist campaigners.

On the high ridge of land across the village, the church of St Oswald was built about 1100. The church was enlarged about 1470 and re-roofed by Mr F. H. Fawkes who also installed the beautiful shepherd window, a century ago. Some of the old box pews remain as screens. In the nave there is a Saxon door with rare antique ironwork.

Across the road on the same ridge of land are the almshouses. The charity was founded by Anne Hitch in 1769 in memory of her brother. Originally it was a school to educate young and old in the village, a home for the master and four flats. Local residents still act as trustees and they are let, where possible, to residents in the Lower Washburn parish, as wished by the donor.

As a starting point for beautiful walks, Leathley is increasing in popularity, although the village contains no shop, no cafe, no pub, nor any commercial building. The village green is in constant use as a parking area.

Leeming 🦋

West of the river Swale in the old North Riding of Yorkshire, Leeming
has Leeming aerodrome, now a Tornado Air Defence Wing on the east
side and the new A1 motorway to the west. It lies between the villages of
Londonderry and Leeming Bar on what used to be the old A1.

The main street is called Roman Road. The village has developed
around this old Roman road (Watling Street) which ran from London
northwards. Catterick, Leeming and Boroughbridge became important
because of the accommodation they afforded to travellers in packhorse
and coaching days.

It appears that in 1424 a chapelry was built in Leeming, dedicated to St
John the Baptist, for the purpose of reading prayers to travellers. The
present church was rebuilt in 1839 on the site of the old chapelry.

Work started on Leeming aerodrome in 1938 when farmland was
taken over by the Crown for runways and buildings needed for the
operation of aircraft for the coming Second World War. Leeming aerodrome officially opened on 3rd June 1940 and Newton House was taken
over by the military as a tactical school. This was demolished after the
war. During the war years the base saw much action, being the home for
Halifax and Lancaster bombers.

An interesting feature of the village is its mill which has a date of 1776.
It was used for grinding corn in the old days, now it is a farm. This area
as a whole is chiefly a mixed farming community but few farms are
actually left in the village due to the development of the aerodrome, the
A1 motorway and housing development. The older houses in the village
are built of bricks from a local brickworks which closed down in the
early 1930s, when it was flooded out.

Leyburn 🦋

With a population of 1,759 the largest community in mid-Wensleydale,
Leyburn sits high on the northern bank of the river Ure. Until the 16th
century, Leyburn was a hamlet. Wensley, the market town from which
the dale takes its name, was a larger town, having a parish church whilst
Leyburn had only a chapel of ease. Then in 1563, Wensley became
deserted after the plague. The charter for the market at Leyburn on
alternate Tuesdays was granted by Charles II and then in 1686 an
enlarged market charter was granted for it to be held each Friday.

There are three squares in the town – the largest being the sloping,
rectangular Market Place which is late Georgian in character. Small shop
fronts belie the size and amount of stock behind their facades and local
tradespeople try their best to oblige, happily becoming involved in their
customers' requirements. The weekly Friday market always produces a
bustling scene throughout the year, though extra visitors during the

summer months swell the crowds around the stalls. The Leyburn auction mart functions some Wednesdays and every Friday for the sale of cattle and sheep.

Beautiful scenery is all around but the view from a natural terrace to the west known as The Shawl presents a magnificent panorama of river, woods, hills, dry stone walls, sheep and cattle and holds the essence of broad Wensleydale in one glance. It was here on this two mile long limestone scar that, according to local tradition, Mary, Queen of Scots was recaptured, at a spot known as The Queen's Gap, after escaping from Bolton Castle, five miles away, where she was incarcerated prior to her fateful journey to Fotheringay.

Another lady of happier fate with local connections was the *Sweet Lass of Richmond Hill* the lass being Frances I'Anson. She was born in the house of her grandfather, situated in the High Street, and his initials are there still, 'W. I. A. 1746' inscribed on the tympanum over the door. She later married Leonard McNally who wrote the well-known song to her.

Linton-in-Craven

Houses, cottages and barns surround the wide rectangular green of Linton, which slopes gently to a pretty stream, Linton beck, crossed by three bridges and a shallow ford. The graceful 14th century packhorse bridge was repaired in the late 17th century by Dame Elizabeth Redmayne. It is said that the local farmers refused to contribute to the cost of repair, so she added a narrow parapet to prevent their carts from crossing.

Linton's name is probably derived from the flax (lin) grown in the rich alluvial soil of the surrounding fields, and in the village there are still some surviving examples of the massive stone retting troughs in which the flax plant was rotted down to expose the fibres. The spinning of flax was still a major occupation for the women of Linton up to the 18th century.

In about 1660 a young man from Linton, Richard Fountaine, went to London. He became an Alderman of the City of London, and after his death in 1721 he left money in his will to provide an almshouse in Linton for 'six poor men and women'. This striking building, the Fountaine Hospital, stands at the southern end of the green. Designed by Sir John Vanbrugh, the architect of Castle Howard, it seems altogether too grand and imposing a building for such a tiny village. His name was also given to the Fountaine Inn, a white painted building overlooking the green.

Down the hill, half a mile from Linton village, stands the little hamlet of Linton Falls. Here the river Wharfe cascades over the North Craven Fault to create the falls which give the place its name. A mill stood here for many centuries, powered by water channelled from above the weir; originally a corn mill, later used for the manufacture of worsted and cotton. Although the mill and chimney have been demolished, two rows of cottages remain: known as 'Botany', these were originally built for mill workers.

At the end of the lane stands Linton church, the parish church of St Michael and All Angels. This beautiful long, low building has 12th century Norman arches. Footpaths meet here from the villages of Grassington, Threshfield, Hebden, and Linton; all served by one parish church.

Linton-on-Ouse ❧

Linton is a small village in the Vale of York, ten miles north of the city and three miles south of Aldwark toll bridge. It is low lying, with the Ings often flooded in winter. Flax is said to have been grown here for processing in a mill at Newton, hence the name Lin-town.

It was mentioned in the Domesday Book and was later owned by a Catholic family called Appleby who sold it in 1706 to Dr John Radcliffe, Queen Anne's physician. He bequeathed it to University College, Oxford, stipulating that the rents from the cottages and farms should be used to provide scholarships for two medical students. So from 1715 the village remained mainly agricultural in character until the 1950s, when all but five farms were sold to the sitting tenants. Before this there had been, in 1936, a great change with the coming of the RAF, when several farms were swallowed up in the construction of the aerodrome. Former farmworkers and their wives and families found occupations on the camp.

At present there is only one village farm and three outlying. There is a new school, one public house, the College Arms, and a post office and general store.

On the Ouse between Linton and Newton there is a lock, a deep weir and a salmon ladder. This is now Linton Locks Marina and caters for pleasure craft. It was constructed in 1767 to enable barges carrying coal and lime and other products to get upriver to Boroughbridge and Ripon. A hydroelectric plant was constructed beside the lock in 1920, supplying electricity to York and the surrounding villages. It was closed in 1963 when it became uneconomical to run. The building still stands and will probably be preserved for its historical interest.

Little Ribston ❧

Situated mid-way between Wetherby and Knaresborough on the B6164, Little Ribston is a pleasant village with houses on either side of the road and no modern back-land development; in fact, since the council built twelve houses in 1950, only a few infill dwellings have been allowed.

154

The houses and land were once owned jointly by the Earl of Harewood and the Ribston Park Estate – the latter includes Ribston Hall which has had a long and varied history. Originally a preceptory of the Knights Templars, it was bought by Joseph Dent in 1835. A forward-thinking and good landlord, he built a school at Little Ribston in 1845 and made improvements to a carpenter's shop in the village to transform it into a mission room in 1860. This was later renamed St Helen's church.

The Dent family no longer own much of the village, the houses being bought by the owner/occupiers some years ago, but they still farm many acres and Ribston Hall is still a family home with the Knights Templars' chapel attached and used for a service once a year and on private occasions.

The delicious Ribston Pippin apple originated here when Sir Henry Goodricke planted the first seed brought from Normandy in the 18th century and a stump of a later tree is still preserved in Ribston park.

Records show that the road through Little Ribston was the old Royal Highway to Knaresborough Castle. Certainly there were several inns or licensed premises in the village in previous times though none remain today. Today there are two farmers, a joiner and a horse breeder, but the residents are mainly employed in other professions travelling to the towns to work. Until recently there was a thriving blacksmith's shop but it closed down when the owner retired.

Littlethorpe 🪶

Littlethorpe lies two miles to the south-east of the city of Ripon and from many points in the village excellent views of Ripon Cathedral can be seen. Although there is a centre point where the church, along with the village hall and a lot of the older properties and farms stand, new properties mean that the village stretches for almost one and a half miles in all directions. The church was built in 1876 on a plot of land given by the Nicholson family, descendants of whom are still farming in the village.

Littlethorpe Potteries was established in 1831 and over 100 people were employed making bricks, pantiles, chimney pots and drainage pipes. Kitchenware was also made, ie jugs, bread crocks, baking bowls etc. Littlethorpe Potteries has its own supply of terracotta clay which is still dug by hand. Over the years it has had to diversify into making garden pottery. Recently the Pottery has been made into a Working Heritage Centre and tourists come to see how pots are made and the old machinery working.

Running to the east of the village is the Ripon Canal. A picturesque bridge leads over it from the village to the Ripon Motor Boat Club. This opened in 1931 with four members, and now has apporoximately 250 and well over 100 boats. It is extensively used by visiting craft during the summer months and people can stop off and visit the dales, Fountains Abbey and all the other places of interest in this area.

As in many other villages modern life has brought about closures. The village school closed in 1936 and until 1969 the Harrogate to Ripon railway line passed through the centre of the village (having seen its first train pass through on the 13th September 1848). The Beeching cuts in the 1960s saw the closing of this line.

Although many parts of Littlethorpe are now in close proximity to Ripon there is still very much a 'village' feeling. The beautiful surrounding countryside lends itself to walking and this is something to be enjoyed by all.

Lofthouse 🌿

Lofthouse village, with a population of approximately 75, is situated halfway between the villages of Ramsgill and Middlesmoor in the upper valley of the river Nidd. Although most of the population lives in the newer houses on the main road the older part of the village is to the east along the road leading over the moors to Masham and the Vale of York. As in many dales villages about a quarter of the houses are holiday homes. Even so it can boast a lively village hall with an excellent car park, one of the most isolated village schools in North Yorkshire, a cricket club/ground, a post office/village store, a small hotel and a brass band!

Lofthouse was a stronghold of early Methodism and the chapel, rebuilt in 1882, has been consistently used as a place of worship for over 200 years. There was also a Primitive Methodist chapel, closed in 1903 and now used as a storeroom.

Unlike Wharfedale the stone walls and rocky outcrops are of millstone grit but there is limestone in the valley bottom and here the river Nidd does a disappearing act. In normal weather the river goes down two sumps, Manchester Hole and Goydon Pot, two miles north of Lofthouse, and reappears at Nidd Heads, a quarter mile downvalley from Lofthouse (easily seen from the road). Only in excessive rainfall is there water under the bridge at Lofthouse. Half a mile to the west of Lofthouse is the spectacular How Stean Gorge, made by Stean beck through the limestone on its way to join the river Nidd.

In the 19th century Lofthouse was much more self-sufficient, with a butcher, blacksmith, grocer, joiner, washerwoman, cordwainer, dressmaker, teacher and leadminers, besides farmers and farm workers. Now Lofthouse is mainly concerned with farming and tourism and is the home of many of the maintenance staff of the Water Authority.

Long Marston 🦢

The village lies six miles to the west of York on the B1224 Wetherby road and is on the extreme edge of the Vale of York, nestling snugly under the lee of Mill Hill. It is an agricultural community with the names of the farming families passing through the years from one generation to the next.

Standing squarely on the crossroads at the heart of the village, the Sun inn is the local landmark. Almost next door is the chapel, and the church of All Saints is a quarter of a mile to the south on the road to Angram.

The battle of Marston Moor took place on 4th July 1644 half a mile north of the crossroads, which was one of the most crucial encounters of the Civil War. On the eve of the battle, Oliver Cromwell and his generals stayed the night at Long Marston Hall, and to this day, a bedroom in the south wing is known as 'The Cromwell Room'. The anniversary of the battle is always commemorated by the Order of the Sealed Knot. A local farmer, John Midgeley of Marston Moor Farm, has cannon balls by the dozen ploughed up over the hundreds of years, and still they are appearing. There have been many reports of phantom soldiers being seen around the time of the battle each summer by travellers on the road which runs across the battlefield from Marston to Tockwith.

Another event which gives Long Marston a place in English history was the birth at Long Marston Hall in 1707 of the mother of General James Wolfe, the English General who with his troops scaled the almost impossible Heights of Abraham at the Seige of Quebec. She was Henrietta Thompson, the daughter of a Sheriff of York, whose town house was on Peasholme Green and is now the Black Swan public house. Marston Hall was his summer residence and it was here that many of his children were born and baptised at the village church. To this day their initials are to be seen carved deeply into a window sill in the upstairs drawing room, doubtless executed on a boring wet day!

Long Preston 🦢

Long Preston is a pleasant village running from east to west on either side of the A65 road. Once larger than Leeds, it has stood still while Leeds has hurried on.

The beck flows through the village, joining the river at Cow Bridge. The water from the hills, which is beautifully clear, is the home of numerous small fish and, in autumn, larger fish when salmon come upstream to spawn. Here by Mill Bridge stands Mill Farm. A corn and cotton mill once stood here. The great flood in 1881 washed away the mill dam, making the mill untenable. Traces of the dam wall and mill-goit can still be seen below the bridge at Bridge End.

Many houses have interesting histories; Cromwell House is where reputedly that soldier once rested his head, Town Head the old manor house, Anvil House the home of the former smithy. There's Prison Lane, leading to the house which was once the prison, now called Ross Cottage. Across the road is an attractive three-storey building which once housed weaving frames. The former wool warehouse adjacent to the village green is now owned by a book publishing firm.

Evidence of a Roman encampment is buried beneath the grass near the wall of St Mary's burial ground. This church is a beautiful building, parts of which date back to the 12th century.

Much activity is centred round the village hall (Mechanics Institute) on the edge of the village green, where the annual Children's Day is held. On the other side of the road is the maypole green, for many years called the 'Concrete'. This was the ancient cattle market. The village has three hotels, the Maypole, the Boars Head and Brigantes, the latter being originally the old vicarage.

The village is popular with walkers and cyclists enjoying the country lanes and also the panoramic views from the moors. From the moors the village is seen nestling amongst the trees, drystone walls making a patchwork of the fields. Whelpstone Crag, Pendle Hill and Ingleborough watch over the valley like sentinels.

Lothersdale 🐑

Lothersdale nestles in a valley in the Pennine hills five miles from Skipton, near to the Lancashire border. Although small, with a population of 380, it has a church, chapel, school, pub, post office and general store.

Approaching the village from Skipton, Stone Gappe lies to the left of the road. It was here that Charlotte Bronte was governess for a short time and Gateshead Hall in *Jane Eyre* was modelled on this house.

The group of houses situated at the foot of the hill is known as Dale End. Here is the Hare and Hounds. Opposite is the mill yard and the mill, originally a cornmill, powered by water and later used for cotton spinning then silk weaving. Today the mill is split into units available to a variety of small businesses. The most interesting feature connected with the mill is the water wheel, the largest indoor water wheel in existence spanning 48 ft in diameter. The 90 ft mill chimney still stands.

At the west end of the village is Raygill Quarry. For well over 200 years limestone was quarried here, some of it being burnt into lime in the kilns and some carried away, first by packhorse then horses and carts and finally by lorries. During quarrying operations here in 1880 the bones of hyenas, straight tusked elephant, slender nosed rhinoceros and the molar tooth of a lion were found. Some of these may now be seen in Cliffe Castle Museum, Keighley. The burning of the lime continued until the mid 1950s, the production of dry stone chippings and tarmacadam until the 1980s when the quarry was closed.

Raygill House which stands near to the quarry is very attractive; it is a very old house but has been rebuilt and now has a Victorian facade. The Spencer family who lived at Raygill House developed the quarry over a period of 180 years, eventually selling out to Tilcon.

The Pennine Way passes through the village on the way from Cowling to Gargrave. Before joining the main road in Lothersdale it passes Woodhead Farm which is a typical and fine example of a 17th century yeoman's dwelling. Another interesting old farmstead is the Knott, which has a beautifully designed porch and houses an eleven ft span arched stone fireplace. Over the past 100 years hardly any houses have been built, consequently the village still retains its original beauty.

Low Bentham

Low Bentham lies some 13 miles east of Lancaster close to the slopes of the Pennines, with Ingleborough five miles to the north-east. It is a small village of some 750 population which has developed in the fertile valley of the river Wenning, a tributary of the river Lune.

The late 18th century saw the establishment of a linen mill in the village which continued until, as a result of decreasing trade, it changed hands and direction and started to specialise in the spinning of silk. This continued until 1969 when the mill closed because of the increasing cost of raw silk and the emergence of man-made fibres. There are now no mills in the village although many of the population are employed in the large hose and belting works at High Bentham which is the successor of these earlier 18th century mills.

The present parish church of St John the Baptist was largely rebuilt in 1823 but the church site predates the Domesday records. The chancel probably dates from the second quarter of the 14th century as a replacement for one destroyed in Scottish raids of 1319 and 1325.

The 17th century also saw the growth of Quakerism in the parish and after persecution of early Quakers the Society bought a house in Low Bentham in 1680. Other forms of nonconformity have a long history in the area and Wesleyan Methodism was well established by 1800.

Much of village life is centred on the Victoria Institute, completed in 1904, and the two public houses, the Sun Dial inn and the Punch Bowl Hotel. A small industrial site has developed in the old Low Bentham silk mill and car repair workshops, joiners, farm building manufacture and a trout farm occupy the units. The post office is also a general store and there is another general store close to the primary school. Other shops include an antiques shop, an electrician's, a plumber's and a garage. A restaurant and old folk's home complete the non-residential properties in the village.

Lythe 🦡

This little village standing 500 ft above sea level commands extensive views of the North Sea and surrounding country. Its ancient church, dedicated to the Martyr-King, St Oswald, is a great landmark, perched as it is at the top of Lythe Bank, with sweeping views across the bay to Whitby, four miles away. There is evidence that a church has existed on this site from about AD 900.

Although small, Lythe has some interesting connections. The great-grandfather of Rudyard Kipling lived here in the early years of the 19th century, and there is still in existence a property known as 'Kipling Cottage'.

The majority of those living in Lythe are, or have been, employed on the Mulgrave estate, the focal point of which is the imposing building of Mulgrave Castle, the seat of the Marquis of Normanby.

Within the grounds are the ruins of the former castle built in the reign of King John, named originally 'Moultgrace' for its grace and beauty, the name later being changed to 'Moultgrave' from which Mulgrave is derived. Due to subsidence the ruins are now crumbling and are not accessible, but the mound on which the castle was built is covered in the early spring by a carpet of snowdrops which attracts many visitors.

Lythe has an old custom – that of 'firing the stiddy' on special occasions. The anvil is pulled out from the blacksmith's shop and upturned, when a charge of gunpowder is placed in it. This is detonated by means of a long metal bar heated red hot at one end.

The art of photography figures prominently in this area, and Tom Watson (1863–1957), the son of a Mulgrave estate carpenter, established a studio in Lythe in 1892. He was a contemporary of Frank Meadow Sutcliffe who was one of the very earliest of photographers of national and international repute in Whitby.

As well as being excellent for photographic purposes, the clear air of Lythe is obviously very healthy judging by the number of graves in the churchyard of those who had attained 100 years of age or over!

Malham 🦡

All roads leading into Malham descend steeply into the village. Malham is surrounded by spectacular limestone scenery which emerges as cliffs, scars and crags.

In the Middle Ages Malham was divided into Malham East and Malham West, the beck acting as the dividing line. Malham East was controlled by Bolton Priory, whilst Malham West was influenced by Fountains Abbey.

The village was united again after the Dissolution of the Monasteries and the focus of the village became the village green in front of the

Lister's Arms. Many of the farmhouses and cottages in Malham are built of limestone with flagstone or slate roofs. Mullioned windows, good stone work and date stones show what the village must have looked like in the 17th and 18th century.

It was on the village green where the annual sheep fairs were held. Today only one sheep sale survives and this is held on the Deer Park where Malham Fair was once held. Another agricultural event is Malham Show.

A special feature of the landscape are the dry stone walls. The walls are built to enclose sheep pastures and cultivated gardens. The smallest fields are called crofts. Some of the walls date from the monastic period and wall building continued until the 19th century. Today walls still need repairing and provide valuable shelter for cows and sheep against cold winds and driving rain. A dry stone wall is built without cement and is held together by stones being locked in position. The wall is built on a firm foundation, called a footings, whilst troughs are long stones which cross both sides of the wall to give added strength. The top stones finish the wall and must make contact with each side.

Although Malham is one of the most visited villages in the Yorkshire Dales a community spirit has survived. Villagers lead busy lives and help one another in time of trouble. Many families have lived in Malham for generations, and the village has a working blacksmith and many farms, some of which have diversified into tourism.

Manfield ✣

The remains of an ancient cross indicate a place of early Christian worship here and the village apparently flourished in the Middle Ages before the population was devastated by the Black Death. A recent land and air survey has established, from the uneven pastures within and immediately surrounding the village, that Manfield is a good example of a medieval shrunken village, and it has been designated by English Heritage to be a site of historical interest.

Examples of workmanship from the 13th to the 19th centuries, with earlier fragments, can be found in the parish church of All Saints, which stands on the site of a more ancient church on a slight knoll at the eastern end of the village. The base of the tower at 270 ft above sea level is a bench mark for the Ordnance Survey.

The Manfield Charity was set up to provide boots for poor boys embarking on working life. This still provides help for the needy of the parish. In 1855 work began on restoration of the church, and in time, a library and men's reading room were established. To the traditional buildings of stone and river cobbles with pantiled roofing, were added the school, two Memorial cottages and some tied cottages of stone with slate roofing.

All Saints Church, Manfield

Currently, Manfield is a rural village with commuters. It has a population of 225 but this increases to 325 when outlying farms, cottages and Cliffe estate, including the George Hotel, home of the clock that 'stopped short', are added. There is a loop road within the village along which lie many of the new houses built in the 1960s and 1970s. Overall, Manfield is not a picture-postcard village, but there are some pleasing aspects. It is complete with its church, school, cottage-style pub and pretty sub-post office cottage garden.

Marske-in-Swaledale

Marske is more a widespread community than just a village, because it embraces all the farms round about the village for a radius of up to two or more miles. The village is the centre of the community, as it is here that there is Marske Hall, once the seat of the Hutton family, which is now divided into flats.

The church is 11th century, dedicated to St Edmund, the King and Martyr. The church has undergone many changes over the centuries, but now is a haven of peace in its antiquity. It has box pews, and a special Hutton pew which faces the chancel.

Marske is about the mid-point on the Coast to Coast walk. Hundreds of people do this walk each year, but cause little disturbance to the village. Others come to walk up the valley of Marske beck, out onto the moors where once lead mining took place. The Swaledale Fell Rescue Group is housed in the Old Stable Block, which belongs to the village and which is also the village hall.

There is stability and continuity as nearly all the farms are still farmed by the same families as 50 or 60 years ago. In 1938 nine farms were sold to the military, for ranges and other army training and are still administered by the Ministry of Defence today.

The village is on the old road, and the shortest route from Richmond to Reeth. The Dormouse inn in Marske was the halfway resting place for the carters and their horses, when upwards of a dozen horses and carts would stop for refreshment. In the early 1900s, one 5th November, such a group of carters gathered at the Dormouse. They became very drunk and made a great bonfire from gates, fencing and anything else that would burn, causing an uproar that the Huttons would not tolerate. The consequence of this 'riotous behaviour' was that the pub lost its licence, the Dormouse became the Temperance Hotel and the house that was the pub is now the farmhouse of Temperance Farm. Marske has been very quiet ever since.

Marton

The oldest part of Marton consists mainly of terraced, albeit very different, houses without front gardens, opening straight onto the footpath which skirts the village green. The village is situated within a large loop of the river Seven and at each end of it were the watering places for the village cattle.

Many houses are built of Spaunton quarry limestone but the chapel and some others are constructed of brick from the local brickyards. The area within the boundary of the river has been declared a conservation area. It was originally an agricultural village with four farms and three smallholdings and many of the houses were homes for farm workers. There are now just two full time working farms and one smallholding. Two of the houses – originally smallholdings – are known as the 'Old Longhouses' with barns and cattle sheds attached to the dwellings. One is a cruck house dating back to 1704. Supporting the farming activities there used to be tradespeople and craftsmen who included two saddlers, two joiners (also undertakers), a blacksmith and several different shopkeepers to keep the villagers supplied with their needs. Now there is the post office, a garage and the public house, the Appletree, built in 1771 and originally called the Spotted Cow. In recent years, several self-employed people have begun their own small businesses.

Most of the cottages had well-stocked orchards, especially with gooseberry bushes, and gooseberries were Marton's claim to fame. Usually in the last week of June and first week of July, everything stopped for 'Berry Picking'. In the middle of June the man who bought the berries for a Leeds jam factory came to inspect the crop and estimate the yield. Shortly afterwards, he would deliver hessian sacks to the growers and tell them when to start picking. Twice a week until picking was finished, he would come to 'gather up'. After the war, there was no longer any sale for them and over the years the bushes have been taken up and the orchards have become gardens or building plots.

Augusto's Miniature Circus has its home in Marton and travellers passing through are frequently surprised to see llamas tethered by the roadside and grazing the verges. These belong to a family whose origins go back through many generations of circus folk and are now an integral part of the Marton scene.

Marton-cum-Grafton 🦚

The parish of Marton-cum-Grafton lies three miles south of Borough-bridge between the A1 and the York road. The parish is situated on high ground and can be seen from both main roads, the water tower in Grafton being the well known landmark.

Although there have been new housing developments in both villages, there has probably been more activity in the repairing, renovating and converting of old and derelict buildings. All this activity helps to preserve the ancient charm.

Christ church is situated on the village perimeter. The present church celebrated its centenary in 1976. Still surviving from the Norman era is a bell said to be the second oldest in England, which swings open to the weather in a little tower of its own.

Whilst chapels come and go, one establishment which has had many moments of glory in its 400 year existence is Ye Olde Punch Bowl inn in Marton. One such glorious moment was many years ago when landlord Eddie Shine integrated into the Punch Bowl's veteran fabric, fittings and character a modern motif – that of motoring. It became the notorious inn to which many motorists drove to 'Please Park Pretty' before entering the hostelry to have a pint of beer drawn from a miniature petrol pump!

Grafton's public house, the Shoulder of Mutton, is a great favourite with the locals. Its interior decoration remains in character with village life.

Once a sand and gravel quarry existed in the Grafton area, but it has long since been levelled and grassed to provide a place for many orga-nised sports activities and for more informal play and picnicking oppor-tunities for local children.

Martons Both 🦚

The two villages of East and West Marton, collectively known as Martons Both, lie a mile apart on the busy A59 near the Lancashire–Yorkshire border. At East Marton the road crosses the unique double-arched bridge which spans one of the prettiest stretches of the Leeds–Liverpool Canal.

The Roundell family featured prominently in the history of both villages. In 1899 the Roundells built a dairy capable of processing 500 gallons of milk a day from the farms on the Gledstone estate. From this beginning the dairy prospered and later became Associated Dairies, from which title the supermarket chain ASDA derived its name.

A native of West Marton, Mr Cecil Southwell, remembers the time early in the century when the road was so quiet it was possible for a local man named 'Goose' Tetley to drive his flock of geese along it to sell in Bradford. The first car in the village, a Daimler bought by the Roundells, arrived in 1910 though the local doctor and vets travelled the country lanes on horseback or motorbike. At this time the villages were self-supporting, though coal had to be brought by canal, then collected and distributed by the estate horse and cart.

Sir Amos Nelson bought the estate in 1919. His original plan was to modernise the old hall but he abandoned this idea on the advice of Sir Edwin Lutyens, designer of the Cenotaph in London, whom Sir Amos met on a cruise to India. The new Gledstone Hall was started in 1923 to Sir Edwin's design. The gardens were laid out to plans prepared by Gertrude Jekyll and the beautiful gates designed by Sir Edwin were wrought in the village smithy by Wilf Hoggart.

The Nelson family lived there until the early 1970s then moved to the renovated stable block now known as Old Gledstone. The hall is now a nursing home.

Masham 🐑

Masham lies beside the river Ure. It is a very picturesque place with many old buildings and narrow roads. The land rises gradually to high moors where the red grouse live and on up to the dales.

The heart of Masham is its wonderfully spacious Market Place with houses and commercial properties mainly dating from the 18th and 19th centuries, on all sides. The ancient church of St Mary stands in one corner, the school founded in 1760 in another and at its centre the market cross stands amid cobbles, trees and flowers. Here a market is held each Wednesday. This derives from a charter granted by Richard II in 1393 to Stephen le Scrope.

Theakston's Brewery is famed for its Old Peculier brew. The brothers Thomas and Robert first practised the brewer's art 150 years ago at the Black Bull Yard and the brewery is now a major employer in Masham. Adjoining the brewery is a recently developed visitors centre. I'Anson Bros and 'Jamesons', both agricultural feed merchants, are also major employers in the area.

The last weekend in September Masham holds a Sheep Fair, an event revived a few years ago by Mrs Susan Cunliffe-Lister. Up until the First World War the sheep fairs were great events in Masham. The fair used to last for three days and the Market Place and the side streets would be full of sheep, horses and cattle. Farmers from the dales and more distant wolds, pedlars, carts and dogs would join the Scottish and Irish drovers who had driven countless thousands of sheep from all parts of Scotland and Northern England.

Skeletons keep turning up in the Little Market Place and beyond! The last time skeletons were found was in the 1980s when the new public toilets were being built. Others have been found in front of the police station and at a nearby pub. The older inhabitants of Masham say they remember kicking bones and skulls when they were children, before the market place was cobbled!

Melsonby 🌿

Melsonby lies at the junction of crossroads running from the Roman Dere Street and Scotch Corner. The village enjoys a pleasant aspect of an elevated character; the chief landmark from the four roads leading into the village is the Norman tower of St James' church. Limestone outcrops are a feature of the neighbourhood and limestone quarries, copper mines and agricultural employment provided the main source of income for the villagers up to the 1920s.

Scots Dyke Close, a housing estate on the south-east edge of the village, perpetuated the name of an ancient earthwork passing over Gatherley Moor, across the A66 to the Swale at Richmond. Gatherley Moor was a renowned hunting ground and race course until the 1816 enclosure act.

In front of the Old Rectory are the foundation remains of a Benedictine nunnery which was dissolved before the Reformation. An earlier church stood to the west side of the present site and a few Saxon remains are now housed in St James'.

The former church day school (now the church hall) carried an endowment by William Cockin from about 1759 to be used for the education of six poor children. This fund, now the Cockin Trust, continues to be administered to provide extra educational facilities for village children.

Until the 1940s there were eight farms and eight smallholdings in the village. Only one farm remains today, the remainder have become private houses and the land bought by outlying farms. A stream runs through the village and the old rectory and church hold commanding positions on opposite banks of the stream. The older part of the village is a conservation area and has interesting terraces of cottages and many Grade II listed buildings. There is a row of cottages which in the 18th century were the almshouses. The village has now an increased population due to new housing estates, retirement bungalows and council houses.

Mickley 🐚

Mickley is a small village about six miles from Ripon. It has only one main street, no street lights, no mains sewerage, no shops and no pubs, but in spite of this, or maybe because of it, it is a very pretty and friendly village. A mobile shop, fishmonger and butcher call every week and a mobile library calls each fortnight.

There is a small church which was built in 1841 through the generosity of the Dalton family of Sleningford Grange in memory of Elizabeth Dalton. It is built of cobblestones taken from the river Ure, which runs the length of the village on the north side. Many wild flowers, both common and rare, grow in the churchyard and a photographic record of these is kept in the church. There are a number of gravestones of Irish Catholics in the graveyard. These are of immigrants who came to work in a flax mill near the river during the potato famine in Ireland in the 1840s. The ruins of the flax mill can still be seen.

After the dissolution of Fountains Abbey, a deed conveyed the manor and premises to certain persons in Mickley, who were to hold this property in trust for the tenants of Mickley. A Court Leet is still held every three years. There is a steward but the office of pinder has lapsed. The Court Leet is held in the village and at a nearby inn all the freeholders attend in the capacity of lords of the manor. A jury is formed from residents who rent and do not own their premises. This jury, after being sworn, views the different properties of the manor and draws up a report in the form of a verdict on the state of the properties and advises what repairs should be done. This verdict is presented to the lords for their consideration and decision. The proceedings are always accompanied by a dinner paid for out of the accumulated rents of the property, at which the Loyal Toast and that of the Manor of Mickley are drunk.

Middleham 🐚

Middleham is renowned for history and horses. Much of the history is bound up with the castle, which dates from 1190, has a keep second in size only to the Tower of London and was owned by Warwick the King-maker and that most controversial of English kings, Richard III. It is still impressive and attracts over 27,000 visitors a year. At dusk in the winter when deserted it is more than slightly sinister.

The monks of Jervaulx introduced the first Wensleydale cheese, made from ewe's milk, and founded Middleham's main industry by training their horses on the Low Moor, just above the village. By the late 18th century there were race meetings on the moor and the first of the racing stables were established. The horses brought prosperity to Middleham.

The Low Moor is still in a place of great activity every morning as strings of horses make their way to the gallops.

Middleham has two market crosses, one in each of the squares. The Top Cross, also called the Swine Cross, is surmounted by a stone animal, said to represent the White Boar, emblem of Richard III, but it is so weathered as to be unrecognizable. Set in the road beside it is the Bull Ring, a relic of the brutal days of bull-baiting. The Jubilee Fountain is a handsome piece of Victoriana and commemorates the Queen's Golden Jubilee. There are four pubs, the Black Bull, two Swans, Black and White, and the Richard III.

St Alkelda, who shares with St Mary the dedication of the parish church, was martyred by two heathen Danish women who strangled her. In the fields a little spring is called St Alkelda's Well and the water was believed to cure eye troubles. The church was granted collegiate status by King Richard, an honour commemorated by the red robes worn by the choir. Another well is known as the Talking Well; housewives used to fetch water there, until the new-fangled oakpipes spoiled the opportunity of a good gossip.

Middlesmoor ✑

Middlesmoor is situated at the head of Upper Nidderdale, eight miles from Pateley Bridge and about 20 miles from Harrogate and Ripon. It is reached via a narrow winding road, which runs past Gouthwaite reservoir and in some places alongside the river Nidd.

The village consists of a cluster of stone-built houses placed in a random manner and linked by narrow, cobbled roads and ginnels. The roofs are of gray or blue slate giving protection against the inclement weather which often occurs at the height of just over 900 ft above sea level.

An early preaching cross with the inscription 'Cross of St Ceadda' (Chad) can be seen in the church. It is thought to date from either the 10th or 11th century.

The present St Chad's, which was rebuilt in 1866, contains many interesting features. At the rear of the church is a massive font, the bowl of which could be Anglo-Saxon or Norman. The church is also fortunate in possessing a fine peal of six bells, which were presented in 1868 by Mary Anna Barkwith as a memorial to her great uncle, Mr Simon Horner. She also left £3 to be paid yearly towards a children's annual festival to commemorate the opening of the peal of bells, 'provided no rude games were permitted'. This festival has been held annually ever since and is now held on the Saturday nearest to St Barnabas' Day.

The closure of school and chapel have come about because of a decline in population – in 1881 there was a population of 104 in Middlesmoor, in 1950 there were 72 people and in 1990 there were only 35. At the moment, there is still a post office combined with a general stores, the Crown Hotel and a butcher, baker and greengrocer call once a week. There are many visitors, though the road peters out into a rough track at the top of the village. It is a very colourful village especially in the spring, when there is a marvellous show of daffodils.

Middleton ✍

On leaving Pickering by the A170 road to Helmsley, the first small village encountered is Middleton, spreading to left and right of the road.

The Manor house mentioned in the 11th century, was situated behind the present New Tavern (until recently and from its origin in the 17th century known as the New Inn). Rosedale Priory ran the Middleton manor house until the Rosedale nunneries were abolished in the 16th century. Since that time the site has been known as Nuns' Garth and earthworks were uncovered in a nearby field.

Opposite Nuns' Garth is the church of St Andrew. The lower part of the west tower is early 11th century, often termed Saxon but it is really Viking. Grave markers set around the district result in the display of several Viking crosses in the church. One particularly fine example shows a Viking warrior bearing a sword.

The most unusual feature of St Andrew's church was the chantry of Our Lady. After the dissolution of the chantry in 1547 it was decided that the revenues be applied to education and they supported a Middleton grammar school until the 18th century. Between 1702 and 1871 Middleton children, perhaps those of the grammar school, climbed the church tower to mark out the shape of their shoes on the lead of the church roof, with their initials and date. At least 400 are recorded.

Next to the rectory is Middleton Hall, a stone-fronted Georgian building with a balustraded parapet. The present owners and residents in the Hall are Sir Charles and Lady Richmond-Brown.

The original blacksmith's forge had made way for a delightful stone-built bungalow and garden named Forge Green, and further along an old manor house still exists with its walled garden and farmland.

Middleton Tyas ✍

Middleton Tyas is situated a mile to the east of Scotch Corner. The road drops downhill to give the village a sheltered position.

Middleton lies midway between two other ancient settlements, Moulton and Kneeton, though the latter no longer exists as a village. This position between two settlements may account for the situation of the church, St Michael's, which is well away from the main part of the village at the end of a long and beautiful avenue of lime trees.

There are two inns: the Shoulder of Mutton, or the 'top pub' and the Bay Horse, or the 'bottom pub'. These designations are not related to their quality but to their position on the hill on which the village stands. There is a junior school with a happy and lively atmosphere, and a village shop which is also a post office. A market garden supplies excellent fruit and vegetables, and a butcher, a fishmonger and a baker visit the village regularly.

Some wealth came to the village in the 18th century when copper was mined in fields near the church. East Hall, one of the 'big houses' of the village, was built by Leonard Hartley in 1713, and it was he who was responsible for the mining. His son George had a grander house, designed by John Carr of York, built on the outskirts of the village and known as Middleton Lodge.

The remains of wells which served the village until a piped water supply was brought to the whole village in 1955–6 can still be found. The most curious of these is a dropping or tumbling well. A spout set in a sheltering arch pours water into a stone trough with stone slabs at the sides on which to stand containers. According to long-standing residents it has never been known to fail, and even today caravan dwellers from Scotch Corner come down to it to fill their churns.

Church of St. Michael & All Angels, Middleton Tyas

Milby 🦋

Milby lies to the north of the small market town of Boroughbridge, along the bank of the river Ure. Strategically positioned at the point on the river where the Romans built a ford from the settlement at Aldborough, Isurium, there must have been activity there from very early times.

Now a small agricultural settlement, it is hard to imagine that Milby once supported four public houses and was the dockland for the area, handling many centuries of river traffic as goods from North Yorkshire were shipped downstream to York, Hull and the rest of the world.

Aldborough declined in early medieval times and the ford fell into disuse. A new bridge was built upstream by the rapidly growing new town of Boroughbridge. The opening of the canal in 1770 to overcome the weir enabled Knaresborough to trade by river directly and, culminating in the arrival of the railway in 1847, Milby's life as a river docks and trading centre declined.

Today there is very little evidence of Milby's past. It has reverted to its agricultural role as a sleepy farming village.

Monk Fryston 🦋

Monk Fryston is a charming village situated seven miles from Selby on the A63. It was in existence before AD 900 and was known simply as Fryston, derived from the words 'free stone' and it is thought that this reflects the number of quarries in the area.

The lands of Fryston were given in 1109 by Archbishop Thomas of York to the Benedictine monks; these lands included both the church and manor (now Monk Fryston Hall Hotel). The abbot had a master of works based in the village and it was he who supervised the quarrying of the stone, much of which was used in the construction of Selby Abbey.

St Wilfrid's church is probably as old as Monk Fryston, parts are pre-Conquest, particularly the lower part of the tower. Other parts were added until it was finally completed in 1444 and dedicated on the 12th May of that year. Much restoration was put in hand towards the end of the 19th century, chiefly through the generosity of the Hemsworth family whose memorial tablets can be seen in the church.

Monk Fryston Lodge, an elegant mansion reputedly designed by the famous Yorkshire architect John Carr, is situated on the York road and used to house various members of the Hemsworth family. After a succession of owners, the Lodge was sold to the CEGB in 1964.

For many years the village was mainly a farming community, but it has now changed and with the building of new houses has become a dormitory for the surrounding towns. In spite of this, village life still goes on in much the same way with many local activities. The increase in population has given new life to the charming village school which is also a listed building, recently restored to great effect.

Morton-on-Swale

Travelling west from Ainderby on the A684 you come to Morton-on-Swale – the two villages have not quite joined up. Originally just one street with houses mainly on the south side, it is a straggling village which ends well before it reaches the river Swale. Apart from the Manor, few of the houses are distinguished, but there are a lot of well-kept pretty gardens and the overall impression is of neat prosperity.

The 1913 edition of Kelly's Directory lists a wheelwright, a blacksmith, a joiner, a grocer and a butcher (who also kept the public house, the Royal George); there was a ropemaker as well. Of these only the butcher remains, though there is a good village shop, which also houses the sub-post office, transferred from Ainderby in the 1980s. White's is known as one of the best butcher's for many miles, built up over four generations. There has been a lot of development in Morton, with three new housing estates since the 1960s.

Morton Hall, now a farm, is mentioned in 1346 when it had a communal oven and a windmill. There were brick and tile works, used in living memory, down Potter's Lane; bricks made here were used for cottages at Ainderby.

There are two public houses in the village: one until recently known as the Non-Plus (named after a famous race horse) is now the Swaledale Arms. The other is the Old Royal George, named after a ship.

The stone bridge over the Swale was built in 1747–8 to replace a previous wooden bridge, which was probably the successor of a manorial ferry. A murder was committed near here in 1759: Mary Ward, a servant girl, discovered that her boss was the leader of a gang of counterfeiters at a time when counterfeiting carried the death penalty. She told this secret to her sweetheart and the gang, learning of her knowledge, lured her to a lonely spot near the new bridge, attacked and brutally murdered her. Her ghost is reputed to haunt the bridge; it is said that her body was never found.

Muker

The village of Muker lies at the foot of Kisdon Hill in Upper Swaledale where two valleys meet. Its grey stone houses huddle in a group around the church of St Mary which is the focal point of the village. There was a church here in 1590 but much of the present day building dates from 1890.

In the 17th and 18th centuries the people earned their living by lead mining. The population was much greater, people living in cramped conditions with large families and lodgers packed into small cottages. There were three public houses but now only one remains. When the industry declined towards the end of the 19th century many people moved away to find work in Lancashire, Durham and America. The ones who remained stayed to farm the land, with others earning a living as tradesmen.

In the days of lead mining people supplemented their income by knitting. All the family took part; father, mother and the children, and dealers travelled the dale leaving wool at the houses and collecting garments later. Today Muker once again enjoys some prosperity from wool. Mr & Mrs D. Morris established a cottage industry when they opened Swaledale Woollens in Muker. Local people hand knit the wool, which has been spun from the local Swaledale sheep.

Farming plays a large part in the life of Muker. Most farmers own their land and families continue the tradition. Sheep and cows are reared on the hills and hay is made in the meadows where during May and June are to be seen an abundance of wild flowers. This is an area of outstanding beauty and is designated environmentally sensitive.

The high spot in the farming year is Muker Show which is held on the first Wednesday in September, when folk who have moved away come back for the day. The local band plays in the village and on the show field most of the day. The band was formed in 1897 when some of the local men got together and bought a few second-hand instruments.

Muker

The first mention of Mustone is in the Domesday Book where it is shown as a dependent of Hunmanby, and throughout most of its recorded history it has been connected with this neighbouring village.

Situated in a hollow at the foot of the wolds, the infant river Hertford flows through the village on its way to join the Derwent, then the Humber.

A Roman road must have passed through the village on its way to the signal station at Filey. Its exact location is not known but a later signal, or beacon was built on Beacon Hill to the east of the village. Its duty was 'to take light from Speeton and pass it on to Staxton'. Just to the east of Beacon Hill stands the stump of a brick windmill tower. The first miller recorded was in 1341 and the last in 1913.

The main street is formed by the road from Folkton which then joins the coast road, this is also joined by Hunmanby Street with the base of a three-stepped medieval cross at the junction. Across the road is the only surviving inn, the Ship, as the Cross Keys ceased some years ago. A feature of the buildings in the village are the six 18th century houses, all with date stones.

The church, along with many others, was given to Bardney Abbey in 1115. There is still a 12th century font. Until Muston got its own graveyard in 1828, burials took place in Hunmanby. It is believed that the steep hill between the two villages, marked on the map as 'Heather-stay' is really 'Hithersta' – a point of rest for the pall bearers.

At the beginning of the 19th century the village gave its name to the 'Muston and Yedingham Drainage Scheme', a plan for draining the peaty carrs along the Vale of Pickering. Farmers still pay a rent to this scheme.

Myton-on-Swale ✺

The small quiet parish of Myton-on-Swale (population 125) stands at the confluence of the rivers Swale and Ure.

Historically, the most notable event was a skirmish between the English and the Scots in 1319. While King Edward II laid seige to the town of Berwick, the Scottish Lords Douglas and Randolph, with 15,000 men marched into England to plunder the north. While they were crossing the river the Scots set fire to haycocks. Confused by the smoke the English were routed with the loss of 3,000 men. Many monks and priests were killed with the result that it became known as the White Battle or the Chapter of Myton. One or two stones which probably formed part of the bridge remain.

St Mary's church is a Norman foundation with an Early English chancel and tower. It was almost totally rebuilt in the 17th century and heavily restored in 1888. The porch was added in 1908. The church is said to have been built of stone taken from ancient Isurium (Aldborough) and still has marks of fire on it. Although only a very small parish the church is in regular use and well maintained.

The famous crusader Roger de Mowbray was buried for a short time in the churchyard. For 600 years he was interred at Byland Abbey which he founded. In 1819 Martyn Stapylton, who owned Byland Abbey, learnt from ancient manuscripts the exact spot, had the bones disinterred and reburied at Myton. However, some 24 years later the bones were again exhumed, taken at night and reburied at the abbey.

At the beginning of the 20th century practically the whole of the village was owned by the Stapyltons and most villagers worked in the village and on the estates. Now most of the houses are owner occupied and few work in the parish but travel to surrounding areas for employment.

Naburn ✺

On the banks of the river Ouse and six miles south of York is the village of Naburn. It is situated off the A19 on the B1222. If you travel by car you could go under the railway bridge, pass the boats at the marina on your right, count to 20 and be leaving the village past the church.

The tiny village green, more like a traffic island, has a maypole that is usually used as a flagpole on special occasions. Not far away is the local pub, the Blacksmith's Arms, and at the end of the street is the slipway for the launching of boats. It used to be a public slipway, but now it is run by the little yacht club.

The railway line has been closed and the rails and sleepers removed. However there is a cycle-track in its place and the more fit cyclists can get as far as York.

In the mid 1970s the landowner died and his heirs sold the farms to their tenants. From then on the village has had new houses built, including two new estates. It meant that there were more children to swell numbers at the school, which is no longer in danger of closure.

Being near the river, there is a problem with flooding. There are fields just up river from Naburn Locks that are called 'ings' which are really water meadows; it means 'liable to flood'. When the river gets very high, as in winter and at high tides, it comes over the banks onto the ings and the roads.

Newbiggin-in-Bishopdale 🐑

Newbiggin means new buildings; the village was not listed in the Domesday Book and was first mentioned in documents in 1230. It is a hamlet now of 31 houses and an inn, strung along the base of Wasset Fell with farms at each end.

The Grange has extensive views over to Thoralby and faces Newbiggin House, which was rebuilt early in the 20th century from two ling-thatched cottages (ling is heather). Tom Heseltine, the last in a long line of masons, did the work. He also put in the water supply from Millbeck for Thoralby and Newbiggin in 1906, for the princely sum of one penny farthing a yard.

During the 19th century there was a much larger population, at least three times as many people as now: they included leadminers who worked on Wasset Fell, three tailors, a cobbler, two shops and a smithy as well as farmers, though some, like the innkeepers, ran farms as well. The Street Head inn, situated at the north end of the lane still has a thriving trade.

Situated by the bridge is a sheep fold; during the 19th century the sheep washing which took place here in mid June heralded the beginning of three days fun and feasting. Fell races and sprints up and down the village were held and the bands played by the smithy.

The present population is 47, the numbers increase in summer as the holidaymakers arrive. Tourism has burgeoned in the dales since the 1950s when cyclists and walkers used to stay at farmhouses. Now there are eight holiday cottages and a guest house and bed and breakfast accommodation, as well as the inn.

Along Turnsyke lane was found one of the massive millstone grit gateposts with holes and slots for wooden bars. They are quite rare in Wensleydale although there is another one in Newbiggin. Also along here were discovered in the stone wall, broken up gravestones thought to be from a Quaker burial ground nearby. One of the buildings on the left was reputed to be a brewery long ago and produced 'Newbiggin lemonade'.

In summer it can take an hour to post a letter as neighbours meet and catch up with news and while away some time in the sun. Winter is different, people use their cars and dash about, glad to be inside again against the cold and wet and visitors to the village think the place is deserted. Not so, the village thrives.

Newby ✑

Newby is a small hamlet situated just off the A65 road between Clapham and Ingleton, and forms part of the parish of Clapham. The original settlement was about a mile to the south of the present position, but the population was decimated by the Great Plague of 1664–65. After this the survivors moved away and reformed the village in its present position, and many of the oldest houses date from this time.

For many years it formed part of the lands of Furness Abbey and the monks carried on a wool trade and cultivated a walled garden, which is still in existence as a small croft at the head of the village. In the Victorian era, Newby was a thriving community, weaving being the main industry with nine weavers working in their cottages and being assisted by their numerous children. But by 1871 the cottage industry had gone, due to the weavers moving to Lancashire to work in the mills, or changing their occupations.

In 1873 a Methodist chapel was built, designed to hold 150–200 people. It remains a well supported chapel, with two services being conducted every Sunday. There has been a school in Newby for a longer period than the chapel, probably as early as 1721.

At the present time Newby has a population of about 60 persons, which is gradually increasing with property development. However the only public facilities are a post box and a telephone kiosk, the nearest shop being in Clapham, one and a half miles away. This results in Newby remaining an isolated, but traditionally friendly, hamlet.

Newby Wiske ✑

Newby Wiske stands on the banks of the river Wiske, four miles south of Northallerton and linked to the A167 by the road which winds through South Otterington.

This picturesque village still retains its post office and shop, also a small Methodist chapel, but the thriving station, once used especially by farmers to transport sugar beet and grain, was an early 20th century casualty.

Many of the cottages date back to Tudor times, but the school was built in 1860, for girls, by William Rutson of Newby Wiske Hall. Both he and his family took great interest in the school. Earlier this century it was amalgamated with the boys school from South Otterington and continues to flourish in the centre of the village.

It is said that the two public houses once existing in the village were closed down by William Rutson following the over indulgence of the locals.

Newby Wiske Hall in the 19th century was the home of the Rutson family and is said to contain a ghost. It is that of a young girl, who, when prevented from seeing the man she loved, leapt to her death from the attic window. Her ghost still wanders the upper floor of the building. The Hall is now the headquarters of North Yorkshire Police and many officers live in the community.

Newton-le-Willows

Newton-le-Willows was for centuries under the jurisdiction of Jervaulx Abbey. There was a quarry at Lindale Lodge, now a farm, and stone was quarried there for the building of the bridge at Bedale.

The railway came to Newton in 1850 and the station was opened in 1856 and called Newton-le-Willows. However, this led to confusion with Newton-le-Willows in Lancashire where guests of Lord Aylesbury to Jervaulx Abbey would arrive by mistake so the name of the station was changed to Jervaulx. The railway had overtaken a canal system that had been planned for Wensleydale in 1815. This enterprise only got as far as Bedale. At the station there was a cattle dock, signal box and timber yard. Now it has all been demolished and houses have been built in the station yard, although the railway line itself is still open and used by quarry trains as far as Redmire.

Aysgarth School originated at Aysgarth, hence its name, but it was moved to Newton-le-Willows where it was purpose-built for 'the education of gentlemen's sons' in 1890. For many years the village men and women have found employment at the school in one capacity or another.

The old Bobbin Mill Cottages bear witness to an industry long past. They were built in 1770 to house the workers at the mill. Behind the cottages there used to be a foundry and a trough beside the road outside Bridge House is said to be the only remaining piece of foundry work that is left in the village.

The village pub, the Wheatsheaf, was built when Aysgarth School was established to house visiting parents and relations of the preparatory school boys. Previously there had been various brewhouses in the village and on the site of the Wheatsheaf there had been a row of cottages and a reading room.

Records of days long past tell us of the existence of village shops, a bakery, shoemaker and the presence of a petrol pump. 'Cocked Hat', now a road junction, used to be an inn on a drovers road that ran from Ulshaw Bridge. There is no church in Newton but two chapels.

Newton-on-Ouse

On 30th November 1957 Lady Edith Enid, Countess of Chesterfield died at Beningbrough Hall. An era in the history of Newton-on-Ouse ended. Since the completion of Sir John Bouchier's baroque mansion in 1716, gentlefolk of different generations of Bouchiers, Dawnays and Chesterfields had driven through the park and into the village to attend services at All Saints' church.

The folk of Newton were to miss Her Ladyship, whom they regarded with an affectionate respect and deference. From 1917, when as a young bride of great beauty she had bought the Hall and Park for £15,000, she had over the years become a familiar figure, emerging through the gates to inspect 'her village', and sometimes arrogantly to suggest improvements and deliver reprimands.

The Saxons built a church by the river side, the foundations of the tower of which still exist. The Normans added to it and the later rebuilding in the 19th century preserved a Norman arch and pillars between the nave and tower, to which a graceful spire was added, to be a landmark for miles round.

From the door of the Methodist chapel can be seen one of the best views over the green and along the Avenue. The chapel was built in 1924 on the site of some demolished cottages. The bricks for the building, delivered by boat to Newton Landing, formed one of the last consignments in a declining river traffic. The railway skirting the parish to the east had won the competition for freight.

The Ouse borders the village to the west, flowing lazily in dry weather between steep sandy banks, but heavy rain in the Pennines transforms it into a raging torrent, bursting its banks and spilling over the ings and flatts, obliterating its normal course.

Two public houses, the Dawnay Arms, which was an inn and coaching house, and 'The Blacksmith's' are popular social venues and refresh passing visitors who come in increasing numbers to visit Her Ladyship's last home. What would she have thought of people tramping through her bedchamber, boudoir and bathroom? No doubt she would have made some acid remarks!

Nidd

A casual visitor to Nidd will find nothing other than a quiet, attractive well-ordered village. Its place in North Yorkshire's ecclesiastical history, however, is well established.

In a solemn ceremony in Rome in November 1987, Cardinal Basil Hume, Primate of England and Wales, handed Pope John Paul II a scroll bearing the names of those who died for their faith 400 years ago. They were declared Blessed – the second stage in a process by which a person is eventually recognised to be a saint, and included two local men. Peter Snow was born in Ripon. He was arrested for celebrating mass at Nidd Hall and suffered death at York on 15th June, 1598. Ralph Grimstone was born at Nidd Hall in 1535. He was imprisoned in 1593 in York Castle for harbouring priests. He was released, but arrested again for accompanying Peter Snow from Nidd to York and both were condemned to death.

This ancient parish's ecclesiastical importance reaches far back into the past. According to the Venerable Bede, it was at Nidd that the synod was convened for the reinstallation of Wilfrid to his possessions in Northumbria and Mercia in AD 705 and to the building of the Minster at Ripon soon afterwards.

Nidd then became a 'lost village'. It is probable that emparkment was the cause of its decline – clearing to establish a hunting park and privacy within an estate. This seems to have taken place between 1811 and 1821 when the population of Nidd fell from 120 to 86. Nidd Hall Park was enlarged in two stages and the Ordnance Survey Map shows that by 1841 the extension of the park was complete.

The village was revived again when the Hall and estate came under new ownership. The village institute is now privately owned as a house, as are the pub (Ass in a Band Box), the Station Hotel, the children's home and the school. The Hall is now an hotel and Home Farm is now a racing stud.

Along the 'sunken road', which leads northwards, you eventually come to the church of St Margaret and St Paul built in 1866–1867.

Normanby

Normanby is a small village situated in Ryedale on the road from Malton to Kirkbymoorside, and on the banks of the river Seven. There is a population of about 100, with the main occupation being agriculture.

The village has been in existence since Norman times, and was a resting place for travellers (and their horses) from Teesside to the Humber. It is recorded that at one time, there were as many as 14 alehouses. Most of the original houses are built of limestone brought from Spaunton quarry, three miles away, with later ones built of bricks made in local brickyards.

The parish church of St Andrew was first established in Normanby in 1150 and was rebuilt in 1718. The two bells and the church roof have been renovated recently. The path in the churchyard goes past the church door to a kissing gate in the hedge and thence across a field to the river. It was along this path on Sunday evenings that village men used to carry buckets of water for the womenfolk to use on their Monday wash-days in the days before mains water was brought to the village. There is still an old iron tap at the roadside.

The Methodist chapel built in 1876 sadly had to close in 1988, as did the blacksmith's shop – it has been converted into a small bungalow. There is still a public house – the Sun inn, a very old building which has been modernised to provide catering facilities for locals and tourists alike.

Within the parish of Normanby there is the hamlet of Thornton Riseborough, which nowadays consists of three farms, a cottage and Riseborough Hall. There is little remaining of the village of Riseborough as it once was, or the church which existed there, apart from some uneven mounds in some of the fields which were the foundations of long since demolished buildings, the inhabitants having died of the plague in the Middle Ages.

North Cowton

North Cowton is a charming village nine miles equidistant from Darlington, Richmond and Northallerton on the B1263 road.

North Cowton must have often been involved in skirmishes in medieval times between English and Scottish soldiers. The battle of the Standard was fought on 22nd August 1138, also known as the battle of Cowton Moor, and there is still a field called Scots Graves near the village.

The population in 1988 was 435. Today the older properties are centred around the village greens, the greens being maintained by the parish council. There is very little employment in the village, residents having to commute to the towns for work. The village has one post office, a garage, a joiner/undertaker, a public house, and a petrol filling station.

The present Methodist chapel was built in 1827. The parish church of St Luke was built as a pastoral centre in 1968, the parish church then being St Mary's, South Cowton which has been taken over by the Redundant Churches Fund. The Bishop of Ripon consecrated St Luke's as the parish church of North Cowton on October 21st 1990.

North Deighton 🌿

If you leave the A1 travelling north at Wetherby, then two and a half miles along the road to Knaresborough you will come to North Deighton, a village where little has changed over the years except for infill of a few dwellings.

It has more than 90 inhabitants and originally comprised seven or eight farms and cottages to accommodate the farmworkers, forming part of an estate. A lovely village, the green still exists, flanked by the manor and Manor Farm originally owned by the Inglebys of Ripley Castle.

The Old Hall Farm on the Spofforth Road is probably the oldest property (listed), possibly 17th century, and one part has still the old mullioned windows. There is a story that an actress, together with her two children, was imprisoned in a panelled room where she scratched with a diamond on a pane of glass. This pane of glass is now being preserved by the present owner and though the inscription is very faint the following words can still be made out – 'For 18 months these walls enclosed, echoed my footsteps as with even pace I went around this prison'.

Howe Hill Farm takes its name from the big mound at the back of the house, supposedly the burial place of the soldiers killed at Marston Moor in General Howe's regiment, the soil being carted from Marston pond which is situated at Westgate Farm. Howe Hill was excavated in 1938–1940 and various things were found there, ie Neolithic potsherds, flint tools, flint implements and an urn of the Bronze Age. Certainly it would appear to be some sort of a burial ground.

North Duffield 🌿

The village of North Duffield lies in the Vale of York between the rivers Derwent and Ouse, and is mentioned in the Domesday Book, being known then as Duffeld.

The village must have had some importance in the 13th century, the lord of the manor, Roger of Thurkelby, having been granted a market and fair by Henry III. These fairs continued into the late 19th century when the school closed for a week's holiday. They were held on the large village green, sadly reduced by four acres at enclosure in 1814. The Knights Hospitallers had a hermitage and eight houses here between 1190 and 1280; and there was a fishery on the Derwent still being recorded in the 18th century.

A number of mills including a horse-mill were in action from 1320 to 1872, and there was a brickworks in the mid 19th century; but the main industry was agriculture and most of the population were farmers or farm servants, or worked in related trades.

North Duffield Village

North Duffield is in the parish of Skipwith and although always the larger of the two villages has never had an established church, Christian worship taking place in the lovely old church in Skipwith, till the building of a chapel in 1821.

Two named licensed houses were first recorded in 1822. The Cart and Horse closed in 1950 but the King's Arms still flourishes by the green. During alterations some years ago, a 400 year old fireplace was discovered and the original stone hearth and beam over it can still be seen. The old smithy across the road is now a ruin.

For the last 150 years the population remained constant at around 300 to 450, but the village has been designated an area for expansion and with the building of many new homes the population is increasing dramatically, whilst agriculture is tending to decrease. Nevertheless, North Duffield is an attractive and lively village, the product of a thousand years of English history.

North Otterington

The hamlet of North Otterington is situated two miles south of North-allerton, on the A167. Consisting of only about 15 dwellings, most of which are farms, it would be easy enough to drive though without even noticing it, except for the church of St Michael and All Angels, which stands on ground above the level of the road and is surrounded by snowdrops and daffodils in the springtime.

The present North Otterington church is the oldest in the parish, and was built with money from Hugh Pudsey, Bishop of Durham in the middle of the 12th century, the first building having been destroyed by William the Conqueror in 1069. It is thought that the original church dated from Saxon times, AD 800 and that burials have taken place on this site for over 1,000 years. In the 19th century the tower and spire were added and in 1874, during major restoration work, the discovery of a stone coffin revealed skulls and some Saxon crosses. Marks can be seen in the porch where soldiers sharpened their swords and there is also an ancient mass dial on the front of the porch.

In 1880 a human skeleton was found in a gravel pit and was thought to be of prehistoric origin and once covered by a burial mound. In 1970 another skeleton was discovered in the garden of one of the houses. However, this time the lady had only been there for eight months and it resulted in her lodger being tried for murder!

For many centuries, St Michael and All Angels was the 'mother' church of the area and two corpse roads still exist from nearby Thornton-le-Moor and Thornton-le-Beans.

Another noticeable building is Otterington House, with its turretted, castle-like appearance, and looking across the river Wiske towards the church is Solberge Hall. There are traces of a medieval village nearby and it is believed a building has existed here from at least that time. A brickworks once existed at Solberge. It has also been a police training college but is currently a popular country house hotel.

North Stainley

North Stainley is situated on the A6108, four miles from the cathedral city of Ripon. Houses flank both sides of the busy main road.

At the heart of the village lies the parish church of St Mary The Virgin which in 1990 celebrated its 150th anniversary. The church is adjoined by the village school, built at the same time. North Stainley Hall, the home of the Staveley family, is a listed building. Mr Robert Staveley is the owner and developer of Lightwater Valley Theme Park at the southern entrance to the village. At the north end is Slenningford Grange which is believed to have belonged to Fountains Abbey. The fishpond, walled garden and well that the monks are supposed to have used, are still in existence.

The village lies in the middle of rich farmland and has two working quarries, the one to the west being a limestone quarry where there were lime kilns some years ago. There is a gravel quarry on the banks of the river Ure, which forms the eastern boundary of the parish, and also on the river bank is the High Batts nature reserve.

Beyond the recreation ground are the old people's bungalows and The Shepherdies which is the oldest housing estate. There are two new estates named Roseberry Green and Beatswell Lawn, the former having won an award for excellence. At the centre of the village is a garage and combined post office and shop, as well as a very pleasant pub, The Cross Keys, and a fine new restaurant called The Spit Roast at the Staveley Arms. There is a village policeman resident at the police house.

In a field just outside the village is the site of a Roman villa called Castle Dykes. It was excavated in 1895, but all that can be seen now is the grassed outline of the foundations and the moat, the water for which came from Lightwater.

Norton-on-Derwent 🦢

Norton is situated at the foot of the East Yorkshire Wolds, bounded by the river Derwent and the town of Malton on the north side. It used to be known as the second largest village in Yorkshire, Cottingham being the largest.

In 1901 Dr Bostock came to live at Norton Manor House Farm, now known as The Elms in Commercial Street. To this day the buildings which were the granary and barn are at the back of the house and the little cottage in the garden was the surgery. Dr Bostock was a 'fresh air fiend' and because children had been drowned swimming in the river he recommended that an outdoor pool should be built in the crypt of the demolished St Nicholas' church, so that there would be a safe place for them to swim.

St Peter's church is a comparatively new building, being built to replace the old St Nicholas' church. Norton also has Trinity and Bethel chapels and a Salvation Army citadel.

The drinking water at Malton was contaminated by a tramp in 1932 and there was an outbreak of typhoid during which 27 people died. Norton had its own water supply from an underground lake at Howe Hill and so was able to supply Malton with clean water during the epidemic. The spring water is very good and at that time Norton had the cheapest water rate in the district.

Horse racing and bookmaking are still some of the chief occupations of Norton inhabitants but the bacon factory employs a lot of people and there is the Yorkshire and Northern Wool Growers, the clothing factory, Bright Steels, Bells Haulage Contractors and other light industry on an industrial estate. Horsley's have their own nurseries and also recently their own flower shop. Two supermarkets and one small shop have taken the place of eleven grocer's shops in the Commercial Street area.

Old Byland 🐏

The name Byland is derived from the Old English 'Bega's land' which suggests that there was a community living and farming there at least 1,200 years ago. In 1143 Roger de Mowbray made a grant of land to monks from Furness who planned to build an abbey near the river Rye, but after disagreements with the monks of nearby Rievaulx Abbey they built their abbey at Byland and maintained the land at Old Byland as an abbey grange.

As shown by the Domesday survey, the original church was built before the arrival of the monks. There are early Norman fragments around the porch entrance and the chancel arch with its carvings like rams' heads is also early Norman. The original invocation is not known but after the church was restored in 1909 it was dedicated to the honour of All Saints.

The village is small and most of the dwellings cluster round the green which used to be the site of the stocks and a Norman font. Throughout its history Old Byland has been mainly a centre for the farming community but in 1610 John Blanchard had a paper mill which by 1635 had become a fulling mill for local weavers. Today the residents are mainly farmers, farm workers and retired people and a few who choose to live in this peaceful spot and travel to their work, including an architect whose wife has put looms in converted out-buildings where she designs and weaves a variety of textiles.

Oldstead 🐏

Oldstead has the distinction of having had two other names in the past. The Cistercian monks of Byland who lived there from 1144 to 1177 named it 'Stocking', which meant a clearing in the woods used for pasture. When they moved to Byland in 1177 the settlement was known as 'Veterum Locum' – the old place, and that is the origin of the name we now use.

The village, with a population of around 50, lies immediately below two protruding ridges of the Hambleton Hills. On one stands a tower built to commemorate Queen Victoria's Coronation by John Wormald of Oldstead Hall. From the top of the 'Mount Snever Observatory', as it is called, the view extends almost across northern England – from Staxton Wold near Filey in the east to the fells of Westmoreland in the west.

The other hill is called Scotch Corner, a name which commemorates the battle which took place there in 1322 between Edward II's army and an army of invading Scots. Edward was defeated and fled to York, leaving the Scots to ransack the Abbey at Byland.

Oldstead has a former Methodist chapel, now a house, and a very good pub – the Black Swan, where the motto is – 'Don't drink the beck dry, call at the old Oldstead inn instead'!

Surprisingly, the village once had a Catholic church and cloister built by the monks, but it fell down long ago and the only sign of the once extensive buildings is a few mounds in a garth near the Hall.

In spite of its idyllic rural setting in the wooded valleys of the Hambleton foothills, Oldstead has not become a retirement village. It contains a good proportion of working families and is a pleasant place to live.

Osbaldwick & Murton ᘏ

Tucked away behind the houses on the north of the York to Hull road, two miles from the city centre, you will find a quiet village green. The beck is a favourite breeding place for mallards, and willows lean over the water. Eighteenth and 19th century brick houses face each other, leading from the pub to Osbaldwick Hall, the old school and the church. This part of the village is protected by a conservation order.

St Thomas' church, of Tadcaster stone, dating from the 12th century, was restored in 1877/8 and enlarged in 1967/8 when the village had expanded enormously. Inside, a huge gravestone commemorates Mary Ward, 1585–1645. Mary's dream was to found a Roman Catholic religious community for women who would teach but not be enclosed. She was buried in Osbaldwick churchyard, but secretly, because at that time Roman Catholics were not allowed to be buried in consecrated ground.

Electricity pylons stride over the fields round Osbaldwick from one of the major transfer points of the National Grid, situated on the Hull road.

Recently the last market garden closed, and houses cover the fields which once grew raspberries and strawberries. The blue flowers of flax no longer border the road to Murton, but you can still see cows, sheep, horses and geese in the fields, and potatoes, beet and vegetables are grown.

A mile to the east is Murton, which has not so much residential development. On the corner of the village street is the Georgian Hall, where in the 19th century lived Mr Ridsdale, a successful racehorse trainer until his fortunes collapsed in 1836. The pub opposite was originally called after one of his winners. The little stone church of St James has a Norman font, transferred from Osbaldwick in 1950.

Up to the 1950s cattle for York market used to be pastured overnight at Osbaldwick and driven into the city on the hoof, causing chaos on the road and consternation in the village when an animal escaped. Then the Murton Livestock Centre was established, a lively place with a well landscaped approach, banks and offices. Next door is an abattoir and then the Yorkshire Museum of Farming, a most interesting and popular museum.

Osgodby

Osgodby is three miles south of Scarborough, off the A165 coastal road to Filey.

In 1928 when the Old Farm estate was put up for auction by the owner Mrs Seaton, who was moving south, the housing stock was only about twelve dwellings and five farms. At the auction there were 64 lots, 54 of them marked for housing. Lot 52 was the field behind Stewart House with a windmill and pond, but there is no sign of these today. In 1932 the first stage of modern houses and bungalows were built.

In the early 1960s building began again until Osgodby has now grown to a village of about 600 houses. The oldest house, Stuart House, is dated 1615 but is no longer a farm. The two Hall farms have been converted into a public house, named the Barn, which was originally the farm's cowshed, and a restaurant, the Wishing Well. These two farms were built on the site of the original manor house, mentioned in the Domesday Book, together with a chantry. There are still two walls of St Leonard's chapel remaining, one showing an arch, it now being part of a barn. When Scarborough & District Archaeological Society excavated in 1963 they found the site of the medieval village of Osgodby on either side of Osgodby Lane, near the Barn.

Osgodby does not have a church, chapel or school, but most residents attend the ones at Cayton village, a mile away. There is a community centre which opened in 1976 and caters for all age groups.

Osmotherley

Osmotherley is one of the most beautiful villages in the North Yorkshire Moors National Park, which has some of the finest stretches of heather moorland in England. Features that make the village so attractive include the golden colour of many of its stone cottages, and their roofs of red clay pantiles. In the village centre may be seen the market cross and a barter

The Market Cross and barter table at Osmotherley

table from which in days gone by various products were sold at the weekly markets. Also (with an internal garden carefully tended by a local inhabitant) the village pound still exists in which stray animals were kept until claimed, and after a fine had been paid!

John Wesley preached in the village on several occasions, and in the old Methodist chapel (built 1754) may be seen the stool on which he stood when preaching, as he was rather short in stature.

The village for many years from the 19th century, and into the 20th century, was famed for its weaving and spinning mills and for a related cottage textile industry. Mining also played a part in providing employment, and alum, jet, ironstone, and even coal mines existed in the vicinity, some of them over a number of years. There were also a number of stone quarries from which building stone was obtained for local use: some of the stone was used for making railway sleepers. Those villagers who preferred to make a less honest living indulged in smuggling, and there are many tales of secret stills being operated on the moors nearby and of caches of contraband spirits being hidden in the village.

Every summer many villagers are involved in the Summer Games, which under other titles date back to at least the early 18th century. The village is also the starting point for the famous Lyke Wake Walk of 40 miles across the moors, which those undertaking are supposed to complete within 24 hours.

Oswaldkirk

Oswaldkirk is situated at the east end of the Hambleton Hills and lies at the base of a south-facing, hanging wood known as 'The Hag'. The North Yorkshire National Park boundary runs along the centre line of the village street, so that the land and houses north of the street are in the park but not those to the south. The whole village, however, is one of Ryedale's conservation areas and is included in the Howardian Hills Area of Outstanding Natural Beauty.

The name of the village derives from the small church of St Oswald which was originally a Saxon wooden building and is now built of stone, dating from the Norman and later periods. The church is in a beautiful position overlooking the lovely valley to its south.

At present there are 90 homes in Oswaldkirk. There is little employment in the village apart from the seven farmworkers employed by the seven working farms. The large public school in Ampleforth (the neighbouring village) is a big employer and several Oswaldkirk residents work there.

There is one public house in the village, which used to be the coaching inn and which now attracts visitors from all over Yorkshire during sunny weekends. The post office with its shop closed during the 1960s but the clock on the front of the building features in many treasure hunts.

In 1913, one of Oswaldkirk's main attractions was built by Colonel Musgrave Benson, who owned the Hall and estate at that time. It was an impressive stone village hall with a beautifully sprung dance floor, said to be the finest in Yorkshire. The Colonel included in the hall a special balcony so that he could sit there and oversee the behaviour of the dancers! There were dances every fortnight and people came to them from as far away as Middlesbrough. Eventually, however, the occasions became rough and there were frequent fights so that the dances had to be discontinued. In 1987, after much discussion, it was decided to demolish the old hall, build two houses and with the proceeds of their sale, erect a smaller hall.

The Ouseburns 🦜

The name Ouseburn comes from the beck which flows between the two villages, Great and Little Ouseburn, and then joins the river Ure just before this river becomes the Ouse.

Anyone passing through the two villages will be struck by their similar linear development, their warm red North Yorkshire brick buildings and their obviously Victorian nature. Indeed much of what is visible to the discerning eye will testify to the Victorian flowering of the villages which were part of the Kirby Hall estate.

The two villages are part of a three-church parish, combined in the early 1970s, and each church of the Ouseburns would repay any visitor's glance. Holy Trinity church in Little Ouseburn contains several interesting Charity Boards. Great Ouseburn's church, St Mary's, with origins circa 1170, has some of the finest church plate in the North of England. In the wall by the gates are the remains of an old preaching cross.

Little Ouseburn's church is an attractive, ancient structure of stone with indications of Saxon work in the tower. It was to this church that the most well-known figure associated with the villages made her way. Anne Bronte was for five years in the 1880s a governess to the Robinson family at Thorpe Green. Anne made a fine drawing of the church, wrote a poem in the Long Plantation on the Kirby Hall estate and used facets of the area in her novel *Agnes Grey*. She introduced her brother Branwell, that fated man of talents wasted by drinking, as a tutor to the family.

Pannal 🦜

Pannal, whose Old English name suggests a damp hollow, lies to the south of Harrogate on the southernmost boundary of the ancient forest of Knaresborough. Early medieval records mention a church, mills, a fair and a market. Today the village is still dominated by the early 14th century church, retains the remains of at least two mills and a weekly

The Village of Pannal

auction market still functions although cattle compete with cars for selling time! Modern intrusions include a large Dunlopillo factory adjacent to the Victorian railway station and recent housing development.

The thatched post office has disappeared, the old house 'Rosehurst' has been demolished for housing, the blacksmith's cottage removed for road widening and two of the village shops have closed – all remembered by many with affection. Only the post office, a butcher's and a newsagent's shops remain to serve the community.

The graveyard provides links with the time that Pannal served Low Harrogate in the last century including graves of famous Harrogate hoteliers like Jos. Thackwray of the Crown and, reputedly the 'Queen of Harrogate Wells', Betty Lupton. The large coffin-shaped stone inside the churchyard was used to prevent body-snatchers (who are said to have visited Pannal in 1832!) from plying their trade.

A favourite children's pastime is feeding the ducks on the millpond, the beginning of a popular beck-side walk to Burn Bridge, a residential area that merges into Pannal village. Burn Bridge boasts a pub and a restaurant whilst drinkers in Pannal can choose the Spacey Houses pub or Platform One, the converted railway station, home for an enviable collection of railway memorabilia.

Pateley Bridge with Bewerley ✍

This large village nestles on either side of the river Nidd, surrounded by sweeping hills to the north, steep farmland to east and west and the winding river to the south. It is a bustling and popular summer visiting place, with its varied shops clustering along the steep High Street.

Some of the original buildings were around St Mary's church on the hillside, as land in the river valley was swampy. Sadly, the church is now a ruin but attracts visitors by way of Panorama Walk from where one can enjoy magnificent views. The newer church of St Cuthbert was built further down the hill. The lovely old monastic chapel at Bewerley still stands and is in regular use.

Much was owed to the Metcalfe and the Yorke families for the development of Pateley Bridge. They were involved in building houses, flax milling, breweries, railways, roads and George Metcalfe helped to set up the Pateley Union in 1837. The workhouse provided for 36 inmates and was considered a model in its time. The building is now a wonderful museum, manned by volunteers and containing a wealth of exhibits of life in the dale.

The 'bridge' at Pateley is an old-established crossing place thought to have been used by monks from Fountains Abbey. It was originally a ford and was superseded by a wooden structure in the 16th century. The present stone bridge dates from the 18th century.

The purpose-built Methodist church was the first in the dale. John Wesley had visited before the present one was built but the actual pulpit from which he preached is preserved in the present building.

Patrick Brompton ✍

As the A684 makes its way from Bedale to Leyburn, Patrick Brompton is situated about five miles from Bedale, clustered on both sides of the main road, a huddle of dwellings; Hall, manor house, old vicarage, church and cottages. The village was recorded in the Domesday Book in 1086 when there was no mention of a church but of a mill. St Patrick's church was built in 1100 by Bardoff to the memory of his parents.

Until the Industrial Revolution the village was under the jurisdiction of the estates at Hornby Castle and the monks of Jervaulx Abbey. In 1801 the census records the existence of 35 households. Most men were employed by the Duke of Leeds at Hornby Castle and most cottages had smallholdings rented from the Castle. In 1856 the Northallerton to Hawes railway line was opened and in 1890 Aysgarth School was built at Newton-le-Willows and so two more advantages for employment came in to the area.

Patrick Brompton claims four vicarages. The original home for the priest was in what is now the Green Tree inn, which was built in 1600.

Later Laurel House became the vicarage in Georgian times and the present 'Old Vicarage' was built in 1890 in the centre of the village. In 1975 the present one was built in the orchard. The original school which still stands beside the church was built in 1717 and is a great village asset for community events.

Pickering

Pickering is a small market town, which, according to legend, takes its name from the fact that a ring was found inside a pike caught in the stream which runs through the town.

In the past there were many local customs and events each year. On Shrove Tuesday the Pancake Bell was rung at eleven o'clock heralding the closure of schools and businesses for the day. The beginning of July saw all the Church Sunday schools congregated in the Market Place for the annual rail outing to Scarborough, while November saw the gathering of all the local farmers for 'The Hireings' when all the labour needed for the coming year was hired. This was accompanied by the Michaelmas Fair with stalls, roundabouts, fortune tellers etc. Pickering can boast a unique event when in mid-December two local characters – The Waits – journeyed round the town greeting each family with the words 'Good morning Mr & Mrs . . . and family, past two o'clock and a fine morning' to the accompaniment of carols played on a melodeon.

The once thriving cattle market in Eastgate now provides a Tourist Information Centre and parking spaces for the numerous visitors and tourists. St Peter and St Paul, the 15th century parish church, has some very fine medieval wall frescoes. The Beck Isle Museum was once home to William Marshall, author of *Rural Economy of Yorkshire* and it housed the first agricultural college in the country. It now holds many examples of local crafts, machinery and the rural way of life on the North Yorkshire Moors and surrounding area.

To the north of the town stand the remains of a very fine castle complete with moat, bridge towers and dungeons. Steam trains are still run by the North Yorkshire Moors Railway, whose scenic journeys take passengers up into the moors past the local trout farm and limestone quarries.

The popularity of Pickering is indicated by the influx of new residents which has doubled the population to nearly 6,000, proving that the 'Gateway to the Moors' is an ideal place to live or visit.

Pickhill ⚘

Pickhill lies one mile to the east of the A1 and twelve miles from Boroughbridge. It is a pretty village built round a village green with a beck running through.

The village is dominated by the church of All Saints, built on a hill, dating back to the Saxon period. There is a most beautiful Norman doorway and arch leading to the chancel. During restorations in 1876 an effigy was found under the chancel, thought to be of Sir Andrew Nevill who used to live at Pickhill Castle; there is no trace of the castle now.

Pickhill used to be a thriving village. In 1890 there was a toy dealer, three grocers (one included a butcher's shop), a joiner's shop, a saddler, two tailors, a blacksmith and three pubs. In fact in 1307 Pickhill was granted a market on Saturdays and an annual fair each September which lasted eight days. Pickhill used to have a feast every Easter when the village was crowded with gipsies.

The Misses Hutchinson used to live at Church House in the village and they had a bull which was treated as a pet and they often yoked it to the plough. It is said that a neighbour called and found one of the ladies sewing up a gash in her knee with an ordinary needle and thread!

One old custom in the village was that the men going to funerals wore their hats in church. No one seems to know why, perhaps it was because it was cold!

The village still has two pubs, a hairdresser and village shop. The railway line Northallerton to Ripon used to run through the village but was closed in 1966. In 1988/9, 30 houses were built on the old ballast yard, almost doubling the size of the village.

Plompton ⚘

Plompton is situated south of Knaresborough and is an ancient parish. It includes the manors of Plumpton, Rudfarlington and Brame, the first of which is described in the Domesday survey as held by Eldred de Plumpton, from whom it was passed from father to son for 700 years. The family is said to have fought on every battlefield and taken part in every political movement of their times.

After the death of Robert de Plumpton, the last male heir of the senior line, a private Act of Parliament was obtained by his four aunts to disentail the estate despite other interests. The estate was broken up and Plumpton Towers, besieged and battered after the battle of Marston Moor, was destroyed. His great-great-great-great grandson is the present lord of the manor of Plompton and owner of Plompton Rocks. Plompton Rocks and Lake is an area of outstanding natural beauty. The Rocks are open to the public on payment of a small fee. The original fish pond was extended by a dam designed by John Carr of York; this dam, the boathouse and gatehouse are listed buildings. Plompton has ancient woods, notably Birkham, and Turner painted in the grounds.

A small square of former agricultural workers' houses are now privately owned and these form the hamlet known as Plompton village. Lodge gates lead into the former parkland, and High Grange Farm has some interesting architecture. A public footpath runs through the park eventually passing through Birkham Wood, which has been the subject of recent controversy in connection with the construction of the southern bypass road round Harrogate. There is no place of worship in Plompton and no inn, although one house in the square was an inn in the 18th century.

The Poppletons

Nether and Upper Poppleton, both Domesday Book entries, are two separate villages each with its own parish council. There the separateness ends. Both are situated on or near the banks of the Ouse four miles north of York. After the Second World War fields separated the two communities, but each village has been extended by the building of houses. Even the beck, which marked the boundary, has been culverted for most of its length so there is now no visible dividing line.

A maypole 64 ft high, painted red, white and blue and topped with a four ft high copper weathercock, rises from the village green at Upper Poppleton. A 'time capsule' was buried at its base in 1968. There is dancing round the maypole annually by village schoolchildren on Spring Bank Holiday Monday.

The present All Saints' church on the green at Upper was built in 1890 and fragments of 13th and 14th century stone have been incorporated in its construction. An unused area of the churchyard has been turned into a small nature reserve.

After a visit by John Wesley in 1757 a Poppleton Methodist Society was formed. The chapel erected in 1889 has been sympathetically extended and looks delightful in amber floodlighting on winter evenings. Both church and chapel have halls which are used by many village organisations.

In the oldest area of Nether Poppleton lies St Everilda's church, with only one other in England of the same dedication – ie at Everingham. Its foundation is circa 1130. Stones left over from the building of York Minster are believed to be incorporated in its structure. Nearby is Manor Farm with a 500 year old tithe barn where Prince Rupert rested before the battle of Marston Moor in 1644, crossing the Ouse on a bridge of boats the following morning. In this barn too, in 1660, Lord Fairfax lodged his 300 men-at-arms before proclaiming Charles II King in York.

The moatfield behind shows signs of an early Saxon settlement. The small square building near the farm was the old tithe gaol where defaulters were held before being tried in York.

Potto ⟨⟩

There are many 'howes' or burial mounds in Old Cleveland and the name 'Potto' may derive from a corruption of one such howe which contained a pot or funeral urn. The parish also includes the hamlet of Goulton.

The most prestigious dwelling was built in 1768 and under the name of Potto Grange has been in the hands of the same family over several generations. Another large landowner, George Edward Copley, built his own Victorian gentleman's residence known as Potto Hall in the 1860s where he and his wife lived with their ten servants in attendance.

John Wesley preached in one of the two old chapels in 1790, but these are now dwelling houses. An Anglican mission hall was erected in 1893, but when this accidently burnt down just before the Second World War, it was replaced by a neat little church which still clings traditionally to the 1662 service in the Book of Common Prayer.

Throughout its history Potto has relied on a rural economy. This has included the weaving and bleaching of linen including a bittling mill. In the 19th century there was a brick manufacturer and a chemical manure and size company. The greatest revolution must have come with the opening of the railway from Picton to Stokesley in 1857. This included a station at Potto with a mineral line running to nearby Swainby to remove ironstone to the blast furnaces in developing Teesside.

The last passenger train left in 1954 and with closure was lost the rail access for industrial workers to come out to the villages to enjoy unpolluted air and beautiful scenery. The premises were taken over by 'Prestons of Potto', a local haulage company making full use of the disused accommodation for a growing fleet of road waggons. The sheds also house an array of steam traction engines and fairground organs which always make a great attraction when en route to shows all over the country.

Today there are no shops or services apart from the Dog and Gun public house. A herb grower occupies the gamekeeper's lodge. The villagers' pride and joy is the village hall, built in recent years by the efforts of this small community.

Preston-under-Scar ⟨⟩

The village of Preston-under-Scar has its back to the wall. Its one street sits on a shelf on the side of a lofty outcrop of limestone which is an outrider of the quarry which lies behind the village.

The earliest written evidence of Preston occurs in the Domesday Book of 1086, but a walk through the fields to the east of the village reveals evidence of a much earlier, Iron Age settlement. The appendage 'under-Scar' is first recorded in the 16th century, and the picture it evokes of the village hugging the hillside under the limestone outcrop has changed little in the succeeding four centuries.

The lead mines around Preston were once some of the richest in the dale, and the remains still give a distinctive character to the landscape, from Cobscar smelt mill chimney on the top of the moor behind Preston, to the Keld Head smelt mills two miles lower down in the woods to the east of the village. They were connected by the longest flue, or horizontal chimney, in the country, which both drew the noxious fumes away from the village area and provided what must have been a tremendous draught to the furnace.

Preston did not have a church of its own until 1862 and was spiritually linked to Wensley over the preceding centuries. However, in common with other dales villages, nonconformism took a strong hold and in the 18th century people of this village became earnest followers of John Wesley, building their own chapel in 1805.

Despite the importance of lead mining, Preston, in common with all rural villages, has its roots in agriculture. One feature of this was the long-standing use of the common land above the scar, known as Preston Pasture. Traditionally the tenants of the village were allowed to graze a

Preston-under-Scar

certain number of cows on it (renting what was known as a cow gait), and employ a herdsman, known as a 'by-law man' to carry out necessary work on the land. The men joined together in a 'Cow Club', paying a yearly subscription which provided the wage of the by-law man and any required expenditure such as the purchase of a bull. This use of the common pasture continued until 1939.

Rainton ✿

Rainton lies off the A1, approximately four miles from Ripon and approximately six miles from Thirsk. It is a farming village, and is especially picturesque when its mature trees (chestnut, limes, copper beech, maple etc) are in leaf. There are two village greens bordered by farms, houses and cottages, mostly built of stone. New private residential homes have to be built in stone or brick with approval from Harrogate Planning Committee.

Rainton Methodist chapel, a stone building, is over 100 years old. There is also the original Rainton Church of England mission built of stone in 1872. By arrangement with the Church Commissioners this building was extended to be used as Rainton village hall.

Rainton is well served by two inns, the Bay Horse and the Lamb. It also has a village shop with post office.

Ramsgill ✿

Ramsgill is a pleasant old village of 21 houses clustered around well kept greens. The small church, built in 1842, is simply furnished and has 'mouseman' altar rails. The well-appointed hotel, the Yorke Arms, is covered in virginia creeper which glows red in autumn. It faces across the lower green towards the village hall.

Most of the cottages were built between 1840 and 1850 to replace thatched cottages, although the row behind the church was built in the mid 1770s. Interesting details are the pound, and the porch shelter in front of the Hall which was added to celebrate the Coronation in 1953. Over the doorway is a small stone head, reputedly found when the original Gouthwaite Hall was demolished. Built into the side of the Hall is a strange carving, considered by some to be pre-Roman, maybe the horned head of the Sun-God! This was rescued from the debris of one of the thatched cottages.

Many visit Ramsgill because the notorious Eugene Aram was born here in 1704, his father being gardener at Newby Hall. In 1758 Eugene was arrested in Kings Lynn and brought back to York to be accused and tried for the murder of one Daniel Clark in Knaresborough some 13 years before. He very cleverly conducted his own case and it became something of a cause celebre. One of his erstwhile friends gave evidence against him and he was convicted. He was executed and his body brought back to hang from the gibbet in Knaresborough. Much has been written and sung about this affair, including an over-romanticised version by Sir Bulwer Lytton.

The Yorkshire artist Stephen Dennison lived in the Old School House for many years and died in Ramsgill in 1965. He was churchwarden and helped with the restoration of the church in 1950. The area is a popular venue for artists and photographers.

Several grouse moors surround the Upper Nidderdale area and the running and upkeep of these gives work for gamekeepers and, alongside sheep farming and some dairy produce, now provide a source of income. With the increase in tourism, especially since the Nidderdale Way was established, Ramsgill has become a popular centre for leisure pursuits.

Rathmell

Rathmell is a little village about two miles from Settle. There are many pleasant walks by the river Ribble or through the Waterfall Wood and over the old packhorse bridges, or up to Whelpstone Crag. It has a Methodist chapel, a school and a church.

Holy Trinity church was built by local craftsmen with subscriptions large and small from local people. The font lid was carved from a holly tree grown at Hollin Hall Farm, and the carved oak panels of the chancel were a gift from the Geldard family of Cappleside. The wood was grown on farms in Rathmell.

One historical building in Rathmell is a little row of cottages known as College Fold. In the 17th century Richard Frankland had an academy here, the first nonconformist college. At one time there were 50 students. He died in 1698 and was buried at Giggleswick church.

Rathmell has many old farms. The Green Farm is dated 1689. Huggon House has a coat of arms over the doorway of the Lion and the Unicorn. New Hall had a new house in 1880; the old house is today represented by a shippon with a magnificent doorway. The Lumb Farm near Little Bank has old mullioned windows and an inglenook fireplace. At New Hall and a field west of Little Bank – called Coney Garth – you can still see burrows of old dwellings from the Bronze or Iron Age. There are many signs of early sites of earthworks at Swainstead Farm and ring dwellings near Little Bank.

Ravenscar 🦅

No-one just 'passes through' Ravenscar. There is only one road into the village and visitors must leave the same way they came in. Ravenscar is situated on the east coast about halfway between Whitby and Scarborough and has superb views across Robin Hood's Bay to Baytown itself.

The village is more of a scattered settlement than a conventional village. This is due to the failure of efforts initiated in 1896 to create a small town. Having laid out some of the roads for the proposed town, and put in main drainage, a series of auctions of over a thousand plots of land was organised. Cheap excursion trains were laid on from the Leeds/Bradford area to attract potential buyers. However, despite all their efforts, only one or two plots were sold, and these were widely scattered over the area. Hence the 'spread out' nature of the village. The consortium went bankrupt and the project was finally abandoned in the 1920s, the remaining land, except for some of the laid out roads, being returned to agriculture. The remains of these roads, including kerbstones, can still be seen and walked on.

Originally called 'Peak', the name was changed to Ravenscar in 1897, when the ill fated development was initiated.

Ravenscar has a small Church of England church with adjoining church rooms and a larger village hall which is regularly used for a variety of activities. There are only two shops in the village, the post office and the National Trust Information Centre and shop, which is open in the summer months only. The only building of any size is the well-known Raven Hall Hotel which boasts a nine hole golf course, crown green bowling and an outdoor swimming pool. Local legend has it that George III visited it to recover from his recurring bouts of insanity, when the building was a private residence.

Ravenscar lies on the Cleveland Way and is also the termination of the Lyke Wake Walk, so it is not surprising that it is a honeypot for ramblers.

Ravensworth 🦅

Ravensworth lies in the 'forgotten dale' of Holmedale. The area is not marked on maps as Holmedale but older residents of the district remember using this name.

The broad pleasant green is surrounded by houses dating mostly from the 18th century. The annual fair is held on the green. Among the buildings round the green is the old Church of England school, now converted for use as a community centre. The school was in use between 1841–1967.

The Methodist chapel was built in 1822 and is the oldest chapel in the Richmond circuit. Next to the chapel is a whitewashed house on a site which has been used since 1643. From 1745 until the early 1800s it was an inn known as the Sportsman. The adjoining corner cottage was known as 'The Ranter's Chapel'.

The Bay Horse inn stands on a prominent corner by the green and is believed to date from 1857. Opposite the inn is a house which in 1909 was an inn called the Two Greyhounds, in later years known as the Hare and Hounds. The old brewery standing behind is visible from the gate.

Until the later 1970s a timber-framed house known as the Cruck House stood on the corner of Mill Close. This has now been dismantled and may be seen in the Richmondshire Museum at Richmond.

The remains of the Fitzhughs' Norman castle are south-east of the village. There is believed to have been a castle on the site in 1180 but the present ruins suggest a 14th century building. It would have occupied the whole of a raised platform surrounded by a moat. At the present time only one gable, traces of the wall of the great hall and portions of three towers remain. In 1391 Sir Henry Fitzhugh had licence to empark 200 acres of land around the castle. The bounds are still traceable and some of the wall remains. The surrounding marshland provides habitat for water and wading birds. The castle is privately owned and there is no public access.

Redmire ❧

Redmire, in mid Wensleydale, is sheltered by the Scar from the north and faces the long expanse of Penhill to the south. In a thousand years the village may have occupied at least four sites. The distance of the village from the church suggests one move, perhaps at the time of a great plague in 1563 when its neighbour, Wensley, was almost completely depopulated.

The green's attractive appearance is to a great extent due to the trees planted long ago, mostly to commemorate coronations and jubilees. The most ancient of all is the old oak, supported by props. It is thought to be over 300 years old, and it is a local tradition that it provided shade for John Wesley to preach, on one of his two visits in 1744 and 1774. Another feature is the monument erected at the top of the old steps in celebration of Queen Victoria's Golden Jubilee. Sometimes called the Cross, mistakenly for the village never had a market, it used to be more generally known as the Stocks, and it is almost certain that the stocks were once set at the top of these steps. The old pump and pinfold are other reminders of the past.

A quarter of a mile to the east of the village is the old Norman church. Dedicated to St Mary, it was built in about 1150, and its best features are a partially restored Norman doorway and a good oak-beamed Tudor roof.

Half a mile away is the river Ure and the Falls. Close to the river, below

Mill Farm, are the remains of an old manorial mill. Nearby is an area known as Well Bank and formerly as the Spa. The spring of healing water was walled round and it was the venue of many excursions until after many years the flow stopped.

Lead was mined for centuries on the moors above Redmire, and outcrop coal was dug. Now there is one large limestone quarry, opened about 70 years ago, half a dozen farms, and a growing holiday complex.

Reeth

About half a mile above the confluence of the rivers Swale and Arkle lies the township of Reeth, surrounded by the curving shoulders of the Pennine range, with the 1,599 ft Mount Calva forming a striking background.

The mining of lead, begun by the Romans, formed the staple industry of the district for many years; but with a combination of foreign competition, rising costs and difficulties of production, the mines gradually closed and the emphasis fell on agriculture. The Swaledale sheep are well known, although cheese and butter making have almost died out in favour of milk selling. Chert, a mineral used in the manufacture of pottery, was mined on Fremington Edge which lies to the east of the township, and at the Old Gang Mines above Healaugh, barytes, used in paint making, was reclaimed from the heaps of rubble which mark the old mine workings.

On the plateau to the west is the Reeth Friends' school; erected in 1862, it replaced the old Quaker school which was built in 1780 at the expense of three brothers, George, Leonard and John Raw. It was under the will of the son of the original John Raw that the present school was built, and a proviso in the will stipulated that the school was to be visible from all the parishes which it served, hence its commanding position.

In 1695, Philip, 4th Baron Wharton, obtained a charter for a weekly market and four annual fairs to be held at Reeth. One of these fairs being held on 'the Thursday and Friday next before the Sunday next preceding the feast of St Bartholomew the Apostle' became known as the 'Bartle Fair'. Between 1831 and 1881, when the population of England was almost doubled, that of Reeth fell from 1,456 to 998. Before the close of the 19th century, the Bartle fair was just a memory.

Reeth today, as the largest village in Swaledale, attracts many tourists who admire its expansive central green, and visit the Folk Museum which depicts the life of traditions of Swaledale. Reeth and District Agricultural Society holds its annual show on the last Wednesday in August when Reeth Brass Band are in attendance, and Reeth Young Farmers Club continues to flourish and is a force to be reckoned with in local and county competitions.

Richmond 🐏

Richmond, North Yorkshire is the original Richmond and has given its name to over 50 other 'Richmonds' throughout the world. It is the principal town of Swaledale, though with a population of about 7,500 it retains a village atmosphere. Markets are held on Thursdays in the Victorian Market Hall and an outdoor market is held in the Market Place on Saturdays.

Richmond is dominated by the castle, built by the Normans in 1071. The castle keep and ruins stand proudly on the rising ground overlooking the fast flowing river Swale and the town's fine large cobbled Market Place. One of the old customs peculiar to the town is the ringing of the curfew bell from Holy Trinity church, standing in the town centre.

Richmond has a special affinity to nearby Catterick Garrison, so it is a fitting tribute that the Green Howards Museum is now established in Holy Trinity church. The parish church of St Mary, built in the 12th century when Holy Trinity church became too small, is situated on the road leading to Catterick near one of the two bridges crossing the river Swale. This bridge is known as Station Bridge as it was close by the now extinct Richmond railway station. The old station sheds have been put to excellent use for a garden centre and nearby the Richmond swimming baths were erected.

The other bridge upstream is known as the Green Bridge, as it is near Richmond Green; a delightful area surrounded by Georgian and Victorian cottages. Overlooking the green on the hillside is the Culloden Tower built to commemorate the defeat of the 1745 Jacobite rebellion. It stands on the site of Hudswell Pele, a fortified mansion. Other special landmarks in Richmond are the market cross in the Market Place and the tower of Greyfriars which is now enhanced by the beautiful Friary Gardens, so colourful and well-tended at all times of the year.

Frances I'Anson is renowned as being *The Lass of Richmond Hill*. A ballad was written for her by her husband, Leonard McNally and is universally known.

Rievaulx 🐏

The name Rievaulx is a French translation of Ryedale. The narrow part of the Rye valley where the village now stands was wild, forested and uninhabited in 1131 when twelve French Cistercian monks arrived to found a new monastery. They were sent by St Bernard, from Clairvaux, his abbey in Burgundy and led by their own first abbot St William, a Yorkshireman who had been St Bernard's secretary. They were given land in the valley by Walter l'Espec, the Norman lord of Helmsley. Within 30 years of their arrival, Rievaulx had become the most celebrated monastery in England. The fortunes of the community declined after some bad bouts of sheep disease, fierce attacks by the Scots and then the Black Death in 1349. When Henry VIII dissolved the monastery in 1538 there were only 21 monks and a number of servants left.

The ruins of the abbey are one of the most spectacular medieval sights in England, the beautiful 13th century choir of the huge church and the earlier refectory and cloister surrounded by many other monastic buildings. The small village, built mostly of stone taken from the ruins, clusters round the abbey. The mill with its three ponds and the bridge over the Rye have monastic foundations, as does the village church built in 1906 and incorporating the abbey's ruined gate-chapel.

Most of the cottages used to be lived in by Helmsley estate workers (foresters, gamekeepers, generations of millers who worked the Rievaulx mill till 1962) and some still are, though most are now the homes of people working on, or retired from, neighbouring farms.

The Methodist chapel, opened in 1877, and the WI which meets in the village hall, are the social focus of the village, which has not had a pub for over 200 years. The little school near the abbey built for the Earl of Feversham in 1845 and run first by a village schoolmaster and then by the nuns, closed in 1960, and the children go to school in Helmsley, where nearly the whole village population goes to market every Friday as it always has.

All those lucky enough to live in Rievaulx, and the many thousands of visitors who come every year to see the abbey and the 18th century Duncombe terrace, with its temples above the valley, think that it is one of the enchanted places of England.

Ripley ✖

A charming estate village three miles north of Harrogate clustered around Ripley Castle, home of the Ingilby family for over 600 years.

The cobbled square leading down to the castle is bordered on one side by the ancient parish church of All Saints, built around 1400 by a Thomas Ingilby, an ancestor of the present Sir Thomas who still worships there. The marks on the east wall were caused by bullets fired by Cromwell's soldiers as they executed Royalist prisoners after the battle of Marston Moor.

The whole village has had a somewhat chequered history belied by its peaceful appearance today. By the 1820s the village was dilapidated by years of plague and pestilence and was rebuilt by Sir William Amcotts Ingilby in the style of a village that worthy gentleman had seen during his travels in Alsace-Lorraine. The stone terraced cottages standing well back behind deep grass verges and the inscription on the village hall proclaiming it to be the 'Hotel de Ville' are an indication of their French origins but must puzzle a lot of first-time visitors, set as they are, in rural

Yorkshire. The stocks and the weeping cross in the churchyard are also signs of the days when the lives of villagers were totally dependent on the rule of the lord of the manor, not only for the roof over their heads, but also in matters of punishment for their misdemeanours!

Happily the present Sir Thomas Ingilby is more concerned with bringing his inheritance into the 20th century and is doing so with great aplomb. The castle courtyards now house a range of upmarket shops and tea-rooms, the castle and gardens in their lakeland setting are open to the public and a new luxury hotel has been aptly named the Boar's Head. Aptly, because one of his ancestors saved King Edward III from the unfriendly attentions of a wild boar while the king was hunting in the adjacent forest of Knaresborough and in recognition of this deed the boar's head is incorporated in the Arms of Ingilby of Ripley.

Robin Hood's Bay ❧

The village is Robin Hood's Bay; the parish is Fylingdales, mentioned in the Domesday Book 1068. Designated an area of special scientific interest, it forms part of the Cleveland Way, is the beginning – or end – of the Coast to Coast walk (to St Bee's, Cumbria), and is near the end of the Lyke Wake Walk. The origin of the name, first mentioned in the 16th century, is as much a mystery as the legend of Robin Hood himself.

Fishermen, possibly linked with Vikings, settled in the hamlet of Raw, moving down to the bay to fish from cobles, flat-bottomed boats suitable for rocky beaches. Later, smuggling became a profitable activity, alleys and houses allegedly abounding in secret passages and adjoining cupboards, making escape easy for the culprits and their bounty. The desire of affluent sea-captains for better housing began the spread of development 'up-Bank'.

Cottages in the old part of the village are mainly of stone from local quarries. At one time there were about twelve inns; there are now three down-Bay, two hotels up-Bank and numerous bed and breakfast establishments. Many cottages are holiday lets and consequently often empty in the winter. The old village school closed in the 1960s and is now a hostel for the Marine Activity Centre. The present school is a mile away at Fylingthorpe, in a pleasant, rural setting.

The railway, one of the most beautiful scenic rides from Scarborough to Whitby, fell to Beeching's axe in the 1960s. A new village hall was built on the site, from stone taken from the old hall, which suffered subsidence. It incorporates the old station goods warehouse. The waiting rooms and ticket office were used by a senior citizens club. The signal box is the coal merchant's office and the station master's house, a private residence. The rest of the area is a car park, catering for the considerable influx of summer visitors.

The original Anglican church (late 11th century) – now known as the

Old Church – occupies a prominent site overlooking the village, rebuilt more than once from the original, with three-decker pulpit and box pews. Maiden's Garlands, reputedly carried at maidens' funerals and last used in 1859, are on display. Now in the care of the Redundant Churches Fund, occasional services are still held. The present St Stephen's, built in 1870, holds the original stone font from the Old Church, recovered from a nearby field.

Many ships were wrecked in the wide bay. The most famous rescue occurred when Whitby lifeboat was manhandled overland through waist-high snowdrifts to Bay and down the steep Bank, to save the six crew of the brig *Visitor* in 1881.

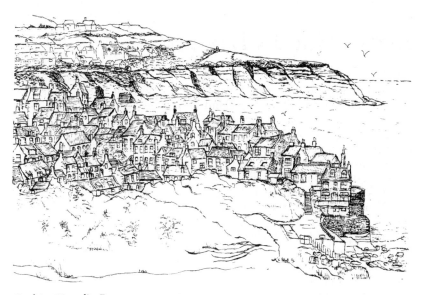

Robin Hood's Bay

Roecliffe

The parish of Roecliffe lies one and a half miles west of the A1 on the road from Boroughbridge to Bishop Monkton.

The church of St Mary, built in the Neo-Norman style, was consecrated on 15th November 1844. Of interest are the chancel floor and steps paved with marble, which once formed part of the pavement in front of the high altar of York Minster.

St Mary's has a notable stone barrel vault also known as 'Waggon Head'. The very nature of this unusual roof gave problems. Soon after being built the weight of the roof caused the walls to bulge and they had to be buttressed. With the problem recurring a decision was made to close the church altogether due to its unstable condition. It was vested in the Redundant Churches Fund in 1986 and extensive repairs were undertaken. The church can only be used for a limited number of services per year. At other times services are held in the village school.

Giving employment locally was a brickyard which flourished in the 18th and 19th centuries. Bricks and tiles were conveyed by river to many parts of the country. This yard was profitable well into the 20th century, but a decline in the industry brought its closure in 1964.

There has been an inn in the village in the same position since the 14th century, and as was usual a smithy next door until the retirement of the last blacksmith in 1955. The Crown inn is well-known and popular.

One of the characteristics of the village, a large pond, began to drain away in 1947. Unsuccessful attempts were made to re-line it, but when the Boroughbridge bypass was built the pond was filled in with surplus soil. Annual events such as Children's Sports Day and Garden Fete are held on this enlarged green.

Romanby ❧

Romanby is a village adjoining North Yorkshire's county town of Northallerton. The name is of Scandinavian origin coming from 'Romund's farm' but the name Romanby has been used since the end of the 14th century. The village is bisected by a Roman road linking Thirsk and Catterick, with evidence of a former Roman military station thought to be provided by the mounds and entrenchments of the Castle Hills area reached by crossing the packhorse bridge, a scheduled ancient monument at the far end of the village green, itself a conservation area. The pretty village green has a number of houses of historical or archaeological interest and a post office cum village store. Nearby is the Golden Lion public house, built on the site of an original 17th century inn.

Spital Farm, on Thirsk Road, was the site of a hospital founded by the Bishop of Durham in 1135. This provided 13 beds for the sick and poor and was looked after by a warden, five brothers and three lay sisters. When St James' church was built in Romanby in 1881, the foundation stone was taken from the old St James' hospital. A Methodist chapel was built in 1964.

In 1903 a dairy was built by the North Eastern Railway Company to encourage rail transport of milk. It now trades under the name Dale Farm Foods. From a small three-storey unit, it has been extended over the years to a compact modern complex.

Northallerton passenger station linking trains to York for Edinburgh and London, is in Romanby, opposite the imposing County Hall, headquarters of the County Council. This was built in 1903 in beautiful grounds on the site of a former racecourse.

Although Romanby has grown considerably since first recorded in the Domesday Book with a population of 250, and skirts the town of Northallerton, it still retains its 'village' identity.

Rufforth 🐝

Rufforth is a small village some four and a half miles to the west of the beautiful and historic city of York. Straddling the B1224 York to Wetherby road, it has at the east end a wartime airfield now used for gliding, micro-light craft and some small industries. At the west end there is a large modern equestrian centre.

Once a thriving farming community, now regrettably the orchards and farmyards are filled with modern houses, whose occupants commute to York, Leeds etc. In the 1950s there were some 14 or 15 farms in the village, but now there are two and these on the extreme edges.

Almost at the centre of the village is the beautiful church of All Saints, built of stone in the 1890s by the benefactors of the village, the Middlewood family. The church stands on the site of a Norman church, parts of which were incorporated in the new building.

Although Rufforth has grown in numbers of houses and population over the last 25 years it still keeps a little of the characteristics of a village: no village green but several small spaces of common land, a pinfold or pound where stray animals were confined until claimed, a small garden beside the village pump – the trough of which now holds plants and flowers instead of water. In spring crocus and daffodils bloom on the road sides to bring a little cheer to passers-by.

The village pond once used by farmers for watering their cattle is sadly overgrown but efforts are being made to improve the area. A small nature reserve has been formed from the long disused sandpits on the outskirts of the village – the sand was once used in the upkeep of the roads.

The blacksmiths, butchers, greengrocers have long since gone – but thankfully there is still a village shop and post office, along with two pubs to keep a village atmosphere for future generations.

Ruston, Wykeham & Hutton Buscel ✤

Eastward along the A170 and about seven miles from Scarborough, is the village of Ruston.

Ruston now has 97 inhabitants, and all except four of the houses belong to Wykeham Estate. There are now only two farms, formerly there were three and nine smallholdings. Cows from these holdings are driven through the village, into the cottage cowpasture after being milked, and home again in the evening. Three roads turn like spokes of a wheel in the centre of the village where a bridge over the beck and a watersplash are side by side.

On leaving Ruston and rejoining the A170 in the direction of Scarborough, one almost immediately enters the village of Wykeham, dominated at that point by the Downe Arms and the church.

The Downe Arms has grown much in size over recent years, but the residential part dates back to the 17th century when it was used as a coaching stage. The church however is a comparatively recent construction having been completed in 1853. It was designed by William Butterfield, the architect of Bradford Cathedral.

All Saints is remarkable for its bell tower, which is completely separate and was constructed from the ruins of an old tower on the site, ornamented by a spire designed by William Butterfield. The adjoining vicarage, which is now a private house, and the school on the south side of the road are also of Butterfield design.

Wykeham Abbey, which is the home of the 11th Viscount Downe, stands in beautiful parkland to the south of the village, adjoining agricultural land which is owned by Wykeham Estate and largely farmed by them. The estate is the largest employer in the area, as it also runs a tree nursery of some 100 acres, and has a large touring caravan park to the north of the village.

Again turn left from the main A170 and up into Hutton Buscel. The original manor house was burned down but some of the outer walls remain forming the entrance to the old school. The walls too remain of a two acre walled garden, the Thomas Farside tythe barn built in 1693, an ice house, and the restored village pound.

St Matthew's church stands to the south of the village, and there is also a Methodist chapel.

At present there are five farms and three commercial businesses. The school, shop and post office have all closed in the last 30 years and the pub, the Old Roadhouse, closed in the 1930s; however the village is well supplied with mobile services.

Ruswarp 🦢

About two miles inland from Whitby lies the village of Ruswarp, situated at the foot of a steep hill on the banks of the river Esk at its tidal limit.

In the Domesday Book the mill mentioned to be in the manor of Whitby is thought to refer to a mill at Ruswarp. A water mill was erected by the river Esk in 1752. In 1911 the mill was severely damaged by fire. It was rebuilt and remained a working mill until 1989 when the business was consolidated at Northallerton. The mill, a dominant feature of Ruswarp, was sold and is now converted into luxury riverside flats.

The township of Ruswarp encompassed much of what is now part of Whitby town. To avoid the heavy shipping assessment of old Whitby, many shipowners moved to the south of Whitby manor, ie into the township of Ruswarp which was exempt from this tax. One such family was the Bushells who had the Hall built in red brick with stone dressings and with a seven bay frontage. It later became a farmhouse and is now an hotel. The post office nearby was the stables and on the cottages opposite the Old Hall Hotel one can see signs of archways to the coach-houses. Before a church was built one of the rooms at the Old Hall accommodated congregations of up to 100 people: the present church, dedicated to St Bartholomew, was built on the hillside in 1869.

There has been a livestock auction market at Ruswarp since 1900. It was originally run by farmers who walked their animals across fields or used the railway's cattle trucks. The mart was taken over by Richardson and Smith, the current owners in 1930.

There is one inn in the village, the Bridge, by the river opposite the now unmanned station. Nearby is the present village school (built in 1873) and the village hall. The first school for the village was the small stone building (now a cottage) along the Carrs, opposite the boating station – its name plaque now covered over.

During the summer Ruswarp is very popular with both visitors and local people. They can be seen rowing, canoeing and taking trips on the steamboat. There is fishing too in the Esk – a salmon river. A golf course with a tea garden nearby and a newly constructed miniature railway offer pleasant recreation. The area around gives opportunities for walking – unless one spends time feeding the ducks and other waterfowl!

Rylstone 🦢

Rylstone is noted for its pond and ducks and for the profusion of snowdrops in the spring. During 1965 extensive alterations were made to the main road through the village, two bad corners were removed and the road straightened. During excavations numerous finds were made including pottery and the foundations of a Roman road.

Rylstone Cross stands high on Rylstone Fell overlooking the parish from the south-east. Originally it was a large stone in the form of a man and was known as 'The Stone Man'. A wooden cross was erected on the top of the stone pillar to commemorate 'The Peace of Paris', the date on the back is 1885 and the initials DD and TB which are carved on it signify the Duke of Devonshire and T. Broughton, who was land agent to the Duke. The wooden structure has been renewed several times, the last occasion being after the severe winter of 1947.

Church Lane, once known as Chapel Lane, leading from Rylstone to Cracoe was once an important road linking Craven with the North and Scotland. It is now a grassy lane and it still has the base of an old cross marking the boundary between the parishes of Rylstone and Cracoe.

The parish church of St Peter was erected in the mid 19th century. Records show that there was a priest at 'Rilston' in the 12th century and most probably a chapel in 1524, when a Geoffrey Procter paid for chantry masses to be said at Rilston. An interesting treasure of the church is a round carved stone of uncertain age built into the vestry wall. The three bells recently refurbished were re-cast in 1853. They are all inscribed, one bearing the inscription 'Gloria in Excelsis Deo 1658' and another 'God us Ayde'. To the north-east of the church is the site of the old manorial Hall and to the south of that can be seen the old fish ponds.

A building known as 'Fox House Barn' is now converted into a house. It was named after George Fox the founder of Quakerism and was built in 1657 by Quakers for a meeting house. A wall encircles the front of the barn enclosing about 100 square yards and this land is the old Quaker burial ground.

Salton

The parish of Salton covers 2,760 acres and is bounded by the rivers Rye and Dove. In the Middle Ages there was a watermill on the river Dove which belonged to the Priors of Hexham.

Salton's name came from a French word 'Saule' which meant willow. In the 12th century the village was ransacked and the church burned down.

The church, which is at the south end of the village and is dedicated to St John of Beverley, was rebuilt in the 12th century and in the 13th century there was a tower arch inserted and the windows enlarged. It remained like that until 1881 when it was restored and the roofs renewed. It still has a 17th century altar table and the church register goes back to 1573. The village consists of a dozen brick built cottages with several outlying farms.

The old school is now a village hall and the former chapel has been sold for conversion to a domestic dwelling. The village has a green which formerly belonged to the manor, which is now a farmhouse. At the manor there is a bridge over the river Dove which was originally called the Crossau Bridge.

Sand Hutton 🦜

Sand Hutton is a small village of about 200 residents, eight miles north of York. It is a pretty village, with an old well standing on a small green. There is an avenue of mature chestnut trees leading up to the church of St Mary, which was built in 1848 at the expense of the local landowner, Sir James Walker MA. The pews and beams were made from oak grown on the estate.

A row of pretty cottages was built in 1841 and another row in 1926 to house all those employed on the estate; these are now owned by the Church Commissioners.

In 1910 Sir Robert Walker constructed a 15 inch gauge private railway in the grounds of Sand Hutton Hall, which was later extended into the village. On the death of Sir Robert in 1930, his son, who had other interests, sold the railway to Wards of Sheffield, and gradually the line disappeared. Traces of the route can still be seen along the bridleways and public footpaths.

There has been a lot of new building in Sand Hutton, the Hall drive now is full of large houses, the main village street has a modern development, and many of the barns and cartsheds are houses. The woodyard which stood at the centre of the village next to the green is a building site. The old laundry was given to the villagers of Claxton and Sand Hutton by the Church Commissioners for use as a village hall. It is a brick building which had stone flagged floors, but is now modernised and used by many organisations.

There was a public house in the village, the Blacksmith's Arms; but the lord of the manor, whilst a genial host himself, did not approve of his workers taking strong drink, and it was closed. There was a very busy shop and post office, but the shop has ceased to trade, and the post office has very restricted hours of opening. The school has been enlarged and now is used by juniors from the surrounding villages. Very few people are employed in agriculture, and many people are retired, some of them from the estate.

Sandsend 🦜

This picturesque village nestles at the foot of the steep gradient of Lythe Bank, three miles from Whitby. It is in two halves – each spanning a separate valley with rivulets running from Mulgrave Woods, and joined by a seafront promenade with houses and hotels.

211

It is hard to believe that this attractive resort had a thriving alum industry dating from the 17th century when men were employed at the Sandsend works – alum was a chemical very important to the industrial revolution. When the mines closed in 1871 due to new methods of making sulphuric acid and the discovery of aniline dyes, another industry flourished producing a cement capable of repairing a sea wall between tides known as Sandsend Roman Cement. This was made from stones known as 'dogger stones' thrown to one side as they were useless in the manufacture of alum and accumulated over the century at the foot of the cliffs. A mill used for grinding corn, standing in the first valley of Sandsend, called East Row, was converted to cement grinding. The mill building still stands in East Row car park, now known as Mill Cottage. Behind it stands the conical kiln where the dogger stones were burnt before being ground.

The village of Sandsend presented a strikingly different picture prior to 1958 when the railway line from Whitby to Loftus was a very prominent feature with viaducts crossing the two rivulets, and the line built on a shelf on the hillside behind the houses on the sea front. Nowadays for the many summer visitors, Sandsend is a favourite spot for sunbathing on the beach, sailing and wind-surfing in the lovely bay, and the former railway track is very popular with walkers.

The second valley of Sandsend with its delightful small cottages and St Mary's chapel, presents a very peaceful scene and is particularly attractive when the daffodils are in bloom.

Sawley 🦢

Sawley, five miles to the west of Ripon, is a long straggling village. The hardy Saxons spread their homes between Moor Lane and the river Skell. The area being abundant with natural springs was greatly favoured even into Tudor times and beyond. An imposing Tudor manor was built on high ground there and in 1612 when the Lacon family moved up from Shropshire was named Lacon Hall, as it still is today. On the hill above is Lacon Cross, a medieval market stone.

However, the dampness from the perpetual springs finally took their toll of aching bones and the dwellers from the old timber-framed houses decided to settle on the drier ground near to where the church was being built. This then completed the straggle by joining up with what was left of the Norse and Tudor settlement in Lowgate Lane.

Earlier this century Sawley estate was owned by Sir J. Barran, grandfather of the present Sir John. Most of the farmers were tenants. The village was small before the Second World War, but more or less self-contained, there being a school, shop, post office, church, chapel, inn, village hall, parish room, blacksmith, butcher, undertaker, joiner, clog maker, telephone exchange and market bus.

Since then villagers have seen the closure of the school and shop and the building of council homes, as well as conversions of new houses. The vicarage was sold into private ownership, the Black-a-Moor inn is to be converted into private dwellings and the Sawley Arms changed from a small village pub to a pub-cum-restaurant. One thing that hasn't changed though is the welcome given to everyone who comes to live in Sawley.

Scawton 🌿

The parish lies on the west bank of the river Rye and the road leading from the village through Scawton Howl (a narrow valley) was originally known as Sperragate. It was the route taken by travellers from the North, who for 300 years must have included the monks of Rievaulx Abbey who built the medieval bridge over the Rye that was destroyed in the flood of 1754.

The village church was originally a chapel, built in the 12th century, by the monks of Byland, and obtained the status of a parish church at the end of the 13th century. Although tastefully restored in 1892 the church, dedicated to St Mary the Virgin, has retained the major part of the original Norman structure.

The present-day Hare inn, the village local, was built in the 18th century but there was an alehouse on the site at the beginning of the 17th century where ale was brewed specially for iron workers employed by the Earl of Rutland. There is no shop in the village and only three farms and a smallholding and although the cottages have changed the land will still be much as it was when the monks built the chapel over 800 years ago.

Scorton 🌿

Scorton is an archetypal picturesque English village with ancient buildings surrounding a village green.

The central village green is one of only two raised greens in the country but, at the same time, reputedly the only one on which cricket is played by longstanding cricket teams of both men and women.

The village, although small, with only just over 500 inhabitants was at one time completely autonomous; with country locals like the mole catcher who provided skins for coats and the 'length man' who was responsible for cleaning the village every Saturday. It had its own slaughterhouse, brickfields, malting house and mill. Several schools have come and gone, of which there are still two existing; there are two shops, three pubs, a chapel and a Catholic church; and until recently there was not only a police station but a jail and accompanying magistrate's court house.

Scorton has always had strong connections with all types of sport. It was the home of the legendary Silver Arrow. This was a silver arrow presented to the Oxford Colleges as an archery trophy by Queen Elizabeth I and won at one time by John Wastell, the son of the local manor house. He was somewhat of a reprobate and instead of returning the arrow he brought it back to Scorton where it was stored in the attic after John had been thrown out and disowned by the family. In 1673 it was rediscovered and an archery competition set up which has been shot every year, except the war years, since. Originally the Arrow could only be won by a Yorkshire man but now anyone is eligible, the winner deciding the place of the next venue.

The St John of God hospital started life as the manor house of the village, which was owned by the Wastell family.

Adjacent to Scorton's old railway station and behind the inn is the site of St Cuthbert's Well. The source of this well sprang up where the pall bearers rested the coffin containing the body of St Cuthbert on its journey to Durham Cathedral where he is buried.

Scotton

Scotton lies four miles from Richmond, in the lea of the Eastern Pennines, not to be confused with Scotton, Knaresborough. The old village straddles the crossroads and has a beck flowing along the bottom of the wooded hillside.

Named in the Domesday survey, this was once a large settlement, and often foundations of the old buildings are unearthed when a new garden or house is excavated. Only nine of the grey stoned houses still exist plus farmhouses dotted around the perimeter.

The oldest house is Scotton House. Built in medieval times, it has old mullioned windows and is said to have been used as a hospice. A road known to older inhabitants as 'going down the town', and having an avenue of sycamore trees, leads to the later building of Low Hall.

The growth and history of Scotton has been dominated for the past 75 years by the development of Catterick Garrison, the greater part of which is in the parish of Scotton. Until Baden-Powell decided the area would make an ideal site to build 'the Aldershot of the North', Scotton was a country estate. Scotton Hall, now an officers' mess, its park, Scotton Lodge and Scotton Cottage are surrounded by army barracks.

Until the building of the Garrison the inhabitants had worked on the estate and kept a cow, a pig and poultry on the two or three fields they rented from the landowner. Rose Cottage was once the village pub, known as the Blacksmith's Arms. The last publican and blacksmith weighed in at over 22 stones and was more than six ft tall, and when a horse didn't co-operate could turn it on its back.

The blacksmith's shop disappeared in 1970 when the mini-market was extended, though the fireplace is still hidden behind a false wall.

Scriven 🐝

The name derives from the Anglo-Saxon 'screfen' – a place with pits; there are remains of quarries and gravel pits on the north side. However, from the flints and axes discovered, there was possibly a settlement here about 2,000 BC. In the Domesday survey of 1086, Scriven was one of the eleven berewicks of the manor of Knaresborough. The history of village and town has remained intertwined.

Home Farm, adjacent to the green, dates from the 15th century. It is a substantial, timber-framed, Vale of York house with hip-end roof and three and a half bays.

By the 17th century, linen was being produced, not only for local use but for the market, and many of the cottages had two looms. Scriven Hall, standing in the Park, was partially rebuilt by Sir Henry Slingsby on the eve of the Civil War, and was destroyed by fire in 1952.

In the mid 19th century, a workhouse and six dwellings stood on the village green; no trace remains. There were also at least four inns; there are none, now. And there is no church in the village – the Slingsbys worshipped at Knaresborough parish church. An evergreen oak was planted on the green in 1849 to commemorate the coming of age of the Slingsby heir, Sir Charles.

On Major Slingsby's death in 1962 there were no male heirs so, in 1965, the estate was divided up and sold. A new Hall has been built on the site of the coach house and stable block. The present scene is a triangular green, dominated by the evergreen oak, and bordered by picturesque cottages and farms. Idyllic – except for the lorries which make noisy progress from Lingerfield quarry along the winding roads.

Scruton 🐝

Scruton is situated midway between Northallerton and Bedale, just off the main road. The picturesque centre is an old village green, shaded by great lime trees, and surrounded by pleasing buildings which include a 12th century church, a 17th century manor house and an 18th century rectory.

The tower clock facing the green was given by the villagers in 1920 as a thank-offering when all their menfolk returned safely from the First World War. The tenor bell which strikes the hours, which was old when the 15th century tower was built, was restored by the village in 1987 along with two later bells to commemorate the 1,400th anniversary of the death of the church's patron St Radegund.

For a village with a spirit of community it was a tragedy when Scruton Hall, a modest Queen Anne mansion, which completed the village scene, was demolished in 1956. The Coore family, who had lived at the Hall for many years, had been at the centre of Scruton social life. The old school at Scruton was purchased by the parish council, and became the village hall, taking the name the Coore Memorial Hall.

The old fashioned corner shop closed in 1971, and since that time the village has just had a small post office. In recent years country crafts have emerged in the village. There is a flourishing pottery, two stained glass artists, a wool spinner and a dried flower arranger. There is a motor vehicle repair garage in the village, and a public house, the Coore Arms, which provides meals.

In the last 20 years Scruton has had five small estates built in different parts of the village. This has doubled its original size, the total number of properties now being 180.

Seamer ✣

Seamer is situated four miles from Scarborough in the Vale of Pickering. The earliest trace of a settlement here was in 8,000 BC when Mesolithic men settled on the shore of the lake at Starr Carr, one of only two such excavated sites in England. In fact the lake has now disappeared underground. An artesian bore in the nearby village of Irton brings the water to the surface to supply Scarborough and the surrounding district.

The oldest building in the village is the parish church, dedicated to St Martin Bishop of Tours. Built on earlier Saxon foundations, the nave and part of the chancel of the 12th century church remain mostly intact. To the west of the church, standing in a field is a fragment of ancient stone walling surrounding a 15th century doorway, which is all that remains of the medieval manor house.

In 1383, Richard II granted to Henry Percy and his heirs a charter for a market to be held every Monday and for a fair to be held for six days in July, starting on St Martin's Day. These rights are still celebrated today, although following a riot between gypsies and villagers in 1911, it has been reduced to one day. On 15th July each year the lord of the manor, now an honorary title, strives to maintain the local tradition by throwing pennies to the children of the village, which is preceded by the reading of the ancient charter at the four points which marked the boundary of the old village.

The fair attracts travelling folk from miles around who congregate in the village to carry out their horse trading. The charter also gave villagers the right to brew and sell beer during the fair and one of the cottages in the Main Street still bears an ale hook to which the villagers used to fix a 'branch of ale' stake advertising that beer was available on the premises.

The last landowning lord of the manor was Lord Londesborough. His estate was divided and sold in 1912. Some of the houses in the village still bear his crest and close to the church stands the Londesborough Arms public house. This is an old coaching inn that also did duty as the manor house up until the 18th century.

Sessay 🦋

Sessay is a long winding village which curves round a single street for about a mile and runs almost parallel to the main East Coast railway line. It is situated in open countryside, five miles from Thirsk, and although it is primarily a farming community, with two working farms, many of its present residents travel considerable distances to a variety of occupations. Housing in the village has doubled since the Second World War and the population stands at 250.

The village was originally sited half a mile from the modern village, near to the present church and until recently its outline was clearly definable in what is now a strawberry field.

Although the village can boast several old cottages and a manor house which may be Elizabethan, its most attractive corner is the church and school set beside the village green. There has been a church at Sessay since the 12th century but the present St Cuthbert's was rebuilt on the old site, at the sole cost of Lord Viscount Downe in 1847/48. The village school and head teacher's house were built at the same time, as part of the estate improvement.

The Old Hall, now known as Church Farm, is situated close to the church and was the seat of the Darrell family for four centuries. It then passed by marriage to the Dawnays. According to an old village story the 'Lion's Paw' on the Dawnay crest is nothing more than a 'Miller's Pick'. There is an old legend that Sessay woods was troubled by a cannibal giant who preyed on the villagers. One morning a Dawnay found the monster asleep in the precincts of Old Mills (now New Mills). He seized the miller's pick – which was the only weapon close to hand – and killed the giant. The king made a decree that the giant slayer should always keep hold of the Miller's Pick – by which token all men might know him.

Settle 🦋

Settle (population 2,500) is a small market town on the river Ribble, nestling under magnificent limestone scars. The market charter was granted in 1248 and the market square is still full of bustling stalls every Tuesday. In the days of coach travel, Settle was a well known stopping place, being on the York to Lancaster and Kendal highway. Today, visitors, walkers and cyclists still come to Settle and sample the hospitality of the inns and hotels in the town.

There used to be a set of mounting steps on the side of Garnetts shop, for people to get on and off their horses when it used to be an inn. Then suddenly they were gone – somebody had decided to remove them in the interests of 'progress'. The outcry over their demolition led to the formation of the North Craven Heritage Trust, which has bought and restored several properties, including the Museum of North Craven Life, in Chapel Street.

The building now called Penmar Court was built by John Delaney, who came to Settle from Norfolk to work at Christie's cotton mill. In his spare time John Delaney hawked tea around the ditrict, then he sold coal. When this began to conflict with his mill work and he had to choose between the two, he chose to set up on his own, although he could neigher read nor write. He took the Temperance Hotel in Commercial Yard and bought a small quarry. When Martin's Bank refused to lend him £50,000 to buy a coal mine he became a Quaker and borrowed the money from a Quaker bank. He died a very wealthy man.

Settle has a long history of carnivals, not always in its present form. Fifty years ago the carnival centred around the local cotton mills with a 'Cotton Queen' chosen from each parish in turn. The carnival at Christie's mill started with a procession from Settle to the mill gates where the retiring queen gave each child under 15 an orange, before opening the wrought iron gates to allow the new queen through to be crowned on the lawn in front of the house. The mill is still there but they make paper there now, not cotton.

Sharow ✤

After leaving Ripon, travelling north, the village of Sharow is to be found. The oldest part of the village ie the sanctuary cross, dates back to the 12th century. This is the only surviving sanctuary cross associated with Ripon Cathedral.

There are numerous natural springs in the village and two of them can still be seen today. There are one or two houses which still have 16th century or 17th century features in them, but most of the old village developed around the 1800s when a nephew of Mrs Allanson from Studley was given land to build a house (the Hall). Several small cottages were built at the same time to accommodate the gamekeeper, gardener etc. This was a thriving area with two working farms (now only one), a butcher's shop, a general store and a post office, but alas all have now gone leaving the only commercial venture, a public house.

In 1815 after the battle of Waterloo, a fund was set up all over England to build churches for the areas so lacking. Thus it was that Sharow got its church. In the churchyard stands a pyramid, a memorial to Charles Piazzi Smyth, who measured the Great Pyramid of Gizeh and was Astronomer Royal for Scotland, a post he held for 43 years.

St John's House was the vicarage and the land between vicarage and church was known as glebe land. There was a public right of way between the manor house and St John's to allow the people to go to church, the last piece of this lane can still be seen between the Hall copse and the Grange. In the 1970s, the Church Commissioners sold the glebe lands to a developer to build houses and this at one stroke more than doubled the size of the village and turned the parish of Sharow into a mixture of old and new.

Sheriff Hutton 🦢

In the Domesday Book of 1086, the village was called Hoton or Hotun, Old English for a town on a hill. 'Sheriff' was prefixed on Bertram de Bulmer's appointment as Sheriff of Yorkshire in 1139 by King Stephen. The Sheriff lived in the motte and bailey castle built in 1141 – the site of which is now part of a newly acquired conservation area owned by the village. Substantial ruins of a subsequent stone castle (1382) remain as a landmark for miles around.

Although the church, St Helen's, contains a small Roman stone altar, the earliest architecture is in the Norman tower. Edward, Prince of Wales, son of Richard III, died in 1484 aged eleven and was buried in Sheriff Hutton. His much restored alabaster tomb in the north-east corner is a focal point for the Richard III Society.

St Helen's Church, Sheriff Hutton

In 1377 Richard III granted permission for a weekly Monday market and five day fair to be held on the green. This was eventually replaced by the Hirings Fair at Michaelmas. The oldest inhabitants remember men and women standing there to be hired for the next year. A shepherd, for instance, would wear a tuft of wool in his buttonhole. Now an occasional fair of children's amusements is all that remains. A Horse Fair was held in the second week of April when horses paraded in front of the Pack Horse, renamed the Highwayman inn.

Peg-leg Smith, for many years up to 1939, 'tented' (tended) the cows. Many householders had one house cow to provide milk from which butter and cheese were made. Every morning as Peg-leg passed, the cows came out to join the herd as he took it along a different road each day of the week, grazing the verges. At night when he drove them home again, each cow went straight through its own gate. The roadsides have never since been so neatly mown.

Shipton 🐑

Shipton is situated five miles north of York on the A19. Until 1916 it was owned by the Dawnay family of Beningbrough Hall, as was the surrounding area of farms and some villages. The church of the Holy Evangelists was built and endowed by the Hon Paysan Dawnay in 1849. The vicarage was built at the same time, and is now a nursing home.

There are several farms, a post office and general store, and other businesses include petrol filling stations and a butcher. The public house, the Dawnay Arms, has the family coat of arms over the door, with the motto 'Timet Pudorem'. There are guest houses and restaurants; a novel one by the railway line is constructed of railway carriages, and displays a wealth of railway memorabilia.

The more modern cottages in the village were built in the 1800s with bricks made at the brickworks on the way to Newton. These are long since gone, although the cottages are still there, the large hole from where the clay was extracted is now a lake stocked with fish.

Shipton then was very different from the village of today with the busy A19 running through it. The railway was one means of transport, and Beningbrough station was very busy as most goods came by rail. In spring Irish Johnny would arrive with his gang for the seasonal work, mostly hoeing. They slept on straw in a granary or barn, cooking large pans of bacon and potatoes over the washhouse fire. After the day's work they would draw some of their wage and head for the local. Later, the strains of Danny Boy or Mountains of Mourne could be heard in the still night air!

Sinnington 🦊

Smoke curls lazily into the air as autumn descends on the village. Much needed rain swells the river and the mallards fuss noisily at its banks. Leaves are almost fallen, conkers collected and the bonfire on the village green sits waiting for its smouldering end.

On the hill, overlooking it all stands the church of All Saints, a compilation of styles but first built in the 12th century. Across the road from the church stands the tithe barn, designated an ancient monument.

On the village green, an old horse nibbles contentedly where once goats grazed, and the 'dry' bridge still engenders discussion as to its original purpose. The 18th century road bridge spans the river but the village was severed and bypassed by the building of the A170 road in the 1930s. Also on the green, the maypole, due to be replaced because of rot, is topped by a weathervane in the form of a fox, for the Hunt is reputed to be one of the oldest in the country.

Some old customs still exist, such as the Mell supper, an autumnal event much enjoyed by all who attend. As winter approaches, the village waits, sure in the knowledge that spring will find the river banks covered in daffodils, and the woods will be alive as the seasons turn full circle.

Skeeby 🦊

Skeeby is a small village sitting astride the busy main thoroughfare from the historic town of Richmond to the old Roman Watling Street, and now to the A1 and points north and south.

There were two mills in Skeeby, and one still exists by the side of Skeeby beck, restored and lived in, with the old wooden water-wheel still in position. There are old stone cottages in the village street with two ft thick stone walls dating from the 14th century.

In the early 1600s a small manor house was erected. This is one of the few examples still in existence of a complete small manor house. One of its unusual features is that all four principal rooms, two on each floor, show traces of stone fireplaces as large as that in the kitchen. Sadly, though legends abound – one that it was built as a guest-house for pilgrims to Easby Abbey, there is nothing that can be authenticated.

Almost opposite the manor house there is a restored house which was once the Rose and Crown inn, mentioned in 1688. This is now a private residence, but there is another public house called the Traveller's Rest.

There are records of stone quarries in the 12th century. Just before entering the village from Richmond there is an intriguing grassy hillock known as Halfe Hill, which tempts the amateur historian into hopes of a barrow or tumulus so near to the ancient earthwork of Scots Dyke, part of which bounds the village to the west. Sadly, nothing such is evident, only the remains of stone quarrying, now grass-grown, which was continued into comparatively recent times.

Skelton

Skelton is at the top of a long, gradual incline, three miles north of York in an ideal, dry position above the ings of the river Ouse.

The church, previously called All Saints and dedicated to St Giles only since 1960, is indeed 'a little gem'. The colour of the stones, the proportions and its situation do seem to be in perfect harmony. There is a tradition that it was built with stones left over from the south transept of York Minster in the 13th century which adds intrigue to the beauty.

During the 19th century some cottages for farm labourers and tradespeople were built as well as some larger houses. One of these was the Grange, home of the Place family who had much influence in Skelton and lived here for six generations. It has now been demolished but the name lives on in 'Arthur Place' an unusual name for a cul-de-sac built where it stood.

Skelton folk say that the village used to start at the Blacksmith's Arms and finish at the school, but that was in the days when there were only twelve children and the village water supply was six standpipes at strategic points. There are more houses and more people now but what has really changed? The shop has always been a shop and is now the post office as well. A new school was built and the old one became the village hall. The green, the historic heart of the village, is where roads and people meet just as they have always done.

Skelton-on-Ure

Skelton-on-Ure is situated four and a half miles from Ripon. The river Ure runs to the north-west of the village through the Newby Hall estate.

The village consists of one long main street bordered by grass verges with horse chestnut and lime trees. Visitors are treated to a welcoming sight in spring, when the verges are filled with daffodils. The buildings on each side are mainly cottages and farmhouses and although farming is still the main industry, much of the land once tended by tenants has returned to the Newby Hall estate. The earliest surviving cottages date from 1540 and are built from small hand-made bricks with pantiled roofs.

Situated in the park of Newby Hall is the church of Christ the Consoler, built in 1871 by Lady Mary Vyner, ancestor of the Compton family now resident at the Hall, as a memorial to her son, Frederick, who was captured and killed by Greek brigands. The church is still in use, but

Skelton-on-Ure

sadly, has been declared redundant. Volunteers are now restoring St Helen's church in the village, an earlier place of worship and burial ground, approached through a fine lychgate.

Once a ferry regularly crossed to Bishop Monkton. In 1869 this was the scene of a notorious hunting accident when members of the York and Ainsty Hunt, with their horses, boarded the ferry to pursue a fox which had swum across the river. The horses panicked and the boat capsized. Sir Charles Slingsby, four other members of the hunt and the boatman were drowned.

An important landmark is the Skelton windmill, standing off the B6265 to the north-east of the village. Legend has it that the land passed to Skelton after the parish of Kirby Hill refused to bury a vagrant who was found dead on the site and was finally laid to rest by the people of Skelton.

Skipton ✤

The lines of a Saxon defensive ditch can be seen from the castle walls in a field near the bailey, which disappear beneath the High Street to join the Ellerbeck circling round the vertical rocky cliff on which the castle stands. The Norman lords strengthened this original defensive site at Skipton, commanding the Aire gap. Holy Trinity church, started in 1122 and enlarged in the 15th century, stands next to the castle and together they dominate the north end of the High Street.

A walk down the High Street – the cattle market until well into the 20th century – may remind you of any other commercial street with its banks and building societies, but look carefully and find the plaques. One marks the site of the bull baiting ring and another where the pillory and the stocks were placed. The plaque referring to Caroline Square, the southern end of the High Street, is less easy to find but reminds us that Skipton folk were sympathetic to the estranged wife of George IV. Near here was born Thomas Spencer, the co-founder of Marks and Spencer.

The Leeds Liverpool Canal passes through Skipton. Now used solely by leisure craft, it provides endless interest in the summer months. Bordering the canal is Dewhursts Sylko factory with its commanding chimney a fitting landmark and memorial to our industrial past.

The Yards leading from the High Street, once the gardens of the burgesses' houses, then infilled with small business properties and houses, are today being refurbished to provide accommodation for tourists.

Skipwith 🌿

Skipwith is a flat, low-lying parish about twelve miles from York in the old East Riding of Yorkshire.

This small village has a pretty triangular green at the eastern side where some houses are found – the rest straggle along a main street which peters out at the western end, past the church, to farm roads and tracks. A group of houses here is known as Little Skipwith and another green, Scarrow Green, with a pond is found. The Skipwith family's manor house probably stood on a moated site opposite the church which can still be seen today, although the house is long gone. Local legend says that an underground passage links it to the church. The present manor house, Skipwith Hall, is situated on the main street a little east of the church.

The oldest and most impressive building in the village is St Helen's church. Tradition dates it from AD 960 but it may be even older than that. The oldest part of it is the Saxon tower – now the vestry. The slit-like windows suggest its defensive function. The village cross stands in the churchyard, the walls of which are topped in some places by medieval tombstone lids.

The fields around Skipwith were not enclosed until 1904 and then an area of approximately 800 acres was left as common. This was the site where Robert Aske, in 1536, assembled the rebels who took part in the Pilgrimage of Grace. It is an area of mixed dry heath, ponds and swampy places and woodland. Iron Age axe heads and burial mounds or 'barrows' have been found but it is more notable for the variety of flora and fauna found there. A large part was designated as a Site of Special Scientific Interest in 1954 and since 1968 about 600 acres has been administered as a nature reserve.

The Grocer's shop disappeared and finally the post office in 1989, now leaving only the local builder. Of the three public houses licenced in the 1750s, however, two still remain to lift the spirits of the inhabitants, the Hare and Hounds and the Drover's Arms.

Snainton 🌿

Snainton is a thriving village lying midway between Scarborough and Pickering with a population of nearly 800. The occupations of the inhabitants are varied, the main livelihood being farming with the farms spread around the outskirts of the village.

The site of the old gaol remains and a turreted cottage is said to be the old court house. The pinfold, which was used for stray animals, is still in good shape. The picturesque route to Hackness via Troutsdale starts here and is known as 'The Little Switzerland of The North'. Cockmoor Hall

Farm is at the beginning of this route and in the 1800s was a rabbit warren.

Wydale Hall is in a lovely wooded area and is now a retreat for the Diocese of York. It was previously owned by the Illingworth family for many years, who owned most of the land and farms in the area.

The Knights Templar Hall is said to be one of only two in the whole country and stands by the river Derwent. The Knights Templar settled here at Foulbridge in the 13th century, knowing the value of tolls from travellers crossing the river.

The church was the chapel of ease to Brompton and erected in 1150. It was rebuilt and resited in 1836, after a fire in 1834. It was then St Mary's but is now St Stephen's. The archway at the entrance to the church path is the original entrance to the old church and the lychgate, it is said, was taken from the chapel at Foulbridge and carries beak heads, representing the Templars.

Part of the old railway station is now a garage specialising in accident repairs. The actual station house is lived in by the owners and part of the platform remains. The Coachman inn is an old coaching house used by travellers passing through on the way to York.

In the 1920s on Good Fridays, the parish council bought bread and cakes and the village children delivered them to the old and needy residents. At the present time, instead of bread, coal is given, delivered by the coal merchant.

Snape

The castle dominates the western end of the village and can be glimpsed through an avenue of lime trees behind which lies the quiet unchanged village of Snape. Here cruck and timber-framed cottages stand together with more modern homes surrounding a long, narrow village green which has a beck running through it. The castle has an illustrious history. A famous 'royal' connection was that of Catherine Parr, last wife of Henry VIII. Her previous marriage was to Lord Latimer of Snape, a member of the Neville family who owned the castle for 700 years.

Snape castle has a truly beautiful private chapel, where many of the Latimers and Nevilles were married. The chapel is still used today by Snape villagers for regular Church of England services.

The village pub, the Castle Arms, is one of the oldest in the district and was originally called the Buck, a throwback to the days when deer roamed two huge parks totalling 500 acres created by the Earl of Exeter in the early 18th century. There is still evidence of the wall that surrounded these deer parks and there are still deer roaming in the area.

The present owner of the Thorp Perrow portion of the estate is Sir John Ropner. Here is the world famous arboretum which attracts visitors throughout the year.

In the middle of the 19th century Snape became a thriving centre for wool combing, a cottage industry. However when the trade became centred in the mills of Bradford the village lost this employment.

There is a dovecote still in excellent condition situated at the western end of the village in close proximity to the castle. The interior walls are lined with nesting boxes. The doves would have been an important source of fresh meat during winter months.

South Otterington

South Otterington is situated on the A167, four miles south of North-allerton, a small village which has been extended over the past few years by controlled amounts of house building. This has resulted in South Otterington incorporating Little Otterington with its long green.

The village, on the banks of the river Wiske, is linked to Newby Wiske by a stone bridge. Overlooking the Wiske is the main parish church of St Andrews. The present Victorian church, with its square 'pencil point' tower, is possibly the third building on this site and was paid for by William Rutson of Newby Wiske Hall in memory of his father. Until 1899, when oil lamps replaced candles, the congregation was accompanied by a violin cello.

An Elizabethan terraced manor house once stood near the river and in fact many of the cottages have Tudor origins. The public house at the crossroads is named the Otterington Shorthorn after this pure breed, which was until recently in the village. Most areas had their own local brickworks and South Otterington had two such places of employment. There is also evidence of a mill and two windmills.

On the outskirts of the village stands Otterington Hall, believed to have been built in the late 19th century and owned this century by the Furness family.

Standing next to the church is the rectory. The present building was erected in 1834 and is thought to be the third on this site. It was in the 1930s that the family of the new incumbent met the previous incumbent on the stairs – some months after his death!

Sowerby

A walk through Sowerby village is a delight. Charming old houses intermingle with smaller houses and cottages along wide, tree-lined Front Street. Ancient and modern go hand in hand from the Flatts, an open tract of land on the edge of Codbeck, past the ancient church, to Worlds End.

Although rubbing shoulders with Thirsk, Sowerby is a separate parish with its own boundaries. Considered to be in Thirsk, the police station, town hall, Lambert Hospital, swimming baths and Thirsk school are in fact within the Sowerby boundaries.

Walking towards Sowerby Front street, the attractive little Codbeck flows gently through the Flatts behind the village street. The old village school on the left has been made into pretty little cottages. The ancient church of St Oswald dates back to the 11th century, with more recent additions. Nearby is Manor Farm, where it is thought once stood Sowerby Manor, a gift in the 12th century to the Lascelles family who lived there until the reign of Elizabeth I, when it passed to the Maynells. An ancient dovecote stands in the grounds of Manor Farm.

Opposite the Methodist chapel stands a lovely half-timbered 500 year old house. The chapel was built in 1865 and some years later the ladies of the chapel made a patchwork quilt, each patch bearing the name of a local worshipper. The quilt is now in Thirsk Museum.

Passing some elegant old houses, we come to the end of Sowerby, aptly named Worlds End, where the picturesque old packhorse bridge, built in 1672 with a grant of £10 straddles Codbeck. Before new roads were constructed, this was the only way in to Sowerby from the south, other than through a nearby ford.

Not far away is Pudding Pie Hill, a 17 ft high Saxon burial mound. In 1855 Lady Frankland Russell of Thirkleby Hall, the then owner of the land, had it excavated and the skeleton of a very large warrior was discovered. His arms and legs were crossed, and the central boss of his shield rested on his breast.

Spaunton

This small village stands on a hill top 600 ft above sea level, with Pickering and Kirkbymoorside being the nearest towns. The village looks towards the wolds and the Vale of York in one direction and over the North Yorkshire Moors in the other.

The manor house of Spaunton which stands at the eastern end of the village has been rebuilt several times. Nowadays the Court Leet still sits annually on the first Thursday in October. After swearing in the pinder and twelve jurymen, fines are imposed on people who have encroached on the manor's common land. The pinfold still stands at the western end of the village.

Near the pinfold are the remains of a former chapel, the building now used as a farm store. In medieval times the village had 30 houses, a windmill and a blacksmith. Until quite recently one of the farmhouses in the village was also the local pub. It was frequented very often by the mineworkers from the Rosedale mines in the early part of this century.

In October 1943, a British bomber on its way to a raid in Germany crashed over the village and destroyed the blacksmith's shop and a cottage. The tenant of the Manor farm was killed when the force of the exploding bomb blew the back door into the passage, just as he was going to investigate.

Today Spaunton is still a one street village. Some properties have rights of both turbary and grazing for sheep, cattle, geese etc. The result is sheep roaming loose in the village and they do a very good job as lawn mowers.

Spaunton has no church, no chapel, no pub and no shop, but it retains the Victorian letter box and the red telephone kiosk. About 35 people now live in the village. Spaunton is a working village and although in the National Park, does not have too many weekend/holiday cottages. It is a thriving community.

Spennithorne

The village still retains a quietness reminiscent of a bygone age, although it has moved with the times insofar as new building has been allowed on a limited scale.

The village church is dedicated to St Michael and All Angels, built on the site of a Saxon church. The only remains of the earlier church are two ornamented stones built into the external walls of the chancel and a Saxon monument in the wall of the vestry.

Lost industries to the village include a water mill, brick and tiling industry, quarrying, a blacksmith and a butcher's shop. The village can still boast a joiner, an architectural metal worker who has taken over the old blacksmith's shop, a post office cum village store, a DIY centre, a sawmill and a shop selling wool and related products from the Wensleydale long wool sheep.

The 17th century Old Horn inn, although small provides excellent refreshment as well as accommodation. The oldest houses in the village are those which formed part of an old manor and these are situated in the lower reaches of the village and include Old Hall Farm.

A celebrated Hebraist and philosopher, John Hutchinson was born in the parish in 1675. He became steward to the 6th Duke of Somerset, who was Master of the Horse to George I. He disagreed with Sir Isaac Newton's theory of gravity and one of his theories was that the earth was cubical. Another Spennithorne worthy, Richard Hatfield, fired a pistol at George III in the Drury Lane Theatre, narrowly missing the King. He was later certified as insane.

Spofforth

The village of Spofforth lies on the A661, five miles from Harrogate and three miles from Wetherby.

During the 15th and 16th centuries the manor house at Spofforth was laid waste many times. In 1560 Henry, Lord Percy rebuilt it as Spofforth

Castle, which remained the principal residence of the family until it was ruined for the last time during the Civil War. Today the castle has a constant stream of visitors during the summer months.

Several attempts had been made to build in front of the castle and this was finally forestalled in 1985 when the parish council, village society and the people of Spofforth raised funds to purchase 'The Castle Field'.

Spofforth church, All Saints, is not mentioned in the Domesday survey and it is reasonable to assume that it was originally patronised by the Percy family. Under a canopy in the chancel is a stone effigy of Sir Robert de Plompton, who died in 1323. The tower is 15th century and the main building is thought to have been originally 12th century. In the churchyard is the grave of a local character and roadbuilder, Blind Jack of Knaresborough. The epitaph is a 16 line poem, telling of his life and exploits.

Spofforth used to have five pubs but now there are only three: the Castle, the William IVth and the Railway. The Railway owes its name to the fact that the village had a station on the North Eastern line, complete with signal box and level crossing.

The population declined to about 750 during the 1920s as nearby towns like Wetherby and Harrogate expanded. However the demand for private housing in the 1960s led to an expansion of development in the village. The interweaving of accents from as far apart as Scotland and London has strengthened the fabric of the village and many of the children of parents from Birmingham, Newcastle and other 'foreign parts' are native Yorkshiremen and proud to be so! Even the cricket club has had a Lancastrian captain!

Stainburn

Stainburn is situated on rising ground in the fertile valley of the river Wharfe. It is an ancient hamlet which formed part of the hunting forest of Knaresborough until it was deforested by King John.

There are signs in plenty that Stainburn has been an iron village. In the early tax rolls, bloomers were listed. These were men who melted iron and produced comparatively pure ingots of iron. Stone artefacts of the early Stone Age people have been found in a field near Almscliffe Crag and two Bronze Age palstaves were found under a hedge in the village. These items can be seen in the Pump Room Museum in Harrogate. There are also signs of Celtic and Saxon influence as stone querns of this period were used as building materials in the south front wall of the church. A Celtic cross is also at the west end of the church.

St Mary's itself must have been built in the early 1100s and stands aloof from the village between the two main clusters of buildings and houses which form the settlement, its position giving spectacular views in all directions. It was originally a barn-like structure with slit windows.

The village population in 1378 was one of the most substantial in the West Riding of Yorkshire, being greater than Halifax and not far behind that of Bradford. This gives strength to the belief that there were many more houses and rows of cottages than exist today. Early tax rolls show occupations as varied as weavers, lacemen, charcoal producers, carpenters, masons and general labourers. The Methodist chapel built in 1836 was closed in 1975 through lack of attendance. The village school was built in 1861 and closed in 1966, and like many other village schools, has been converted into a house. The beauty of the village still remains, however, due to its lovely situation.

Stainforth ✖

The village of Stainforth lies below the protective hills and crags of Craven. The Cistercian monks were responsible for the origins of sheep farming here and green tracks were constructed up the hill sides by them. One such track is known as Goose Scar which leads to Catrigg Force, a waterfall of some drop.

The village was largely destroyed during the Civil War and rebuilding was done very simply with local materials and labour. Since then, the substance of the village has changed very little, with only a few new cottages and barn conversions to residential use being added in recent years.

There is a beck running through the village which joins the river Ribble a few hundred yards away. The river divides Stainforth and Little Stainforth. The latter is reached by crossing the old packhorse bridge which is now under the care of the National Trust. A few yards from the bridge, after a series of small waterfalls, the river drops into the Foss. In the autumn season, visitors are often rewarded by seeing the salmon leaping the Foss as they travel upstream to spawn.

Employment in the village is mostly of a farming nature, while a few people work at the local quarries and the paper mill at Langcliffe. In the past there was a small industry for dying cloths. There is a croft by the beck known as Dyers Croft, where the industry took place.

There had been no church in the village before 1842, as villagers came under the care of Giggleswick parish. The money to build the church was donated by the Dawson sisters who had connections with Langcliffe Hall and whose family farmed at Neil Ings as early as 1652. The church was dedicated to St Peter in 1842.

In the past, the village had two or three shops besides a butcher's shop and the post office. Sadly, today there is no shop, though the post office is now managed from Brookfield Farm House. There is one garage and a public house which has served the village over many years.

Staithes ✤

The little village of Staithes lies at the foot of a steep hill, nestling between the cliffs a few miles to the north of Whitby. Its cobbled streets and back alleys evoke an old world charm at variance with the craggy cliffs and often wild North Sea.

The most recent acquisition to the village is the new school, a bright spacious building with playground and playing field. It is a far cry from the old school, an austere Victorian building with a school yard, outside toilets and windows high up in the walls.

The old school opened in 1878 and from the first its history reflected life in the village. The weather could be bleak, and the school log shows that in 1897 great storms of wind 'blew in the windows and destroyed the perimeter wall'. Some of the older boys would go fishing with their fathers during the spring and summer, and every year the children went to the woods to collect ash branches for the making of crab-pots. The children of the miners were particularly poor and many could not afford the school fees.

The number of children at the school fell dramatically during the 1920s, as with the closure of the ironstone mines many families moved away to Middlesbrough to find work. When the new school is a hundred years old, will the log books tell a story, as moving, sad and funny, as those of the old school?

Starbeck ✤

The village of Starbeck is on the old toll road between Knaresborough and Harrogate. There is a large building on the High Street which was once a workhouse, one of the oldest buildings in Starbeck. The town planners of Harrogate needed a workhouse, but not in elegant Harrogate! It served its purpose from 1810–1858 and has a plaque on the stone pillar at its entrance. This fine old building is now used as offices.

Beyond the old railway crossing, near the beck which gives the village its name, there is a precinct of old people's flats called Spa Mews, gathered round an old stone archway and courtyard, with a spring, now disused, as a centrepiece.

Sulphur and chalybeate springs were found in the area and the Prince of Wales Baths (1870) had sulphur water bathing as well as swimming until 1939. This building, now renovated, is Starbeck Baths, a very busy and popular pool.

There is a good library, a shopping centre and four busy churches of Anglican, Methodist, Catholic and Mission persuasions. The Mounted Police Stables are situated off the High Street. Adjacent to the stables there are schools for mentally and physically handicapped children and adults. These less fortunate members of our society are well integrated and cared for.

Evocative smells and scents daily pervade Starbeck. Taylor's Yorkshire Tea have their headquarters in the village; Betty's, the renowned confectioners, have their bakery near the railway crossing and from there wafts the wonderful aroma of roasting coffee; James Dalton, international dealers in spices and seasonings, carry on their business in the same area. Therefore, depending upon the direction of the wind, exotic and mouthwatering aromas inspire the residents in their day to day culinary skills.

On the outskirts of Starbeck there is a riding school, a school for the visually handicapped and a golf course.

An interesting part of the history of old Harrogate hangs in a Starbeck shop. In 1887 an ox, provided by Samson Fox, was roasted on the Stray to commemorate the Diamond Jubilee of Queen Victoria. The head was carefully preserved and can be seen on the back wall of John Horsley's butcher's shop next to the post office in the High Street. Below it there is a brass plaque suitably inscribed.

Starbotton 🐌

Starbotton lies two miles up the dale from Kettlewell, bisected by the busy B6160. It is a quiet village, apart from the noise of the traffic, with just over 50 inhabitants and many holiday visitors. There is one public house, the Fox and Hounds, but no shops or church and the former Methodist chapel is now a holiday home. The grey houses, dating mainly from the 17th century, huddle together surrounded by colourful gardens and a few clumps of large trees. Below the village, reached by a footbridge or stepping stones, runs the Dalesway, here following the course of the river Wharfe.

Today there are two working farms in the village, in time past there were many more. There was also a quarry and a thriving lead mining industry but only their scars remain, also a derelict smelt mill on the hillside, above a beck, which in certain lights resembles a castle.

On the edge of the village a tree-filled enclosure is all that remains of a Quaker burial ground; it is called Sepulchre.

The village's chief claim to fame is the disastrous flood of 1686 when a huge head of water descended from the fells sweeping away many houses and causing much damage, so much that a national appeal for help went out and money was sent, in aid, from as far away as Trumpington in Cambridgeshire.

Starbotton shows to best advantage from above; either from the steep track known as Knucklebone which leads up to windswept Buckden Pike or on the other side of the river on the Arncliffe path. From this bridleway one gets a superb view of a U-shaped glaciated valley with the Wharfe meandering from Langstrothdale to Kettlewell, where in spring the flowers are abundant and very lovely.

Stillingfleet 🌿

Stillingfleet is a small village situated eight miles south of York on the B1222 and has a population of just over 300 people.

Stillingfleet has a history which goes far beyond the 12th century when the church was built. At that time the region was inhabited by a tribe called the Paras. These ancient people coined money before the days of the Romans, and faint traces of their existence are to be found in the various tumuli on Thorganby and Skipwith commons.

In 1833 a great tragedy struck when eleven carol singers were drowned. They were crossing the Ouse when their boat became entangled with the tow rope of a passing barge. Nine were buried in a communal grave, the other two bodies were never found. The story goes that a twelfth man was saved by the fiddle on his back enabling him to keep afloat and reach the safety of the bank.

The hundred year old American harmonium in the Methodist chapel has 'Mouse Proofed' engraved on the foot pedals. Stillingfleet church has often been described as 'the jewel in the crown' and much has been written about its history and architectural beauty. The Norman door takes pride of place after its restoration and is protected by an additional door.

The population has varied little in size but far fewer are now employed on the land. There are two garages, a public house and the shop and post office. Just outside the village is part of the Selby coalfield complex. Subsidence is just beginning to have an effect.

Stillington is now a conservation area so that the lovely rural setting can be protected.

Stillington 🌿

Mentioned in the Domesday Book in 1086, Stillington was part of the see of the Archbishop of York. At that time the village consisted of six farms and a working mill. The mill is still in the same place on the river Foss, but not working now.

There were two blacksmiths working in 1932 and a candle shop, (the house named by the present owners 'The Chandlers') and four other shops. Souters had been in the family a very long time, but the advent of regular transport to York hit the village shops.

Stillington Hall was set in the middle of eight acres of parkland and was owned by the Croft family. It has been said that Croft Original Sherry was born here. The kitchen garden was a picture and a south-facing wall had a row of hot houses, nectarines, peaches, tomatoes and grapes. Now it is a large housing estate called Parkfield.

Laurence Sterne came here in 1745 as vicar of Stillington and Sutton on the Forest. His book *Tristram Shandy* was written during this time; it was almost lost. He tossed it onto the fire in a fit of petulance, but the squire rescued it. This happened during a social occasion at the Hall. Stillington church of St Nicholas dates back to 1329.

The old post mistress was quite a character and was very proud of her status in the village. On special days such as washing and baking when her hands were wet or covered in flour, stamps of different value were laid on the inner counter and the customer was handed the stamp on the end of a pair of scissors. She never dropped one!

The population has altered completely, with people settling here from all areas, and the dialect has died out. Sometimes though, one hears snippets of dialect such as: 'Sixpence to the shilling', if not feeling fit, or 'Now then missus! what fettle today?'

Stirton 🌿

Stirton is one of two small hamlets, half of the parish of Stirton with Thorlby, approximately one and a half miles from Skipton.

The village obtains its water from springs on nearby Sharphaw Hill, which is piped to the village, consequently there is no mains sewerage

Old Barn at Stirton

only septic tanks. These two factors prevent the village from growing too fast.

Stirton has a number of 'Gentlemen's Residences', some of which were originally farmhouses. They are built mainly of millstone grit and local Flasby Red stone, which makes an attractive combination. The oldest of these houses is Stirton House, built in 1668. Until recently an estate farm, it is now a private house. The outer walls have been stripped of the plaster which covered it, and the lovely coloured stonework is revealed.

There are two very attractive barns nearby with outside steps to the lofts; these and other properties are protected by the National Trust.

None-go Bye Farm is situated approximately two miles from the village crossroads. This was an important coaching house on the medieval road to the North from Skipton.

The crossroads of the villages is the site of a Victorian letter box set into a wall, with the VR at the top. Here are also the remains of the village stocks, where minor offenders would be exposed to public ridicule. Tradition does not tell when these were last used, possibly in the early 19th century.

A field nearby has some old earthworks. No one knows for sure what the banks and ditches denote, but the most popular theory is that it was a cockpit. This is probably so, as the neighbouring hill is called Cock Hill, and it seems an ideal out of the way arena for the sport. This same field is usually the venue for the annual village sports.

Stockton-on-the-Forest 🌿

The village lies four miles to the north-east of York and is at the centre of a parish of over 1,000 acres. The name refers to the Royal hunting Forest of Galtres which covered this area. At present less than ten per cent of the parish is wooded, the rest is in farmland or built up.

It is a street village laid out in a north-east to south-west direction along the line of the road and straggles for about a mile and a half with Stockton Hall at one end and the Old Rectory at the other. This road was at one time the main road between York and Scarborough and runs part of the way along the line of a Roman road. The village street is wide, representing the need in the days before roads were surfaced to allow carts to avoid the ruts in the mud created by vehicles which had passed before. There is also a pond at the side of the street which enabled the carters to water their horses.

Stockton Hall is now a hospital, having formerly been first a clothing factory and then an approved school and community home. The church of Holy Trinity is on the site of an ancient chapel of ease and the present building dates from 1843. In addition there are some interesting houses probably of 17th century date, including the present Fox inn and Church Farm.

The village at one time offered a full range of services with two shoemakers, two tailors, a school, a bricklayer, a victualler, a butcher, a blacksmiths, a cornmiller, a carpenter, a shopkeeper and a surveyor. Today there is a church, a chapel, a school, and two shops (one with a post office). The garage stands on the site of the old blacksmith's shop and the father and grandfather of the present owners were the village blacksmiths. A garden centre is nearby, together with a small unit industrial site and a new golf course has been created.

Stokesley ✍

'Dear old Stokesley' – the words of a small visitor who enjoyed tramping backwards and forwards over the various bridges across the river Leven, which flows through the town. These bridges give access to Levenside where chestnut trees hang over the water, and herons, kingfishers, water hens and water voles have been seen. Today visitors enjoy feeding the ducks. The narrow packhorse bridge has low walls which allowed animals carrying heavy packs to cross the water.

Follow the road eastwards along Levenside passing the Bethel chapel (now a dwelling) to Preston House. Here lived Mr John Preston who made provision in his will for the building of a school. When this school opened in 1834, the master and pupils lived in Preston House. Further on, a plaque tells of the first white woman to settle in Victoria, Australia in 1836. She was a Miss Jane Pace, born at Stokesley in 1817 who later married the Hon George Henty. A footpath leads through the old churchyard, passing the parish church of St Peter and St Paul before entering the High Street.

Narrow roads lead from the surrounding countryside into the wide High Street where the town hall holds a central position. It was built in 1853 by Colonel Hildyard of the manor house at his own expense. Every Friday a market is held on the area in front of the town hall, which is known as The Plain.

Across the Plain, which is used as a car park by shoppers and business people, is the old manor house. After restoration the building now houses the library and court house.

The highlight of the year is the Agricultural Show and Fair, which fill the town with roundabouts, side-shows, people and traffic.

Strensall ✍

Strensall lies some six miles to the north of York, on the east bank of the river Foss.

Methodism came early to Strensall and a local man, William Warriner, became a travelling preacher and then went to Antigua as the first

Methodist missionary to the West Indies. He returned to England and was present at the opening of the first Methodist chapel in Strensall, in 1823.

By 1798 the river Foss had been made navigable as far as Strensall and the existing bridges had been built. An extension canal was dug to Sheriff Hutton Bridge and there was an influx of 'navvies'. The canal's importance dwindled away with the coming of the York and North Midland Railway in 1845. The station is now closed and the inhabitants have taken to the roads once again.

In 1866 a new church of St Mary was built on the site of the old Norman one. It contains examples of the work of Robert Thompson (the 'Mouseman').

To the east and north-east of the village is an extensive area of common land, much of it occupied by a permanent army camp. The land for the camp was purchased in 1876 and it was not without opposition that the villagers relinquished their rights to graze their animals on that part of the common. However, much of the common is still available for recreation and one area is designated a nature reserve. York Golf Club lies to the east of the village and has attracted many residents to the village.

Strensall expanded slowly this century until about 20 years ago when it began to grow rapidly, the present population being about 4,500. It is still a farming area, the tannery which was built early in the 19th century is still operating, and there are some small businesses, but Strensall is now very much a dormitory village of York.

Stutton ✎

Stutton lies about one and a half miles to the south of Tadcaster, a bustling market town which is very famous for the three breweries which between them employ a large percentage of the population.

The village itself is comparatively small, consisting of just over 100 houses, plus a small wooden church, St Aidan's, and a pub, the Hare and Hounds. The village is built mainly of limestone from local quarries and was originally arranged round a small oval field upon which was a pinfold. However in about 1966 great changes took place when the whole of the central oval was built upon, and this and gradual building on side lanes totally altered the character of the village.

An area adjacent to the village is called 'The Willows'. Here willow was gathered and put into 'pies' similar to potatoes, kept damp using water from the beck, then taken into a barn, stripped and laid to dry. At this point they were sold on to a basket maker who made a wide range of goods from shopping baskets to the huge baskets which were, and still are, carried under hot air balloons.

The village also provided a service for the people of Tadcaster in the form of a laundry. This was at one time run by the Wilson family, and is vividly remembered by a surviving member of that family who tells of boiling the whites in a large copper, drying outside, and ironing with flat irons that weighed up to 11 lbs. There was also a collection and delivery service – by horse and cart to the surrounding area.

The three quarries, two of which are still working, are of interest because one of them, 'Jackdaw Crag', provided the stone to build York Minster.

Summerbridge 🦜

Summerbridge is situated on the B6135 between Ripley and Pateley Bridge, about ten miles from Harrogate and four from Pateley. The river Nidd forms the southern boundary of the village, its name owing its origin to the bridge which connects to the neighbouring Dacre.

The settlement developed due to the building of a large flax mill, known as New York Mill, at the western end of the village in 1825. The mill later produced hemp and man-made fibres, being a main centre of local employment until its closure in 1981. Part of the building is now an industrial estate. There was also an iron foundry, run from the middle of the 19th century by Joseph Todd & Sons who made the traditional Yorkshire ranges which were found until recently in many Yorkshire kitchens. The firm now handles farm machinery and sells all types of hardware.

The Methodist church is the dominant building in the Main Street which boasts a wide variety of shops including the post office. There is a public house, the Flying Dutchman, named after a racehorse not the legendary character. The village school is fronted by a pleasant lawn on which the May Queen is crowned.

To the north of the village, up a steep hill, stand Brimham Rocks, now owned by the National Trust. Every year thousands of visitors are attracted to the 60 acres of heathland on which stand a collection of millstone grit rocks which millions of years of erosion has formed into fantastic shapes.

Sutton-in-Craven 🦜

Sutton-in-Craven, mid-way between Keighley and Skipton, is just within the boundary of North Yorkshire. Older residents think of it as the two villages of Sutton Mill and Sutton.

The mill was originally a corn mill (1543), the rent for which was one red rose paid to the Earl of Cork. Textile production started in 1938 and continued to 1970. A few years later the mill was bought by a bedding firm.

Along the Main Street (which links the two villages) are St Thomas' Hall and St Thomas' church, money for the latter provided by the mill owner. The hall was paid for by a joint effort between a later mill owner and the villagers.

Set in the centre of the community, the park is a little gem. Opened in 1912, on land given by two mill owners, it belongs to the village.

After the park comes the older area of Sutton. Greenroyd Mill, which once turned raw wool into finished yarn, now houses health and fitness equipment and a part has returned to the production of speciality yarns. Four 17th century cottages were converted into the Black Bull inn in 1767.

High Street leads past the Manor House and Kings Arms to Croft Shed with its craft workshops. Nearby is a family gear-cutting engineering works which has supplied naval dockyards since 1941, one of the biggest ships being the *Ark Royal*, first replacement for that sunk in the war.

A notable building is the Jacobean-style archway with lodges, one of many listed buildings. This was the gateway to Sutton Hall, now demolished, and marks the entrance to Sutton Clough, a valley carved out by melting glacial ice. Moorland springs flow down this lovely area of woodland where school children have planted bulbs among the bluebells. Now a favourite walk for villagers, this was formerly an industrial site, the remains of an elling-pit and smelt mill are still to be seen.

Ellers Road leads to the Bay Horse inn where in the 19th century the landlord brewed his ale behind the inn and cooled it in the stream in front.

Swainby ✍

We have two names, which sometimes cause confusion. Domesday Book tells us that Whorlton, the original village, was a place of some importance at that time. It lay under the shadow of Whorl Hill, which legend says was called Worm Hill, inhabited by a worm of gigantic size which terrorised the countryside around until it was vanquished by a baron of Whorlton Castle nearby. Historians believe the hill was probably a military position in Roman times, and a hoard of 4th century silver coins and ornaments ploughed up by a farmer in 1810, with fragments of Roman pottery discovered in the churchyard during excavations, suggest Roman settlement.

Today Whorlton consists of a ruined Norman church, the gatehouse, earthworks and site of a castle built by the de Meynells, four farms, and two or three houses.

The name 'Swainby' first appears in documents in 1368, having been a planned and laid out village in the 13th century. It is thought that the Black Death was responsible for the migration down the hill, and the 18th century brought settlement along the banks of the stream.

Little evidence remains of the ironstone mining which took place in the mid 1800s, resulting in a burst of prosperity and a dramatic increase in the population figures, and only the small shale heaps along the hillside in Scugdale on the outskirts of the village reflect the activities of jet miners in Victorian times. Stone quarrying has always been a local industry, and one family of stonemasons working today have been carrying on the business for eight generations. The busy A172 road cuts across the old droving road at the entrance to the village. This winds up the hill, passing Black Horse Farm which was originally a wayside inn used by the drovers, and which is romantically if unreliably associated with Nevison the highwayman.

Swineside 🦡

Swineside is a small hamlet situated on a ridge on the hillside at approximately 1,000 ft. It consists of four houses – in earlier times all small farms; one is now an hotel, two are private houses and one is still a farm with the house and land rented separately.

The hamlet is approached from West Scrafton by a road that crosses the moor bottom – as late as the early part of the 1950s this was a gated track but is now a good metalled road with a cattle grid. It is one mile from West Scrafton and the road ends at Swineside. Good bridleways, tracks and paths continue in all directions. Earlier this century children walked one of these tracks to go to school at Horsehouse – now the school minibus picks them up at their own gate for their journey to Middleham.

The water supply is from springs on the moor and apart from very dry summers the supply is good. The houses are all built of dark stone with stone slate roofs presumably quarried locally. They all retain most of their original characteristics externally but have been altered internally and have all the modern conveniences.

Terrington 🦡

Terrington is a small picturesque, stone-built village situated about 15 miles north of York and eight miles west of Malton. It lies at the head of a valley on a ridge in the Howardian Hills.

Undoubtedly the most important building in the village is the church of All Saints, the fabric of the building dating in parts from Saxon times. In the churchyard lies the grave of Richard Spruce, an outstanding botanist, who grew up in Ganthorpe. Spruce is perhaps best known for his expedition in the Amazon jungle between 1848 and 1862, where he studied and collected around 700 species of plants, including over 400 previously unknown species of flowers.

The village may have had some early religious significance as covens of witches were said to gather there during the 17th century. Old customs and festivals have now largely died away, though few, if any, would have been exclusive to Terrington. Many customs were connected with marriage, one of which was for a race to be held in the main street, with the winning tape being held by the newly wed couple. Another, which was last carried out in about 1926, was for the bride and bridegroom to be greeted by the firing of gunpowder on the blacksmith's anvil. If a man committed adultery, his effigy was placed on a cart and set alight in front of his house, whilst the villagers chanted a rhyme – it is thought that this was last carried out in about 1890.

Present day Terrington follows the plan of the original village, being compact around three parallel streets. At the west end of the main street is a triangular 'green' occupied by a ring of trees known as The Plump. Where the village pond originally stood, on the south side of the main street, is now a triangular area containing the village store and post office and a couple of holiday homes.

Theakston

Theakston is a hamlet comprising some twelve houses, and is situated to the west of the A1 motorway and about a mile north of the village of Burneston.

A thoroughbred Race Horse Stud came here in 1892. During spring and summer, the mares and foals run out in the fields and are a delight to watch.

Theakston is a very peaceful place to live, and as the flowers appear, has quite a pretty outlook. The houses are surrounded by fields and during the spring and summer are visited by numerous birds mating and nesting. All the activity of the village is centred around the stud and the cattle.

Thirkleby

Thirkleby consists of two villages which, in the past, were owned by two families. Great Thirkleby, marked on old maps as High Thirkleby, was the home of the Payne-Gallway family and was an 'estate village'; whilst Little Thirkleby was owned by Lord Downe until 1918 and had within it several farms let to tenants.

There is no road between the villages but they are connected by a pleasant bridlepath crossing the beck by a narrow footbridge. In times long past coaches and horses would pass through on the way from York to Coxwold. In a corner of the field adjacent to the ford is a cobbled area (now covered by grass) where the horses and coach would stand to be washed down, a forerunner of today's carwash!

At the beginning of the 20th century Sir Ralph Frankland Payne-Gallway lived in the mansion (built in 1780 and replacing an Elizabethan house). The rule of the estate was very strict. Tenants were not allowed to have children! This rule was eventually relaxed but children were not allowed to play in the village after 3 pm and were ordered to attend church and Sunday school. Failure to comply incurred the parents' dismissal. There were various tradesmen in the village; a joiner, tailor, blacksmith, miller and a seamstress, also farmers. Today there are still farmers and two brothers who are the third generation of their family to have the joiner's shop. The village fortunately still has a shop and post office, situated in old farm buildings.

In 1928 the Hall was in ruins, the fine interior fittings were sold and the buildings demolished. The stable block and West lodges remain. These now lead to a flourishing caravan park giving opportunities for people to enjoy the peace and tranquillity of the countryside.

Some still recall former village life and taking a horse-drawn 'rolley' to sell eggs, butter and garden produce, including fruit from the many orchards each autumn. This money enabled people to pay the rates. Many of the fruit trees still stand although some have blown down in recent gales and it is calculated that they were almost a hundred years old.

Thirlby 🦋

Five miles from Thirsk off the A170 road, nestling under the Whitestone Cliffe lies Thirlby village, half in, half outside the North Yorkshire Moors National Park.

The oldest house possibly dates back to the 12th or 13th century and has a preservation order on it, and there is at least one house which is a cruck house and was originally thatched. When one of the new houses was being built a kiln from the 13th century was discovered complete with pottery. The kiln and contents can still be seen at the Ryedale Folk Museum.

Thirlby also had its own brickworks, the bricks being two inch in size. The house which was called 'Brickyard House' is still used, although with a different name, as a holiday cottage, and the brick ponds can be seen in the field close by.

Gomire Lake which lies behind the village is one of only three natural lakes in Yorkshire. It is renowned for its interest to the botanist for its flora, and by lovers of the countryside for its quiet beauty.

At one time the village had a shop and a public house. The public house had no name but this rhyme:

What sign this is
No man can tell,
Yet 'tis a sign there's ale to sell.

This was closed by the local landowner of the time.

The village had eight farms – now there are four working farms varying in size from 16 to 200 acres within Thirlby's boundaries. Other than the farmers there is a woodcraftsman and blacksmith-engineer working within the village.

Thirsk ✤

Thirsk is situated at the foot of the Hambleton Hills, lying approximately half way between York and Darlington to the east of the A1 trunk road.

A prominent feature of Thirsk is the parish church of St Mary which was begun in 1430. Taking half a century to complete, it is a fine example of Perpendicular Gothic architecture. Traces of a preceding Norman church can be seen in the south aisle walls of the present church.

Apart from a cobbled market square, Thirsk can boast of having two greens, St James' Green and the Little Green, the latter being the site of the first markets which date from the 12th century. It is reported that in 1623 this green was also the site of the ducking stool, the stocks and where elections took place. Bull-baiting used to take place in the cobbled market square where the twice-weekly market is now held.

Thirsk's market place saw the first draper's shop in Britain, established in 1580 by Bartholomew Smith and Son. The site is now occupied by a menswear shop and a chemist. Another famous name which started life as an ironmonger's in Thirsk is that of Purdeys, probably the most famous gunsmith for shotguns in the world.

Horses have always been important to Thirsk. Indeed, George III decreed that Thirsk was one of the few places allowed to have horse racing in an organised way. This, no doubt, led to the establishing of the existing race course in 1854, with the first race being run on 15th March 1855.

During the days of stagecoach travel, Thirsk was one of the main posting stops on the route between London and the North. Two coaching inns of the time, the Golden Fleece and the Three Tuns, still flourish with the help of locals and tourists alike.

Tholthorpe ✤

Tholthorpe is a small rural village with a population of about 170, five miles south-west of Easingwold. It was a watering and resting place for drovers travelling from the North to York. Human bones and Stone Age tools have been found at Ten Mile Hill to the west of the village.

The heart of the village boasts a large green with a duck pond, which is fed by a spring rich in nutrients. Sometimes in bright sunlight an algae called *Eugleana Sanguena* turns the pond from bright green to red.

The Methodist chapel, built in 1844 of red brick and a grey slate roof seats 120 people and is the only place of worship in the village. Pond View Farm, 1790, is a Grade II listed building. It has long passages on both floors and the original beams in the kitchen have been retained.

Occupations of the present inhabitants are many and varied. About a dozen are employed in farming but many people commute to York each day. Several people have their own business – a carpenter, second-hand car sales and repair, and a fishing reel manufacturer. There is a village shop and sub post office, a butcher, who has his own abbatoir, the New Inn and Restaurant, a residential home for the elderly and a plant hire company. There is a small industrial estate and a straw plant which converts straw into animal food to the north-east.

In 1939 the Air Ministry requisitioned farmland and converted it into a grass airfield. A memorial made of Canadian granite was unveiled on the village green in 1986 with an inscription in English and French. A line of oak and Canadian maple trees was planted along both sides of the road towards the airfield as a reminder to future generations.

The village's charm has led to bed and breakfast and cottage accommodation being made available for holidaymakers.

Thoralby

Thoralby, with a population of 130, stands on the north slope of Bishopdale facing its sister village of Newbiggin on the southern slope.

Bishopdale beck runs close by Thoralby and indeed powered a three-storey corn mill. This mill has since been used as a piggery, a cheese store and later for chickens. Today it is divided into three holiday flats. The weir and mill race are still visible.

The medieval chantry chapel of All Hallows was founded in 1316 by Lady Mary Neville. A house which was called Chapel Close and later renamed Chapel Garth now stands close to the site of the chapel. Monks are known to be buried in the adjoining garth or paddock. Chapel Close is now a row of senior citizens' cottages on the opposite side of the road.

Lead and iron-ore were mined on the High Scar and Thoralby mine is well marked on an ordnance map of the area. These industries would have accounted for the employment of part of the population and farming would have occupied the remainder. Yeoman farmers would have produced wool which everyone knitted, thus a dales tradition and export industry was started.

There were once three inns in the village, the present day post office and store being one and the eastern part of a house on the north side of the green another, which was then known as the 'Loyal Dales Volunteer'.

Today only the George inn remains and is a busy meeting place for villagers and visitors.

Today the main source of income is from farming of sheep and cattle. Visitors often pause to watch herds of cows going in for milking and marvel at the silence of scores of hooves. Thoralby lies within the Yorkshire Dales National Park, a sleepy haven between two popular holiday routes.

Thorlby

Thorlby is a hamlet situated two miles from Skipton and part of the parish of Stirton with Thorlby.

The old York to Lancaster coaching road and the Keighley and Kendal turnpike road converged on the outskirts and passed through the hamlet. The new Keighley and Kendal Trust road runs to the south of it.

Bay Horse Farm, an old inn, stands at the side of the old turnpike road. Where there are now attractive gardens in front of the long fronted house, there were cobbles. Rings in the house front wall still show where the horses were tied. Ghyll Cottage and Bay Horse Farm were both subject to severe flooding until the present farmer diverted the water from the culvert under the garden. One story tells of the occupier of Ghyll Cottage being met by his piano floating out of the door.

The toll house for Thorlby is still occupied. It was built on the Gargrave side of Holme Bridge. The Leeds and Liverpool Canal was completed here in 1816, and the Bar House was removed to the Skipton side of the canal in 1820.

There are six modern, and eight old houses in the actual village of Thorlby, four of these are holiday cottages. Other houses and farms are spread over an area away from the village, but are still in the parish.

Thornton-in-Craven

Thornton-in-Craven stands on the Pennine Way and enjoys commanding views of the surrounding area. On its boundary is the church of St Mary, built in the 12th century. Unfortunately exact dates are not available as all records were accidentally burnt by a retiring rector! The village still has a manor house although this is not the original, which was razed to the ground by Royalist soldiers shortly after the visit of Oliver Cromwell who stayed here to attend a wedding. The present manor house was built on the opposite side of the road. Five almshouses are part of the community and were built in 1815 by a Joseph Smith in memory of his wife Rachel; he was a native of the village who became a City of London banker.

Employment in the late 1800s and early this century was mainly in the quarry, now disused and full of water. The depth is unknown but it is used now by local frogmen for practice.

The community work well together in keeping the village attractive and have been awarded the 'Dalesman' Best Kept Village award several times and in 1989 won the Britain in Bloom award for small villages.

Thornton-le-Beans 🦞

Thornton-le-Beans (usually shortened by the locals to TLB or simply 'The Beans' to distinguish it from the nearby Thornton-le-Moor) is a small, attractive village in the heart of rural North Yorkshire, lying half a mile to the east of the main Northallerton–Thirsk road. The village street contains several 18th century houses, but a number of modern houses have been built in small cul-de-sacs on either side so that the rural atmosphere is unspoiled. All around is gently rolling countryside, with small patches of woodland and scattered farms.

The village street runs from east to west and at the west end stands the small church. Originally a chapel of ease it was rebuilt in 1776 on the site of an earlier chapel built in 1208.

The welcoming public house now named the Crosby after a well-known locally trained racehorse, was formerly the Shoulder of Mutton. It has many horse racing associations. One landlord was the trainer Chris Bowser, another the jockey Alec Jack, who altered the building to include horse-shoe shaped entrances to the alcoves.

Hawnby House in the centre of the village is probably the oldest building remaining. Built about 200 years ago it comprised a dwelling and joiner's workshop. A large well at the rear supplied most of the villagers with water until the mains supply came to the village in the early 1950s. Other services came later – street lighting was installed in the early 1960s and sewerage only in 1969.

Among recent housing developments is 'The Stonebow', containing 18 dwellings, which was started in 1968. Here, by the junction with the main street stands a four ton granite rock, believed to have been carried to the village from Shap Fell 70 miles away long ago, in the Ice Age.

Thornton le Dale 🦞

This attractive village so well known to visitors and holidaymakers has a long and interesting history. Material evidence points to an early settlement many hundreds of years before the Domesday records of 1086. There are tumuli to be seen on surrounding moorlands. Flint workings and remains of primitive pottery have been found, also some Romano–British brooches.

The church of All Saints stands on high ground and has been rebuilt

Rose Cottage, Thornton-le-Dale

several times down the centuries. It is believed that the medieval mystic and hermit, Richard Rolle had an association with the church in the 14th century. In the churchyard there is the gravestone of Matthew Grimes. He was a soldier who helped to guard Napoleon on St Helena and was even a bearer at the Emperor's funeral.

The lady of the manor, Lady Lumley, founded a grammar school in 1657 in order for boys to receive a classical education, many becoming Oxbridge scholars. The school continued until the beginning of the 20th century when the trustees founded instead the Lady Lumley Grammar School in Pickering. The almshouses close by the school were also established by Lady Lumley for poor people on her Thornton and Sinnington estates. Beck Isle close by has the much photographed thatched cottage. Many years ago it was used as the laundrymaid's house. Priestman's Lane is so named after the family who built the large houses there in the 18th century.

The village cross is known to have been the place where the yearly tribute of 1,500 red herring and 1,500 white herring was handed from the Abbot of Whitby to the Hospitallers of St Leonard's in York. Close by are the stocks, a replica of the original.

In the everyday life of the village a number of activities have taken place. Corn milling, spinning, weaving, fulling and bleaching were known and during Stuart times many cottages had weaving looms. Paper making took place in the neighbouring hamlet of Ellerburn. Shoemaking and tailoring flourished in the 18th and 19th centuries, indeed tailoring continued until the late 1940s. The first known butcher traded in the early 18th century although grocers were rare until the 19th. Two inns and an alehouse were also in existence in the 18th century.

The Thornton beck has been divided into many channels but still flows through the village. Trout can be seen from time to time, also mallards and moorhen on the pond. Rooks still caw and build their nests near the church. Numerous visitors come in the summer months to enjoy the beauty of the village and also the famous home-made ice-cream.

Thornton-le-Moor 🦜

The village of Thornton-le-Moor is mentioned in the Domesday Book as Torentun, from the Saxon meaning fortified place protected by a tower. There is unfortunately no longer a tower in Thornton-le-Moor, but the village continues to flourish.

It lies mainly either side of the road which links the A168 with the A167, about four miles south of Northallerton. It contains the parish rectory, local policehouse and a 19th century public house, but has lost two towers in recent times.

In 1940, the 90 ft tower of Baxter's brewery had to be taken down as it was considered a possible landmark for German pilots. The brewery, which had been a mainstay of the community throughout the 19th century, had ceased production in the 1920s, much to the dismay of the medical profession, which held its ales in high repute for their tonic and stomachic properties. The rubble from the tower became part of the foundations for the Friarage Hospital in Northallerton.

The church tower was removed in the 1980s with the rest of the Victorian church of St Barnabas, as it had become unsafe. This was a very sad occasion, as worship had taken place at that spot for many centuries. Until the building of St Barnabas' in 1868, coffins were taken along the corpse road to be buried at the church of North Otterington.

Before 1840, Thornton-le-Moor was a well known centre for cock-fighting and a 14th century lord of the manor listed a ducking stool, pillory and gallows in his possession. These were fortunately not in use when the school was built in 1822.

Thornton Steward 🦜

The hamlet of Thornton Steward lies on the north side of Wensleydale opposite Jervaulx, commanding the most glorious views towards Witton Fell. Its most interesting building situated at the east end is a small castellated square tower with side wings built by Capt G. Horn for a store-room and armoury for the corps of volunteers stationed here during the troublous times of the French wars 1804–1815.

Don't be deterred by the gates across the public road leading to the simple church – St Oswald's – one of Wensleydale's oldest, and mentioned in the Domesday survey. The path then leads on to Danby Hall, the home of the Scrope family, who have been there for three centuries.

Thornton Watlass 🖋

The village of Thornton Watlass lies on the eastern slopes of the valley of the river Ure between the townships of Bedale and Masham, where the river enters the plain of York. The name was mentioned as two separate villages in the Domesday Book.

No mention was made of a church, though the relics of two Saxon crosses and a broken shaft found in the churchyard suggest the presence of a preaching cross. The church of St Mary is a handsome stone edifice rebuilt, with the exception of the tower, in 1868. The tower, like many others on the border, appears to have been used as a place of security in troublesome times. From the top of the tower on a clear day, 30 churches can be seen including York Minster. It contains apartments for domestic purposes. The church has a famous collection of hatchments and a superb carved black Angel lectern – the figurehead of a ship.

Thornton Watlass Hall, which is still the seat of the Dodsworth family after 500 years, is an ancient gabled stone house of two storeys situated in a well wooded park.

Half a mile north of the village is an ancient British barrow, now called Gospel Hill from the early Dissenters having held their prayer meetings upon and around it.

The focal point of the village is the triangular village green with a cricket pitch over a hundred years old. There are unusual boundaries – for example the position of deep third man stands at the front door of the Buck inn. The village has had a school since 1600.

Two stock trees were planted in 1660 at the Restoration of Charles II. The stocks were moved between the lime trees from the churchyard. On the 300th anniversary of these trees (to the day) two walnut trees were planted directly behind them by Cyrilla, Lady Smith Dodsworth. At the present time only one splendid tree remains. The village still retains one of its three village pumps. In earlier times two were for household use and one for cattle.

Threshfield 🖋

Threshfield is a village in Upper Wharfedale situated eight miles from Skipton on the main road to Kilnsey. The old part of the village which remains relatively unspoilt lies directly before the junction with the road to Grassington. Later developments have spread down towards the river Wharfe which forms the boundary between these two villages.

Entering the village from the Skipton direction over a handsome humpbacked bridge, there is a house on the right where the ancient craft of besom making was carried on for several centuries. The last member of the family, called Ibbotson, renowned for this craft died as recently as the 1920s.

The first prominent building of interest to be seen is the Old Hall inn standing well back from the road on the left. It was built in the late 18th century on the site of a much earlier old Hall, parts of which remain at the back of the inn. These form outbuildings dating from the 14th and 15th century and have two unusual mullioned windows. It is thought to be the earliest domestic building in the dale.

Looking across the road from the inn is a small patch of green, remnant of the old village green complete with stocks. Clustered behind it and along two small lanes leading off to the Linton road are cottages, houses, several farms and outbuildings, some of these having lintels bearing 17th century dates and the initials of their original owners.

Quarrying and tourism are the main industries in the village but farming, particularly sheep farming, influences the character of the village and the surrounding countryside.

The village also provides a home for the local well known Upper Wharfedale Rugby Club.

There are many and varied walks in and around Threshfield, several of them passing through the nearby pretty little hamlet of Skirethornes and over what was the old drover's road to Malham. This passes on its way many places of interest including a cave in which evidence of prehistoric dwellers has been found, several ancient settlements and a stone circle.

Thrintoft ❧

Thrintoft is a small straggling village, low-lying and muddy in bad weather. This village, and much of Morton-on-Swale, belonged to the Earl of Harewood; when the estate was broken up in 1922 some of the farmers took the opportunity to purchase their farms. There are four in the village: two of them are dairy farms with fairly small acreages, and the other two are larger mixed farms. There is also an agricultural contractor and an agricultural engineer.

There is a pump at the crossroads, now disused, and halfway along the main village street is a spring which has never been known to dry up. Before mains water was available villagers queued up with pails, and farmers with milk churns, for their supplies.

The North Bridge over Thrintoft beck was built early this century, and in summer is crossed four times daily by Brian Lightfoot's herd of Friesians as they are moved from pasture to byre and back again. There have been Lightfoots in this village for as long as anyone can remember, and Brian's forebears used to 'tent' their cows on the verges of the lane – his cows still stop to graze where they can.

Of historic interest are the village pub, the New Inn, built in 1776, which now has a restaurant attached, and a 15th century Cistercian chapel, now used as a barn, at Thrintoft Grange at the west end of the village. This is one of only three grange chapels attached to Jervaulx Abbey, which had extensive agricultural interests, and was for travellers between Jervaulx and Rievaulx.

Tollerton ✑

The river Kyle or Carr, was the natural boundary of the ancient forest of Galtres. There can be no doubt that the 'road' to York would be hazardous, traversing the forest as it did, and it is thought that at Tollerton a tax was paid for the services of a guide.

There was, up to some 50 years ago, a mound in a field near the river Kyle which was purported to be the site of the toll house. Tollerton would have been in a very important and strategic position being near the Roman road to Aldborough, near Boroughbridge. A skeleton of a vessel, either Roman or Viking (records differ on this) was found some twelve to 15 ft below water level when the foundations of a water mill were being dug in 1815, thus pointing to the fact that the river Kyle was at one time navigable.

The village is very compact, four roads leading from a triangular shaped village green with a tree and a seat in the middle. In 1823 the population was 481, present day around 600.

In living memory there were three shops and a post office, now there is only one, a post office/shop combined. In 1890 five public houses were listed; today there are three.

There is believed to have been a church or chapel of ease at Tollerton at one time, but its whereabouts are lost in antiquity. The first chapel was built in 1794, and in 1869 a larger one was erected on the same site; this was demolished in 1982 and a house built on the site. A mission church (St Michael's) was built in Tollerton in the 1950s.

It is known that up to the late 1800s a Stot Play was performed in the village on Plough Monday. Plough 'stots', dressed in bizarre costumes went from house to house. They depicted Beelzebub, St George, a Clown, a Doctor, Slasher and Devil Doubt. Eventually Beelzebub knocked out the Clown and the Doctor was called upon to administer a restorative!

Topcliffe ✑

The present-day traveller might be forgiven for thinking that Topcliffe is a 'new village', as the view from the bypass is of modern houses with the church in the background, whereas the original route from the west crosses the old bridge and climbs steeply into the older part of the village on the top of the cliff. On the highest level is the church, dedicated to St Columba, built in 1855 but incorporating some of the old church, there having been one on the same site since the 7th century.

The Domesday survey of 1086 describes Topeclive as a large place with many farms, a mill, a church with two priests and the important castle of the Percy family, Earls of Northumberland. The castle must have been immense, judging by the remaining earthworks and moats on a perfect site where the rivers Swale and Codbeck meet, a short distance from the village.

Charters were granted in medieval times for annual sheep and horse fairs on 17th and 18th July, the horse fair, affectionately known as 'Topley Fair', continuing until the late 1960s. Older residents remember how Dr T. Carter Mitchell donned his frock coat and top hat on the evening of 17th July each year and made his way down the hill and over the bridge to the gipsy encampment where he visited each caravan and welcomed the occupants. The following day, the village street was crowded with visitors and horse dealers watching the horses being raced up and down by young men and boys.

The Tolbooth is a very old building, having the former village prison on the ground floor and two rooms upstairs approached from the outside by stone steps. These rooms were, and still are, the Men's Institute. One room contains a huge black oak table, reputed to be where the ransom money of £200,000 was paid to the Scots in exchange for King Charles I. Other places, it has been said, also claim this doubtful distinction.

Topcliffe Mill, possibly on the same site as the mill mentioned in Domesday, produced flour up to the 1960s. At Christmas time, small bags of wheat were given by Mr Lister at the mill, so that the traditional 'frumenty' could be eaten on Christmas Eve. An earlier miller at Topcliffe, Old Mealy Face, was by nature very mean, so before going to market, he pressed his face into the flour bin so that his wife could not use any of the flour in his absence without disturbing the impression.

Ugthorpe

Ugthorpe is a small village situated on the edge of the North Yorkshire Moors eight miles from Whitby. On the evidence of some coins found in a field in the village in 1792, it is thought that a Roman settlement existed here in the 1st century AD.

In the early 1660s, when Roman Catholics were persecuted, Father Nicholas Postgate returned from France to his native Yorkshire. On the edge of the village is a farmhouse known as The Hermitage and it was here that Father Postgate lived for a time and said mass. The villagers knew when this would be when they saw his white sheets hanging out on a hedge to air! He was eventually arrested and executed at York Assizes in 1679. A rally of the Postgate Society is held every other year when up to 2,000 people honour his memory.

As well as St Ann's Roman Catholic church, the village also has an active Anglican church, Christ church, built as St Ann's was in 1855.

A striking landmark, standing in a commanding position at the top of the 'Mill Hill' is the windmill. Once a working mill it is now minus its sails and is used as a dwelling. The views from the top are quite stunning.

In the 1930s there were two cobblers, a watchmaker and joiner. A bacon factory was run by Alice and Dinis Hart who went by pony and trap on Saturdays to Whitby market. Alice died aged 103 years and the business was continued by her son and then her grandson, both Aaron Hart. Originally the slaughterhouse and factory were at White House, later moving to a site near the Black Bull inn. The building, now a dwelling, is still often referred to as the Bacon House.

At one end of the village there are two caravan parks and visitors are often seen strolling through the peaceful village in the summer, passing at the bottom of the hill a piece of ground known as the pinfold where stray cattle used to be kept until claimed by their owners.

Ugthorpe is not on the main tourist routes and so it has retained its quietness and calm which is part of its charm.

Upsall

Upsall has obviously been a larger settlement in the past as there were once more houses and also an inn. The existing village green was once a cobbled market. A group of pine trees towards the top of the village were used as a holding pen by looping rope from tree to tree in which the cattle were left until they were due to be sold.

The Forge & Joiner's Shop, Upsall

The present day castle was built in Victorian style in 1924 on the site of two previous castles. The original belonged to the Scrope family whose ancestors still live in the county. In 1768 it was bought by Dr John Turton, physician to George III, and he left it to the youngest son of Rev William Peters who assumed the Turton name and coat of arms. It is still occupied by his descendant, Robin Turton, Lord Tranmire of Upsall.

The village is unusual in its architecture, some of the houses having very ornate chimneys, patterns on the roofs and the majority having fancy eaveswork, some more elaborate than others. They are all of a basic style although built at different times. The forge has an unusual horseshoe-shaped doorway, presumably to depict the type of premises therein, and connected to this is the joiner's shop which is still used as such today. Further up the village is a Methodist chapel, a red brick structure, erected in 1887.

The population of the village is about 40, the majority of the adults being employed by the castle or tenants on the estate land. Only two of the 14 houses are not owned by the estate.

Warlaby

Warlaby is a small hamlet – it has a letter box, but no telephone kiosk. It is worth visiting in February when the roadside near the Hall is covered in masses of snowdrops. It is approached by two narrow lanes leading from the A684, and a few modern houses have been erected along these. The river Wiske forms its east boundary.

Warlaby achieved a measure of fame among cattle breeders because of the prizewinning herd of Warlaby Shorthorns; the breeder, Thomas Booth, came from Catterick to Warlaby in 1819. The herd has been dispersed, since this breed of cattle has become unfashionable. There are a few houses, some quite large, and three farms as well as the Hall, which would have created employment in bygone years. The Hall is now divided into two houses.

Wass

The hamlet of Wass lies 600 ft below the south escarpment of the Hambleton Hills. It faces south across a shallow valley which links the Vale of Mowbray with the western edge of the Vale of Pickering. The hamlet is partly tucked into a broad cleft in the hills, with steep wooded slopes on three sides, sheltering it from northerly winds. It is a place of great natural beauty.

Present day Wass comprises about 40 houses with just over 70 people living here. It is a community which boasts its own church, village hall, shop and post office, and village inn. It is a living, thriving community.

Wass, however, is an ancient place. On Wass Moor are to be found the long barrows, the graves of the people of the New Stone Age.

There is firm evidence of a medieval kiln on the western edge of the hamlet, to the south of modern day Hambleton lane. Many fragments of pottery have been excavated, together with broken pieces of clay pipes, all doubtless produced for the use of the monks of Byland and their lay brethren.

The school was built after 1850 mainly of stone from Byland Abbey, and finally closed in the 1930s. The building that comprised the school and the chapel of ease is now St Thomas's church.

The two oldest cottages in the hamlet, plus the present village inn (the Wombwell Arms) go back to the 17th century. There was a forge near the site of the present crossroads, which was part of the 17th century buildings. There was also a butcher's shop, a joiner's, a village store and post office. The bellows, forge and anvil are still in the forge, and the rim bender can be seen on the outside wall. Opposite is a cast iron water trough with a lion's head spout, built in 1870 and still in working order.

Wath & Melmerby ✒

The manor of Wath was bestowed by William the Conqueror upon Alan, Earl of Brittany and Richmond, and was in his father's possession at the time of Domesday in 1086.

Today, Wath is very little changed. The old boys school built in 1684 and then endowed by Dr Peter Samwaies DD as a free grammar school, closed in 1974 so children now travel by bus to Burneston. The old school is now a village hall and is used for village meetings.

Though the greater part of St Mary's church is the work of later builders, craftsmen of the 12th and 13th century were responsible for the original design.

The George and Dragon inn supplies meals and drinks for villagers and visitors. The main recreation in Wath is the cricket club and for the ladies there is the Women's Institute.

Melmerby is situated one mile from Wath to the western side of the A1. It has a Methodist chapel and a village hall, which is used by the play group and senior citizens' club. Melmerby Hall, previously in private ownership, is now a home for the elderly.

There is also a garage, petrol station, and village inn.

Welburn ✒

Welburn (York) – not to be confused with Welburn (Kirkbymoorside) – is a compact, attractive, Ryedale stone village. It lies conveniently just off the A64 York–Scarborough road and immediately south of the great

Castle Howard estate with which many residents are still closely associated. The character of the village owes much to the long curving main street, in the Ryedale tradition, running east to west from the main road to the Bulmer boundary.

Traditionally, Welburn was part of Bulmer parish but it is now a parish in its own right. There are few records of the village's ancient history but Roman remains have been unearthed and many old names indicate times now past. A listed house is Chapel Garth where monks' coffins reputedly rested on the way from Kirkham Abbey northwards.

The church of St John's spire cuts the skyline to the south towards Whitwell. It has interesting stained glass commemorating the Howard family and is a Victorian construction. The Methodist church lies halfway up the main street and an older resident remembers helping to lay the foundations when he was a schoolboy at the village school. Both churches contribute a lot to the excellent community spirit here.

In the centre of the village is the pub, the Crown and Cushion – formerly the Horse and Groom but renamed after Queen Victoria's visit to Castle Howard in 1850. Next door is Temperance Inn Farm, formerly the Bull but whose licence was removed by the 9th Countess of Carlisle. This family farm and another, Mount Pleasant, to the east of the village, are important working farms and both are still run by the original families. The village and surrounding landscape owe much of their character to the dedication of such stewardship. The village store and post office are vital to village life and it is hoped that such amenities can be retained. Further up Main Street is Welburn primary school, in what must be one of the most beautiful positions of any local school.

Well ✣

The village of Well owes its name to the spring or holy well dedicated to St Michael by early Christians. Occupation of the area however pre-dates Christianity as there is evidence of a Roman villa and bath house in Mill End. A portion of a tessellated pavement was removed and can be seen in the church.

The church of St Michael the Archangel is a memorial to one of the great feudal families of the north, the Nevilles. Ralph Neville was responsible for the building of the present church around 1350, replacing an earlier building. He also founded the Hospital of St Michael in 1342, a charity which still exists under modern regulations and has cared for the poor people of the district for hundreds of years. The almshouses, now called St Michael's Cottages, built in 1758 stand near to the church in Church Street, presently providing homes for two men and two women of the district. Nearby is Well Hall, the north wing of which was the original hospital. This 12th century house has many historic features, notably a magnificent vaulted room.

St Michael's Well is one of several springs which feed the stream flowing into the well frequented duck pond at Holly Hill. The stream then flows down the village, running alongside Church Street, where residents cross the water via their own bridges. Well was once mentioned as 'the village of 90 bridges' though there are now only a handful.

Unlike other small desirable villages in the dales, Well is still very much a working village. The present population of 225 includes a high proportion of families with young children, who are at present working hard to raise money to equip a playing field recently acquired. The public house the Milbank Arms was previously called the Well Ox. There is a post office and shop, which is necessary in a village where the bus calls on only three days of the week.

Wensley 🌿

Wensley is a place of former great importance which gave its name to the dale in which it lies. A charter was granted to Sir Henry Scrope to hold a market in Wensley during the reign of Edward II. The 'town' was struck by the plague in the middle of the 16th century, many of the inhabitants fleeing to Leyburn, thought to be a healthier spot owing to its distance from the river. Wensley never regained its former prominence or population.

The only two surviving medieval structures that can be seen are the bridge and the church of Holy Trinity. There was almost certainly a church on this site in Saxon times, indeed a Saxon cross was found in the churchyard in the 19th century.

The Bolton family pews are a pair of opera boxes removed from Drury Lane at the time of that theatre's refurbishment in the 18th century. The Duke of Bolton fell in love with the singer who played Polly Peachum in *The Beggars Opera*. The Duke kept her as his mistress for many years until his wife died, at which point he married her. Although she produced numerous children for him out of wedlock, she never managed any more. Polly Peachum's Tower is said to have been built for her to sing from because there came a point when the old Duke could not bear the sound of her singing any longer!

In days gone by the commodities of Wensley and the area around it, for home and foreign consumption, were cattle, horses, wool, butter, cheese, mittens, knit stockings, calamine and lead. Today the agriculture is based on dairy, sheep and cattle. Within the village there is a saw yard, a candle-making business and a self employed joiner. Wensley is still an unspoilt village set in beautiful surroundings and long may it thrive.

West Scrafton ✤

Today, with a resident population of 49, West Scrafton can only be described as a hamlet. The village green must be one of the smallest in the country. Eleven of the houses are listed buildings and it is a pretty and unspoiled village, but whilst a local community spirit manages to survive, 14 of the houses, eight of which are barn conversions, are now holiday or weekend cottages.

The village is built on a huge cavern known as West Scrafton pot, the entrance to which is under the Primitive chapel and involves a 40 ft collapsible ladder descent only possible when Great or Red Gill is reasonably low. When the Gill is in spate the water rushes down and makes the entrance impassable. The stream which runs through West Scrafton pot comes out into the river Cover at Otter's Hole after running over a mile underground. Near Otter's Hole is a derelict building known as Tom Hunter's Parlour. Tom Hunter is said to have been a highwayman who prayed on travellers using what was then the main road from London and who hid his loot in this building.

The village has its own water supply which is piped from natural springs near Roova Crag. There was an inn, the Moor Hen, until 1927 when it was purchased by a local stalwart of the Methodist church and the liquor licence was relinquished. Ever since the village has been known locally as the Holy City. There was a local shop for everything including paraffin until 1954.

There was a coal mine on West Scrafton Moor until the turn of the 19th century, the entrance to which is now fenced off and the spoil heaps of which can still clearly be seen. The coal was poor stuff, known locally as Scrafton crackers because it did nothing but spit and crack.

At one time there were nine working farms in the parish. Today there are four working farms which still give the village its traditional farming basis, now concentrated exclusively on milk and beef production and sheep breeding.

West Witton ✤

West Witton is in the heart of Wensleydale on the south side of the dale and under the shadow of Penhill, four miles west of Leyburn.

It is interesting to note that in 1890 there were 24 tradespeople and 20 farmers. Only two farms are still in the same family name and today there are ten farms or smallholdings and one tradesman and no village shop.

The parish church is dedicated to St Bartholomew and is first mentioned in records of 1281. Except for the tower (16th century) the present building was built in 1875 – there are two very ancient bells.

The 24th August is the feast of St Bartholomew. Also on that day the annual Village Feast is held. Prior to 1939 the 'Feast' was a feast of good food, with the traditional Yorkshire curd cheesecakes always being served – there are photographs of some of the village men and women 'cheesecake gathering'. The Feast ends with the Burning of the Bartle. This is an effigy of a man, carried down the village.

A native of West Witton, George Smorthwaite, became a schoolmaster in Twickenham. During the 1950s he bought six properties as they became vacant in the village. These were to be let to elderly people at a nominal rent. On his death he left money to help to ensure the continuation of the feast custom and also a gift of money for all the 70 or 75 year old residents. Today, though there is no cheesecake gathering and no 'Feast', the celebrations are held on the weekend nearest 24th August. The same benefactor provided funds for a green and garden to be created from a pond, and a playing field.

Swinithwaite is a small hamlet about a mile west of West Witton. A short distance further west and part of the Swinithwaite estate is The Temple (farm house), an octagonal three-storey building of Grecian style. A short distance from The Temple are the remains of a preceptory of the Knights Templar. The existence of this site was unknown until 1840 when an earth mound was removed and the ruins and ground plan of the chapel and other buildings were found along with a number of stone coffins.

Weston ♋

Travelling the road from Otley on the north side of the river Wharfe, Weston is the first village. Although the population is only 46 it has two large country houses: Weston Manor, the home of the Vavasours, now used as offices, and Weston Hall where Colonel H. Dawson lives. The Hall goes back at least to the 1500s.

The church of All Saints is adjacent to the Hall and there is proof that the church was here at the time of the Domesday survey of 1086. A stone, The Weston Marc, carved by the Vikings indicates a church before the Norman invasion.

The inside of the church is interesting. There is a three decker pulpit and an orchestra pew, which on special occasions such as Harvest and Christmas was used by visiting Glee singers. The squire's pew houses a beautiful stained glass window depicting a lifeboat scene. This was to the memory of Emma Dawson who worked hard for the lifeboat cause, indeed she gave one to Redcar.

The stocks are still at the top of Church Lane.

Whashton 🐚

Whashton is a small village about two miles from Ravensworth with houses set along the green.

The Hack and Spade public house was converted from cottages, probably by Christopher Blenkiron in 1857. It is thought to be the only public house of that name. There is a Victorian letter box on the side, set in an old window.

Whashton Grange is a fine old farmhouse built in the 18th century on the site of a toft and croft which in 1270 was presented to Marrick Priory with 60 acres of land. York House was used as a police house many years ago, hence the name 'Bobby's Bank' for the hill approaching Whashton. In the field adjoining the blacksmith's shop, which still retains many original features such as an earth floor, hearth, bellows and anvil, there can be seen humps, bumps and foundations suggesting medieval house plots, possibly the site of the village of Whassyington in the 12th century.

From the village green there is a very good view of the surrounding countryside. Noticeable is the rock face of a former quarry from which limestone was dug for roadmaking and limeburning.

Whashton Lodge is an 18th century house where Nicholas Allen ran a so-called 'London school' for a few years until his death in 1749. There appears to be no further reference to a school here until 1840 when Whashton Lodge Academy was founded for boys and girls, day pupils and boarders, by Thomas Wallis. He remained as principal until 1873.

Wheatcroft 🐚

The former village of Wheatcroft lying on the main Scarborough to Filey road, and which is now incorporated into the Borough of Scarborough, was astonishingly called New Brighton a century ago. This name is recorded on the Ordnance Survey map of 1893. There have been two farms in the area for centuries, High Wheatcroft and Low Wheatcroft.

It would seem that a small community developed in the mid 19th century, consisting of about 18 houses with a chapel at the bottom of the hill which was later converted into a cottage. The present church of St Michael and All Angels was opened on 20th April 1880.

Mr George Alderson Smith of Holbeck Hall (now an hotel) was looked upon as the Squire of Wheatcroft. The village had two laundries and at one time it was nicknamed 'Soap Suds City' – it was one of Scarborough's light industrial villages. The laundries, which were all hand-washing and ironing, employed 40 to 50 women who walked in from Scarborough daily.

At the back of the church was a field where a local team called the Brighton Rovers played and nearby there was a chestnut tree. It was claimed that whoever stood under it would become engaged and live happily ever after.

The village had one or two local characters, one being Alfie, the wreck watcher, who lived in a hut at the cliff top. He would be seen going down the path to the sea shore accompanied by a large dog on a huge chain. Another was an old woman who told fortunes.

Present day Wheatcroft has substantial housing developments and is a suburb of Scarborough. It is administratively in the Weaponess Ward. Two modern primary schools have been built in the area and a large golf course is situated on the nearby cliffs.

Whenby ✣

The village of Whenby nestles under the Howardian Hills about two and a half miles to the east of Brandsby. It is a small community comprising three farms and 18 cottages and houses. It has a telephone booth and a post box, but no shop or school. The village has a splendid church which is well looked after by the Redundant Churches Fund. St Martin's stands at the east end of the village and was entirely reconstructed in the 15th century. There is now no trace of the vicarage which was situated near the church.

The manor house, now Manor Farm, stands at the west end of the village and is a substantial building of the 15th century. The village school, situated at the west end, was opened in 1868. It is no longer functional and has been extended and converted into a private residence.

It is likely that at some time in its history Whenby was a larger village than it is today, but evidence to support this is rather sketchy. Meantime it is an excellent example of a small rural community with a determination to preserve its heritage by attention to style of buildings and preservation of the countryside.

Whixley ✣

Whixley, formerly Quixley, is situated on the old Roman road between Aldborough and Aberford, just off the Great North Road and about six miles south-east of Boroughbridge. Stone for the walls of the church is reputed to have come from the old Roman town at Aldborough (Isurium). Similarly, the walls of the Park and of some village houses are partially cobbled, the cobbles reputedly coming from the Roman road when this was dismantled.

The ground is very fertile and for many years the village was famous for its cherries, grown extensively by friars of the priory of Knaresborough. There are verses which imply that the friars were too fond of the sweet fruit. In later times, cherries were sent to Covent Garden for sale.

Villagers celebrated Whixley Cherry Feast on the first Sunday in August, and some elderly folk remember the practice. House names, Cherry House, Cherry Cottage, Orchard House etc, are a reminder of these harvests, although there are few of the old trees still producing fruit, and new houses stand where once the biggest cherry orchard flourished.

For over a hundred years the Tancred family occupied the manor house and Hall. The last of the male line, Christopher Tancred died in 1754. Christopher was an eccentric. In his will he decreed that the estates and investments should not pass to females of the family, although he had sisters, but that a Hospital was to be established in the Hall, where 'twelve indigent and decayed gentlemen' would live and receive £20 per year each. Another condition of Christopher Tancred's will was that his remains should not be buried and at various times his coffin was in the cellar of the Hall or suspended by chains in the dining room. There are references to villagers 'rattling old Tancred's bones'. Today the remains are more appropriately contained in a sarcophagus in the church.

The Trust sold the Tancred lands to the then West Riding of Yorkshire County Council and it was divided into small farms of approximately 50 acres each and rented to returning servicemen from the First World War. Such small farms are not really viable today and many have been combined, so that the few remaining have scattered fields. Root crops are grown, and some stock is kept. The population, between 500 and 600, remains the same as it was during the 19th century, but most workers commute to Harrogate, York or Leeds.

Wigginton 🌿

Wigginton, a village some four and a half miles north of York is mentioned in the Domesday Book as Wichistun. In 1801 the population was 260 and in the 1981 census the population had grown to 2,748 due to some of the farmland having been used for small housing estates.

Mill Lane, which is one of the original parts of the village, was named after the windmill which was just round the corner on the Sutton Road. It was shown on the 1769 Enclosure Map but is not listed in directories of the 19th century. Next to the mill was the Windmill public house. This was pulled down in the late 1930s.

The Sutton Road was a turnpike road and opposite the windmill was a toll cottage, unfortunately also demolished in the late 1930s. A little way from here, in the centre of the village, Westfield Lane follows the line of an old corpse path which in former times ran from Wigginton to Huntington. Nearby Butt Hill was probably a mound used for archery practice.

The parish church of St Mary and St Nicholas dates from 1860, the previous church having been demolished in 1859. It cost £700 and is built on an ancient Saxon site.

There are several shops and the Black Horse public house, whilst the rest of the shoppers' needs are met mainly in nearby Haxby, including the post office. The focal point of the village is the village pond. This is carefully maintained by the parish council and attracts many visitors from the surrounding area when children are brought to feed the ducks, older people sit and watch the wildlife and even wedding groups take their photographs here. The pond certainly keeps alive the rural atmosphere of Wigginton.

Wilsill

This is a small unspoilt village in Nidderdale, two miles from Pateley Bridge on the main Harrogate road. Inhabitants now number about 80.

The village has an Anglican church – St Michael and All Angels, opened on 28th April 1906. Associated with the church there used to be a school called Raikes endowed school, the endowment dating from 1743.

Under the will of Mrs Alice Shepherd each boy at Raikes school received on Easter Sunday every year 'one full suit of clothes of dark cloth with green collars and cuffs, a black beaver hat and a pair of shoes'. Each girl received 'one round gown of dark tammy stuff with green cuffs, a beaver hat and a pair of shoes'. This was discontinued as the children did not like to be classed as 'charity children'. A gift of bread was also given to the poor on Easter Sunday by the church. The school was closed in 1949.

A Methodist chapel was built and opened in 1897, and is still in use. Many village activities take place there and a thriving luncheon club is held there for retired people who live alone.

Bridge House, along with the old school is now an agricultural contractor's premises, and a stone in the nearby stream shows where a wheelwright used to put the wooden wheels to fix the iron rim. The rim would be put on very hot and the cold water would cool and shrink it so it fitted tight onto the wheel.

A row of old cottages and a shop were demolished around the 1930s so there is now no shop of any kind in the village, the nearest being at Glasshouses half a mile away. There is a public house, which it is said, was built as near to Glasshouses as was possible in order to spite the brewer, who owned most of Glasshouses and the mill there, but who wouldn't allow a pub in his village.

Wilton

Wilton is a small village of 44 houses and a population of 119. Lying on the edge of the North Yorkshire Moors in the Vale of Pickering, it is four miles east of Pickering.

The site of the Hall with a moat is next to the church. John de Heslerton made a castle of the Hall in 1335, the tower surviving until the 17th century. The 'Fish Dams' field belonging to Manor Farm is now grazing land, but in medieval times the dams would have supplied fish to the castle.

The church of St George began as a chapel of the neighbouring Hall. In 1252 Archbishop Gray ordained that Ellerburn and Wilton should be a united vicarage, Wilton remaining a chapel of ease to Ellerburn. Wilton inhabitants were carried two miles along 'corpse road' to Ellerburn for burial. Work on rebuilding the church began in 1911.

The Wesleyan chapel built in 1840 was pulled down and rebuilt in 1894. In the early 1900s the author of an article in the *Methodist Recorder* noted 'Time has wrought many changes. The village of Wilton is no longer notorious for vice and drunkenness'. The chapel closed in September 1986, and has been sold.

In the mid 19th century the village had a schoolmaster, blacksmith, shoemaker, wheelwright, a public house (known as the Fox and Pheasant) and a beer house. The public house is now Sands Farm. Some of the cottages had a cow house and pig sty, and with smallholders, the right to a strip of arable land in the Cottage Field and a 'gate' in the Cow Pasture. As this way of life gradually changed the fields were added to larger farms.

Wilton remains a farming village of 1,704 acres, arable and grassland, with large dairy herds, sheep, beef cattle and pigs.

Wistow ❧

Wistow is steeped in history, and was a settlement long before the township of Selby even existed. In area the largest parish in the Diocese of York, it has throughout the centuries been plagued by severe floods, one of which changed the course of the river. When the water subsided a village originally built on and around its banks was left almost a mile inland.

The whole population in those early days depended entirely on the profession of salmon fishing, an occupation that was carried on by one particular family until the 1930s, by which time fish had almost disappeared and agriculture had taken over. The area contains some of the best arable land in the north of England.

The parish church of All Saints, a listed building first used for worship in 1213, dominates the centre of the village. A more beautiful and well kept church would be difficult to find.

The ghost of a horse thief, caught and hanged near 'Boggart Bridge', occasionally wanders around during the dead of night. The little people from nearby 'Elf Hole' appear to have grown more timid and sightings have not been reported for some considerable time.

At the other end of the village, the old 'Goblin Tree' finally succumbed to the spring gales, but would undoubtedly have disappeared much earlier had it not been for the firm belief that anyone responsible for its destruction would, together with their whole family, meet with an untimely end. Reputed to possess evil spirits, it was treated with suspicion and even in the latter part of the 19th century it was a brave man indeed who ventured into the vicinity during the hours of darkness. Only the dead, hollow bole, with peculiarly shaped branches remained of this landmark. The remains of a once mighty oak, which was part of a medieval forest, it is believed to have stood close to the Wistow and Cawood boundary for almost 1,000 years.

Worsall ✍

There are two parishes of High and Low Worsall. It is reasonable to assume that their existence is related to the fact that the river Tees is tidal to a point west of Low Worsall and it may be that the first inhabitants came up the river with the tide, settling at a point near the village green.

There was a chapel at High Worsall at the beginning of the 13th century. Catholicism survived the Reformation and was strong in High and Low Worsall into the 17th century. The chapel was rebuilt in 1710 but only a wall and decaying gravestones now survive. The Wesleyan chapel was built in 1885 and the church at Low Worsall in 1894.

Throughout the Middle Ages and later, Yarm had been the main port on the river Tees. In 1732 however Thomas and Richard Peirse built a wharf at Low Worsall and the produce of North Riding was sent down to Stockton, while imports from Scandinavia and Northern Europe were brought back to Low Worsall. Despite the difficulties of sailing ships above Yarm the enterprise prospered. Thomas Peirse occupied and developed the manor house and a whole community grew out of the trade on the river. For a variety of reasons however the enterprise faltered and in 1779 Thomas Peirse was declared bankrupt.

The facilities were used but little thereafter, the cottages decayed, the granary and the wharfs disappeared and all that is left is Piersburgh Grange, formerly the Malt Kiln inn. The Northumbrian Water Authority now has a pumping station where once was a thriving little port.

Throughout the 19th century High Worsall was a farming community, which it still remains. Of the village which may have existed in the Middle Ages there is no trace. During the same period Low Worsall developed into a community. There was a pub, a school, a shop, a wheelwright, a blacksmith and a shoemaker as well as other trades. Now only the pub remains and it is completely changed from the village inn some remember.

Wrelton ❧

To travellers on the A170 between Helmsley and Pickering, Wrelton is probably no more than an awkward corner to be negotiated, but it has more history than meets the eye. Inhabited long before recorded history, it became, after the Ice Age, a settlement on the edge of the lake of Pickering. During the Roman invasion it stood on the route north from Derventia (Malton) to Wade's Causeway on Stape Moor. Close inspection of some of the old buildings show what good use was made of this source of free stonework.

In Georgian times the people of Wrelton would have seen many travellers, when coaches trundled their way to Scarborough and Whitby. There were then several alehouses and inns – the Red Lion, White Hart and the Buck. Where Croft Head Farm stands there are the remains of the old mounting steps. Methodism had an immediate effect on the village – Wesley discouraged alcohol, and although there had been a long tradition of ale and wine making in the village (Vinery Farm bears witness), gradually the inns and alehouses disappeared, and today only the Buck remains.

The first chapel to be built was the Wesleyan in 1814, followed by the Primitive Methodist in 1840. Both thrived, encouraging reading and basic education in the schoolrooms, which were open seven nights a week. Free meals in the form of bread and broth made from donations were prepared in an old coal-fired copper. The chapels boasted two small orchestras and thriving choirs. Only the Squire at Wrelton Hall was thought to be Church of England!

During the 19th century the foundry – sited in the end of Wrelton known as Goshen (reason undiscovered) – made use of the iron produced in local Rosedale. It specialised in kitchen ranges, some of which still lead ornamental lives in local houses, but the only trace that remains of the foundry is in the name of Foundry Farm and Cottages.

Today village life has almost disappeared, taking with it many long-established traditions. Several farmyards and the grounds of the Hall contain new housing developments and it is now largely a commuter village and an area for retired people. There are, however, still people who have lived in Wrelton all their lives, who can keep alive the memories of the village in a different age.

Yearsley ❧

Yearsley is situated twelve miles north of York and five miles north-east of Easingwold, which is the nearest town. Because it is approximately 550 ft above sea level it is exposed to the chilling north-east winds as they sweep across the Hambleton Hills. The vegetation is generally three or four weeks behind that of Easingwold even though it is such a short distance away.

Sandstone cottages with slate or pantiled roofs huddle down each side of the road which runs through the village. Some houses are faced with stone taken from the ruins of Byland Abbey.

Until 1944 Yearsley belonged to Newbrough Priory, the estate of Sir George Wombwell. There was a general shop, now no longer in use; a chapel, which has been converted like so many others into a private dwelling; a school, which was converted to a village hall but has now been demolished; and a church. The site of the original church is adjacent to the existing church and its foundations were found under the building now known as Trinity Cottage. Yearsley also had a public house known as the Unicorn, a unicorn being part of the Wombwell coat of arms. This pub later became known as the Wombwell Arms and was granted a seven-day licence, that is until Sir George reduced it to a six-day licence because the local Sunday revellers made fun in a rather boisterous manner of the Coxwold curate as he arrived to take the afternoon service. It is no longer open for trade.

Yearsley had a pottery which belonged to the same family who made Wedgwood and some Yearsley ware can be found in the Yorkshire Museum. The site of the pottery is now 'Smith's cottage'.

Forestry now prevails to the north of the village occupying what was once Yearsley moor, and there are fine walks to be found through the woods and down to the three lakes where Yearsley water mill was once situated. Sadly there is now no trace of it.

Yedingham

Yedingham lies on the old road from Malton to Scarborough and there are the odd milestones standing to prove it.

Yedingham is well known for its bridge over the river Derwent. Next door is the 500 year old Bridge inn, which in modern times served for 30 years as the local post office, until closure, but prior to that was a coaching inn.

Nearby is the church of St John the Baptist. The church was controlled by the twelve nuns and prioress of Little Marish nunnery, who were known as the Poor Nuns of Yedingham. They followed the Benedictine rule there for over 400 years. The Priory of Yedingham was founded in 1163 by Lady Helewisia and Roger de Clere and today there is a preservation order on the site. In 1970, when the course of the river was straightened, wolf-hound skulls were unearthed and it is believed these massive greyhound/mastiff cross dogs were kept by the nuns to protect their stock from roaming wolves. In the old wall on the side of the main road into Yedingham, holes are visible and through these, it is believed, the dogs were released.

This once busy village lost its blacksmith in 1967; he died the day before his 500 year old shop was demolished to make way for the new bridge.

The original school was situated on the opposite side of the road to the 'Old School', which was closed in March 1967. At that time there were 36 houses in the village, now there are about 50 with the out-lying farms, and a population of approximately 120.

The river Derwent was navigable as far as Yedingham between 1805 and 1901. Efforts continue today to reopen navigation from Malton to Yedingham, but this may not be feasible. It is not the angler's paradise it once was.

The Methodist chapel, the school, the post office, the shops, along with the cricket team, have long gone. Yedingham now has holiday cottages, a caravan site and low flying aircraft, and, of course, its heritage.

PATELEY BRIDGE

Index